DATE DUE

DEMCO 38-296

RING RESOUNDING

JOHN CULSHAW

RING RESOUNDING

TIME-LIFE RECORDS SPECIAL EDITION

TIME INCORPORATED · NEW YORK

TIME Ⓛ LIFE
RECORDS

EDITOR: *George G. Daniels*
Executive Editor: *Jeanne LeMonnier*
Art Director: *John R. Martinez*
Picture Editor: *Betty Ajemian*
Associate Editors: *David Johnson, Karl F. Reuling*
Researchers: *Lea Guyer; Sally Forbes, Mary Jane Hodges, Sigrid MacRae*
Copy Desk: *Rachel Tuckerman, Greta Newkirk*
Production Assistant: *John Loggie*
Consultants: *Dan Sibley* (Production), *Earle Kersh* (Graphics)

MANAGING DIRECTOR: *Francis M. Scott III*
General Manager: *Peter L. Hoyt*
Sales Manager: *Edmund Schooler*
Promotion Manager: *William C. Kiefer*
Business Manager: *Terrance M. Fiore*
Production Manager: *John D. Hevner*
International Operations Manager: *Charles C. Colt, Jr.*
European Manager: *Robert H. Smith*
Asia Manager: *Beto Yamanouchi*

For GORDON PARRY *and* GEORG SOLTI

AUTHOR'S NOTE AND ACKNOWLEDGMENTS

Because the making of a good gramophone record is essentially a matter of teamwork, I have alternated between the first person singular and the first person plural throughout this book. The use of the latter is neither an evasion of responsibility nor an editorial regality: it refers to the "we" who constitute the recording team in Vienna and who frequently make communal decisions about our work, or to the greater "we" which represents The Decca Record Company itself.

I am indebted to the Chairman of Decca, Sir Edward Lewis, and to Mr. Maurice A. Rosengarten for permission to write this account of how Wagner's *Ring* cycle was recorded for the first time; and I acknowledge with gratitude the permission given to me by the late Kirsten Flagstad's daughter, Mrs. Else Dusenberry of Phoenix, Arizona, to quote from her mother's letters to me during the last years of her life.

J.C.

FOR THE AMERICAN READER:

In most countries of the world, the name Decca refers to records made by The Decca Record Company Limited, whose headquarters are in London, England. Decca has a subsidiary Company in the United States of America called London Records Incorporated, and records made by British Decca are released in America (and in certain other countries) on the London label. It should be understood that all references in this book to the name Decca refer to The Decca Record Company Limited, London, England.

ABOUT THE AUTHOR:

John Culshaw is one of the outstanding record producers of our era. The word "producer" is relatively new to the recording industry. An older term, used mostly by professionals, is "A. and R. man"—the person who decides what is going to be recorded (repertory) and who is going to record (artists). He then supervises the recording sessions and edits the tapes. Often enough the real decisions are made by executives or in financial committees. But the great A. and R. men have been able to impose their visions on executives and committees. It is to them that we owe the finest achievements of which the age of the phonograph can boast. The history-making first complete recording of Wagner's *Der Ring des Nibelungen* must stand near the top of any such list of achievements. And from the first, the *Ring* was John Culshaw's "baby."

Culshaw was born in Southport, Lancashire, England in 1924 and fell in love with music at the age of ten or eleven. He played the piano "about as badly as most kids do" and tried the clarinet too, yet by 14 he was making his first attempts to write about music rather than play it. His first magazine piece was published while he was a navigator-officer in the Royal Naval Air Service. When he left the service in 1946, he decided not to take a university degree: that would merely delay him four years from his goal of getting into the music world. The 22-year-old enthusiast spent a rather bleak ten months knocking on the doors of the music establishment—the BBC, various newspapers and magazines, and the record companies. Finally Decca Records (known in the U.S. as London Records) gave him a job in their publicity department, writing capsulized biographies of performers and program notes.

Young Culshaw thought he had found his niche: the salary was modest, but he was writing about music, just what he had always wanted to do. Very soon, however, he found something he wanted to do much more. His assignments had taken him into the recording studio, where he fell in love with the art of making records. Decca allowed him to transfer to their Classical Artists Department, and for a time he served as everybody's Boy Friday, seeing to schedules, running errands and making tea. Then came that hoped-for recording session when nobody else was available and John Culshaw was sent in to pinch-hit. That was the first step. There followed a natural progression from sessions involving one performer (usually a piano recital) to those involving two (usually violin sonatas), and so on—until he finally made the major leagues: orchestral sessions and operas. He approached the latter by way of Gilbert and Sullivan, recording some of the first D'Oyly Carte productions to be put on long playing records. His first grand-opera recording was a 1951 *Carmen* which, he now says, was not very good. In Amsterdam he recorded symphonies with Eduard van Beinum and George Szell. During his peregrinations he met a young pianist-turned-conductor who was to play a large role in his future—Georg Solti. Other conductors with whom he later worked closely include Herbert von Karajan, Leonard Bernstein, Pierre Monteux, Fritz Reiner, Lorin Maazel and Zubin Mehta. He produced most of Benjamin Britten's operatic recordings up to and including *Billy Budd* in 1967 and also the *War Requiem*.

In *Ring Resounding*, Culshaw describes his later career with Decca, especially as it related to his *magnum opus*, the recording of the entire *Ring des Nibelungen* over a period of seven years. The original plan was to record only *Das Rheingold*, the first opera of the *Ring* tetralogy, but its success was so great that eventually the remaining operas were added. Culshaw initially attempted to write a book about the *Rheingold* recording, on the advice of publisher Fredric Warburg, but as the scope of the recording grew, so did the scope of his book. With the epic labor in Vienna's Sofiensaal behind him, he began his fascinating note-by-note account in 1966. Most of the book was written on "a horrid Greek boat" that went round and round the Mediterranean, loading and unloading cargoes. Since the boat had no swimming pool and few other amenities, Culshaw spent virtually all his time in his cabin, writing. The four-week trip was long enough to rough-out most of the volume. His excellent memory was bolstered by a mountain of documents relating to the project—correspondence with artists, internal memos exchanged with management and engineers, all the schedules, pocket diaries, even day-by-day accounts of telephone calls and telegrams. Among the papers most precious to Culshaw was a packet of letters from Kirsten Flagstad, the great Norwegian soprano who served, in a sense, as the patron saint of the project. Out of all this grew a book unlike anything else in the bibliography of recorded sound. It gives us in-depth understanding of this one grand recording project, but it also takes us into the arcane world of the recording studio itself as no other book has ever done. And it reads like a detective story.

In 1967 Culshaw bid a reluctant farewell to Decca and assumed his new duties as head of television music programs for the BBC. He had scaled his sonic Everest in producing the four operas of the *Ring* and could not view with excitement going back to a routine of *Toscas*, *Lucias* and *Carmens*. His television achievements have included a remarkable production of Benjamin Britten's opera, *Peter Grimes*, taped not in the studio but at the Suffolk location of the opera's action. An even more challenging project was bringing to life another Britten opera composed specifically for television, *Owen Wingrave*. Although busy running his department, he continues to get into the studio himself to try out what he calls his "dotty ideas." He has been experimenting with new ways of televising classical music programs that do not depend upon performers' faces or fingers for their only visual interest. In 1970 he directed a highly praised visualization of Schubert's *Winterreise* and more recently has directed a series of musically popular and visually challenging studio concerts with Andre Previn.

Needless to say, some of Culshaw's experiments have elicited yelps of indignation from the critics, just as his *Ring* recording, with its seminal use of stage sound-effects, angered some of the more conservative reviewers. But controversy has never frightened John Culshaw. He believes that each medium has its own way of saying things and has proved it in his recordings, his television programs, and in this book.

The Editors of Time-Life Records

CONTENTS

ABOUT THE ILLUSTRATIONS:

To produce this special illustrated edition of John Culshaw's *Ring Resounding,* the editors of Time-Life Records dispatched famed LIFE photographer Dmitri Kessel to Vienna to shoot the series of color pictures of Georg Solti and the bulk of the material in the special color essays on the city of Vienna and its Opera House. They also sifted through hundreds upon hundreds of black and white photographs of the *Ring* recording sessions, taken by the late Hans Wild and others, in order to devise a proper pictorial counterpart for Mr. Culshaw's fascinating narrative. The archives of the Bayreuth Festival were a particularly rich source of photographs showing scenes from the *Ring* and many of the recording artists in their roles onstage.

Is NOT THIS FORM capable of further development? Can we not imagine something like the second Act of *Tristan* with silent or only dimly visible actors, the music, helped by their gestures, telling us all that is in their souls, while they are too remote from us for the crude personality of the actors and the theatrical artificiality of the stage-setting to jar upon us as they do at present? . . . Or, to go a step further, *cannot we dispense altogether with the stage and the visible actor*, such external coherence as the music needs being afforded by impersonal voices floating through a darkened auditorium?

—ERNEST NEWMAN, *Wagner as Man and Artist* (1914)

RING RESOUNDING

CHAPTER ONE

The Background

In Vienna, on the afternoon of September 24, 1958, Decca began the first commercial recording of Richard Wagner's *Der Ring des Nibelungen*; seven years later, on the evening of November 19, 1965, every note and every word of Wagner's huge masterpiece had been recorded. Nothing comparable in scope, cost, or artistic and technical challenge had been attempted in the history of the gramophone.

This book is the story of how the recording was made and the people who made it: the aspirations, the failures, the triumphs, the disasters, and even the trivialities which impinged on this huge project. It was not planned by a computer or a mastermind. In retrospect, it is the haphazard aspect of so much of it that seems hard to grasp, for memory has a way of minimizing incidents which, at the time and in view of the cost, seemed appalling. We did not set out with the great idea of putting a complete *Ring* on records for the first time. Rather, a few of us dreamed about it and never really expected it to happen, for the prophets of commercial gloom are two-a-penny, and only too ready to cast their heavy shadows over projects far less risky and expensive than fifteen hours of Wagnerian music-drama on gramophone records.

That it came about at all is attributable to two people: Sir Edward Lewis, the chairman of Decca, and Mr. M. A. Rosengarten, the senior director who has been the principal force and power behind the Decca classical program since its inception. No matter what any of the rest of us contributed in our various ways to the success of the *Ring*, it was their decision late in 1957 to take an enormous risk on the hitherto unrecorded *Rheingold* that provided the foundation for the whole venture. A measure of the extent of the risk was that no other company

Old 78-rpm records preserve something of the vocal splendor of soprano Frida Leider and baritone Friedrich Schorr, Wagnerian stars of the 1920s and '30s.

in the world had even considered the possibility of such a recording, and when Decca's decision became known at least one distinguished competitor prophesied financial disaster.

One of the factors which in my opinion contributed decisively to the success of the *Ring* recording was that it was subject to commercial discipline. We were treated generously; we were left alone to get on with the work; we were never refused anything which might contribute to the success of the recording. But we were also not allowed to run amok and indulge in those pointless extravagancies which sprout and multiply whenever the discipline of a proper budget is absent. (We know of one opera producer who, working in a superbly equipped theater, demanded and got over sixty separate lighting rehearsals for one production of *Götterdämmerung*. With such inefficiency, or perversity, it is no wonder that huge subsidies are required for opera on the stage.) The financial reins which held us were neither taut nor uncomfortable, but we never had any doubt that they were gripped by a firm hand.

Inevitably in a story of this kind the focus must be, rather unfairly, on the artists and the recording studio. Wagner's drama, and the real-life dramas which surrounded it for seven years, make up the substance of this book to the exclusion of dozens of other people without whom the Decca *Ring* would be less good than it is. There are the administrators, the accountants; the tape editors and the men who take such pains to transfer the sound from tape to disk in such a way that the two are indistinguishable; the factory technicians who strive to maintain that quality through a process of mass production; the promotion men and the representatives who get the records into the shops. All these play a part in the history of any recording, and I draw attention to them here because they do not get their fair share of what is coming. The glamorous side of any record company is its studio, because that is where the artists are; yet without the skilled efforts of a cutter or a process engineer working sometimes thousands of miles away from the recording location, the work of the artists could go for nothing.

I am very much aware of a contradiction in purpose between this book and our recording of the *Ring*. In reviewing the records, many critics acknowledged that we succeeded in creating something like a "theater of the mind" which enabled the listener at home to get involved with Wagner's characters and the sweep of his great music-drama, as distinct from the different sort of enjoyment that comes from hearing a particular singer "interpreting" a part. By writing about what happened in the studio, I am open to the criticism of diverting attention to what is relatively unimportant. It can certainly be argued that it is undesirable to know *how* something was achieved if such knowledge then detracts from one's enjoyment of the result. Yet I do not think this will happen, because the power of the *Ring* as drama is too great. Close as I have been to every incident connected with the recording over the past seven or eight years, I still find that when I hear it again it is the characters of Wagner's drama who come to life, and in so doing instantly dispel any memories of artists standing in front of microphones. Hagen is Wagner's Hagen, and not just Gottlob Frick pretending to be Hagen; and it has required a considerable effort of memory to recall the various technical means through which all of us sought to bring about a result in which technology would not obtrude. So I do not think that anything in this book is likely to get between the listener and the recorded *Ring*: the cast and the characters are simply too strong.

It has seemed worthwhile to give an extensive background to the Decca *Ring*, for although it was not *planned* as a long-term venture, it would not have come into being at all had not certain factors, and certain people, happened to converge at the right moment. Would it have happened if, in 1946 Mr. Rosengarten had not signed a contract with a struggling Hungarian pianist, exiled in Switzerland, who hoped to become a conductor and whose name was Georg Solti? Would it have happened if Kirsten Flagstad had not come out of retirement and revoked her decision never to make another record, although her contribution to the *Ring* was, in the end, relatively small? Would it have happened if Decca's recording staff had not included a producer and a first engineer devoted to Wagner? It is because the forces that converged on that autumn afternoon in 1958 to begin the recording of the *Ring* came from so many directions that I have tried to follow their traces as far back as possible.

Tenor Lauritz Melchior and soprano Lotte Lehmann made a memorable recording of Act I of "Die Walküre" with Bruno Walter and the Vienna Philharmonic Orchestra in 1935.

The idea of a complete *Ring* on records was unthinkable until the advent of LP and premature before the invention of stereo. Bits and pieces of the *Ring* were recorded in the days of the 78-rpm record, and some of them are valuable if only to remind us, however dimly, of the great voices of the past. We are the richer because the gramophone has preserved the voices of Leider, Lehmann, Melchior, and Schorr. The most consistent and satisfactory of all such recordings remains the set of *Walküre*, Act One, made in 1935 with Bruno Walter conducting the Vienna Philharmonic and a cast comprising Lehmann, Melchior, and List, although I have never been able to agree with those critics who find this performance irreproachable. Bruno Walter and Lehmann are superb; but Melchior, despite the excellence of his voice as such, seems to me to take rhythmical license far beyond any reasonable bounds.

Flagstad made a lot of prewar 78-rpm records which serve to give some idea of her voice in its prime, though the musical value of the disks is often impaired by the presence of undistinguished conductors; there remains, however, her excellent postwar recording of the immolation scene from *Götterdämmerung*, conducted by Wilhelm Furtwängler.

These, and a few other distinguished examples apart, constitute the main legacy of the 78-rpm era so far as the *Ring* is concerned. Much of the rest is frankly comical. Not long ago a colleague of mine came across an old 78-rpm set of *Walküre* on the HMV label. It contained fourteen records—twenty-eight sides—and played for roughly two hours, which is just over half the average timing for the whole work. It was, therefore, a "condensed" *Walküre*, although the process of condensation seems, from today's standpoint, to be the least of its surprises. Seven sides, or about thirty-two minutes, are devoted to Act One, with Walter Widdop as Siegmund and Göta Ljungberg as Sieglinde. Through the first four sides the London Symphony Orchestra is conducted by Albert Coates, but when we come to sides five and six an anonymous orchestra has taken over, and Lawrance Collingwood is the conductor. (The singers remain the same.) By side seven, which contains the end of Act One, Mr. Coates has reappeared with the London Symphony.

The interjection of another orchestra and conductor in the middle of Act One may seem startling enough today, but it is as nothing when compared with the comings and goings in Act Two. For the opening of the second act the orchestra has become the Berlin State Opera, and the conductor is Leo Blech. There is a fine cast, with Frida Leider as Brünnhilde and Friedrich Schorr as Wotan, and these forces manage to remain constant for three sides, or about thirteen minutes. But when, on sides eleven and twelve, it is necessary for Siegmund and Sieglinde to reappear, the orchestra becomes the London Symphony once again and Mr. Coates is back on the podium.

From that point onwards a state of anarchy may be said to prevail. In the *Todesverkündigung* scene the orchestra and conductor (Coates) remain the same, and Widdop is still the Siegmund; but the part of Brünnhilde has been taken over by Florence Austral. By side sixteen, where Siegmund challenges Hunding, we are back in Berlin again. The Siegmund is still Walter Widdop, who presumably went to Berlin in the hope of meeting his former Sieglinde, Miss Ljungberg . . . but no such luck, for another singer has taken over the part. However, Miss Ljungberg manages to reappear on the very next side to witness the death of her brother, along with Mr. Coates and the London Symphony Orchestra. Miss Austral is still the Brünnhilde, but for the end of Act Two we find a new Wotan, Howard Fry. Miss Leider is back as Brünnhilde for Act Three; Mr. Fry has been replaced as Wotan by Mr. Schorr, and the Berlin forces are again conducted by Leo Blech. Altogether, this is a very confusing set of records.

Another 78-rpm set, devoted to Act Two, is only marginally less complicated. Marta Fuchs sings Brünnhilde for eleven of the twenty sides, but has been replaced by the end of the act. The same applies to Hans Hotter, whose place is taken by Alfred Jerger on side twenty. The Berlin State Opera Orchestra under Seidler-Winkler plays sides one to eleven and fifteen to eighteen, while the others are played by the Vienna Philharmonic under Bruno Walter. How anyone was supposed to get a conception of the piece from this sort of mess is very hard to imagine, but such was the beginning of the *Ring*'s recording history. (There was a similar patchwork *Siegfried*.) Haphazard planning and a shortage of money doubtless governed these hotchpotch ventures; but the real trouble was the format of the 78-rpm record, which could not, by its nature, accommodate this kind of music without fatally damaging its continuity. Indeed, considering all its deficiencies, it is amazing that the 78-rpm disk lasted as long as it did. For almost half a century it *was* the gramophone record, and its tumultuous history has been well recounted by Roland Gelatt in his book *The Fabulous Phonograph*.

The death of the 78-rpm record was sudden and unlamented. With the advent of LP—pioneered in the United States by Columbia Records, Inc., and in Europe by The Decca Record Company, Ltd.—continuity of performance in terms of both playback *and* recording became possible, and the field of complete opera was wide open. Seen in retrospect, one realizes that some strange things happened in the transition period between 78-rpm and the establishment of LP. Thus, although Columbia in America had shown not only what could be done with LP but with opera on LP by producing a really brilliant, imaginative recording of Gershwin's *Porgy and Bess*, the company promptly abandoned its interest in opera and concentrated its classical activity almost entirely in the symphonic field. In Great Britain, EMI reached the odd conclusion that there was no future in LP and devoted itself to a hopeless, last-minute attempt to preserve the 78-rpm format. But Decca, on the instigation of Maurice Rosengarten, plunged into complete operas as early as 1950. In Vienna, Clemens Krauss recorded what has become a sort of vintage *Fledermaus*; and in Rome, Renata Tebaldi made her first appearance in a complete-opera recording with *La Bohème*. A recorded *Ring* was already a technical possibility in 1950, but the standard operatic repertoire obviously took precedence.   ·*Continued on page 8*

Edison ponders improvements in his cylinder phonograph. Machine was run by electric battery at left.

The earliest days of the disc

The art of recording has come a long way since Thomas Edison's invention of the tin-foil cylinder in 1877 and Emile Berliner's development of the first crude disc record and phonograph a few years later. Turn-of-the-century opera stars helped popularize the phonograph because their robust voices were able to ride over the heavy surface noise inherent in the early discs. The original acoustical method of recording, however, reproduced the orchestra badly; and it was not until the advent of electrical recording in the 1920s and the development of LP and stereo in the 1940s and '50s that works like Wagner's *Ring* cycle could be accorded full justice.

This Emile Berliner phonograph (left) sold for only $12 in 1894 but presented its user with the problem of maintaining constant speed. The turntable was rotated manually, and it took a strong and steady arm to keep it going at the correct speed of about 70 revolutions per minute.

Wagnerian contralto Ernestine Schumann-Heink poses with a console that encased horn phonograph in "piano-finished" mahogany.

Soprano Félia Litvinne gets set to record in a Paris studio of the early 1900s. Accompanist is placed on a platform so sounds of her piano will be picked up better by the horn.

It is a sobering thought that if anyone had tried to put the *Ring* on 78-rpm disks, the complete work would have required something like two hundred and twenty-four sides, or one hundred and twelve records. You would have been interrupted thirty-five times in *Rheingold* and over seventy times in *Götterdämmerung;* and most of the breaks would have made musical nonsense. Now, with the reasonable latitude provided by modern dubbing techniques, one can accommodate the whole of *Rheingold* on six sides, *Walküre, Siegfried* and *Götterdämmerung* on twelve sides each, making twenty-one records for the entire cycle, which has a playing time of over fourteen hours.

Although many early LP's consisted of 78-rpm disks redubbed into the new format, it was not long before every record company was using magnetic tape as the basic material for recording. Since tape can be spliced, the era of the "assembled" performance had come into being almost before anyone realized the implications. One might say that the LP could not have been launched seriously without the invention of tape; yet within six years of the arrival of LP the record industry faced another revolution in terms of stereophonic sound. From my position in the studio this was the breakthrough we had waited for in order to record complete operas in a way that might bring the home listener into closer contact with the drama. It was a development for *today's* listener: it could not be expected to appeal (and indeed did not and does not appeal) to those sentimental folk whose greatest listening pleasure comes from hearing ancient 78-rpm records made by the ladies and gentlemen of the so-called golden age. But for the huge, untapped, and mainly young audience interested in opera-in-the-home, and also healthily interested in using modern technology to produce a decent sound from records, the coming of stereo opened a new world of experience.*

It is true to say that stereo changed the whole concept of recorded opera. Until stereo, a record was a document of a performance, and one could not really expect it to be more. In the old mono system you

Dr. Peter Goldmark, pioneer of LP in America, holds an armful of 33⅓-rpm records containing all the music in the eight-foot tower of 78-rpm albums to his right. The advent of LP made feasible for the first time recordings of lengthy works such as the "Ring."

---

*Briefly, and nontechnically, the difference between a mono and a stereo recording is that on a mono record the pickup stylus—the modern equivalent of the old needle—moves in a direction which produces a single sound. On a stereo record the movement of the stylus is more complex, and produces *two* sounds, one of which is fed to the right speaker and the other to the left. Assuming that, as usual, the first violins are deployed to the conductor's left, they will be heard mainly from the left speaker; and whatever is on the right will be heard from the right speaker. With good stereo there should be no "hole in the middle," for this problem will have been overcome by skillful microphone placement in the studio. A sound which emanates from the center of the orchestra (the woodwind, for example) will be recorded on both channels and will therefore, under proper playback conditions, appear to be located in the center, despite the fact that the home listener has no center speaker.

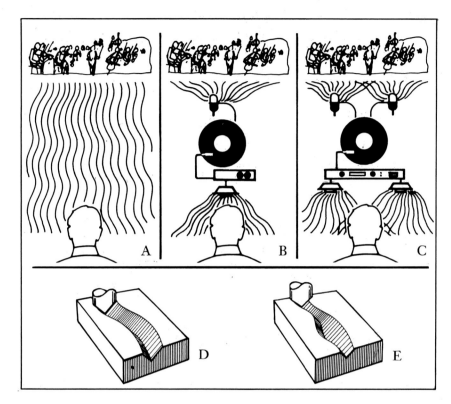

Diagrams at top show how directional apprehension of sound at live concert (A), impossible via mono recording (B), is conveyed by stereo recording (C). Diagrams at bottom show mono record (D) has same information engraved on parallel groove walls which make stylus move only laterally, producing single sound; stereo record (E) has different information on left and right groove walls, making stylus move vertically and laterally, producing two sounds.

could, in a rather primitive way, convey the idea that a character was approaching from a distance—like Don José in Act Two of *Carmen*. You could more or less accommodate all the sounds a composer wrote in his score, but you could do little to suggest the sort of perspectives—the layers of sound—he may have had in mind. (Outside opera, Britten's *War Requiem* is a perfect example, for the perspectives are part of the work and stereo is able to convey them, whereas mono can only suggest their existence.)

It is unfortunately true that only a minority of those who invest in stereo make the most of its advantages, which, from the listener's point of view, are two. First, there is an obvious improvement in sound *quality*, a sense of spaciousness and a lack of strain—though such improvement is dependent on the quality of the listener's equipment. Second, there is stereo's ability to convey *position* in the lateral sense. It differentiates between sounds on the left, in the middle, and on the right, and should cover all points between the extremities of the two speakers. And when handled properly from the recording end, it can seem to convey that certain sounds are actually coming from *beyond* the extremities of the speakers, like the offstage call of Waltraute in Act One of *Götterdämmerung*, or Siegfried's horn call as he approaches the Rhinemaidens in Act Three. Given this possibility to convey position and *movement*, it was obvious to us from the beginning of stereo that operas would have to be conceived aurally for the new medium. It would make no sense at all for the tenor and soprano to sing a passionate love duet while standing several yards apart; and if the baritone has to flee from the tenor's wrath, he must obviously move away from him, and not towards him. Elementary though these examples may seem, it is very funny now to listen to some of the earliest stereo recordings in which one of two things happened: either the cast remained rooted in the same position throughout, which made dramatic nonsense, or the artists moved about more or less as they felt, with equally nonsensical or even downright contradictory results.

Today, movements necessary to convey dramatic action or sense are plotted long before the opera goes into the studio, and the artists are rehearsed in such movements before the orchestra assembles. To help them, it is usual to cover the stage with a numbered and lettered grid, so that an artist who forgets his move can refer to a pencil mark in his score and find out exactly where, on the sound stage, he is supposed to be. An indirect advantage of the system is that it has made artists far less microphone-conscious than they used to be. Once they have gained confidence that the battery of microphones gives an even coverage wherever they stand on the stage, they feel free to move and to *act* in a way that was very rare in the days of mono.

Stereo is therefore a medium to be *used*: it is what you can make of it. At its best, it can bring opera to life in the home in a way that was unimaginable twenty years ago. The effect is nothing like that of the opera house, for several reasons. The listener at home is not a member of a community, and whether he admits it or not his reactions in private are not the same as his reactions in public. I am not claiming that one environment is better than the other, but simply that they are different, and that therefore the reactions are different. The sound of a good stereo recording played under good conditions in the home will tend to engulf the listener, and may draw him psychologically closer to the characters of the opera than when he is in the theater. The sense of being inside the drama is heightened by the absence of a visual element: the listener can hear the words and the music, he can hear where the characters are standing, and he can follow them when they move; but he has to create his own mental image of what they look like, and in what sort of setting they are moving. Instead of watching someone else's production, he is unconsciously creating his own. (Andrew Porter, reviewing *Rheingold* in *The Gramophone*, wrote: "Listening to these records is not like going to the opera house without looking at the stage. In some mysterious way they seem to catch you up in the work—not in a particular set of performers—more intimately than that.")

Composers have been among the first to realize that stereo has transformed the purpose of the classical gramophone record. Britten will devote days to discussions with me or one of my colleagues about how best to convey one of his operas in the stereo medium.* Stravinsky's views on the subject have been extensively published, and in the realm of performing artists there are very few left who maintain that stereo is not a huge step forward. One does not have to go all the way with Glenn Gould in his prediction that within fifty years the concert hall (and presumably the opera house) as we know it will cease to exist, and will have been replaced by the stereo recording played under ideal domestic conditions. But the trend is there, unmistakably. My feeling is that since stereo offers, or should offer, an entirely different experience from that of the concert performance, there is no reason on earth why the two should not exist happily, side by side, for many years to come.

The question of how far to go in producing an opera for stereo is a tricky one. As I have said, it is essential to plot and convey those movements and actions which contribute to the drama. It is essential to handle offstage perspectives with skill and artistry—to respect, say, Wagner's careful instructions about the proximity of the various horn calls at the opening of *Tristan und Isolde*, Act Two, or Verdi's complex demands in the first scene of *Otello*. Such things can probably be better done on a stereo recording than in most theaters. But like any other medium, stereo can be abused; and once it begins to draw attention to itself and away from the music it serves, it can reasonably be said that something has gone wrong—not with stereo as such, but with the way in which it has been handled.

In recording the pub scene from *Peter Grimes*, it is logical to establish the position of the door through which Grimes will eventually make his entrance, and beyond which the storm is raging; but it is not logical to add seagulls to the first act or the sound of surf to the last. It makes

---

* By the same token, a good film of a good play is not a *filmed* play: it is a good film because it conveys the essence of the play in a new medium. A stereo opera recording is not a transcription of a performance, but a re-creation of the opera in aural terms quite different from those of an opera house. It cannot be stressed too often that all records are made with a view to performance at home under domestic conditions, which is why it is almost always impossible to suggest the real qualities of a record by means of a public demonstration in a hall.

sense to use a special acoustic to heighten the atmosphere of loneliness and fear in the short solo scene for Gutrune in *Götterdämmerung*, Act Three; but I would not myself adopt a church acoustic for the whole of the first act of *Tosca*, nor try to emulate an open-air acoustic for Act Three. The fact is that an abnormal acoustic cannot be sustained for long without inducing aural fatigue, and a hint is often enough to convey the point you are trying to make. (In the closing scene from *Aïda*—the von Karajan/Tebaldi version—we used a normal acoustic for the tomb, except for the moment where Radames tries to move the stone which seals the crypt. The mental image of the entombed lovers is assisted by the momentary trick, and remains when the acoustic has returned to normal.) Where any sort of magical business is required—the Wolf Glen scene in *Freischütz*, Alberich's disappearance and transformation in *Rheingold*, Puck's comings and goings in *A Midsummer Night's Dream*, and a host of other examples—the use of a special and appropriate acoustic from moment to moment, although impossible in the theater at present, is valid for stereo. The furthest anyone has gone in that direction is our transformation of Siegfried the tenor into Gunther the baritone at the end of the first act of *Götterdämmerung*. We had to alter the construction of Windgassen's voice in such a way that it would sound vaguely like Fischer-Dieskau's, but without altering the key or tonality of the passage in question. It was an exceedingly difficult business, but the critics did not kill us for it, because it was what Wagner hoped for, according to his stage instructions, and because it came off—which is to say that it fitted into the dramatic context without drawing attention to itself as a gimmick and without interfering with the music.

The sad thing is that so few listeners among those who have equipped themselves with stereo can get anything like a proper idea of what is on the records. Those who have gone to the expense of getting good equipment and the trouble of deploying their speakers properly have found that the experience of stereo, properly played, is remarkable, rewarding, and different.* For them, what someone has referred to as "total immersion" in opera is possible whenever they feel like it. But for the rest, and that includes just about everyone who listens to stereo with both speakers mounted in a single piece of furniture, the improvement over mono is merely that of quality—an agreeable enough improvement in itself,

---

* It is especially different for those who like to listen on stereo earphones. Some people find the effect disturbing, but it is a fact that on good earphones you can pinpoint the position of every instrument in the orchestra and follow even the smallest movements of the characters over the aural stage.

but only the smaller part of what is a huge technical and artistic step forward.

It is pleasing to think that the Decca *Ring* seems to have done much to make people aware of what can be obtained from a modern stereo record. As Alan Rich wrote in the New York *Herald Tribune* on July 4, 1965: "It is not only Wagner and *Götterdämmerung* that are justified by this new album. Suddenly, the whole concept of recorded opera seems to make a new kind of sense."

The advances in technology over the past few years have also brought about a psychological change in the studio. It is still true that all the machinery and all the assembled skills are there for the single purpose of getting the artist's performance on a record; but the means of achieving that end have become far too complex for the artist to command the *method*, as was commonly the case until a few years ago. There was, for example, a famous conductor of the old German school who refused to perform unless a single microphone of a hopelessly outdated type was suspended over the orchestra. Another conductor, involved with an early opera recording, demanded that the entire setup be changed around by one hundred and eighty degrees, despite the protests of the engineers that such a change would make the sound worse, not better. In those days, he was allowed his whim, and an entire session was wasted in proving to him that his theory was wrong.

This attitude derived from the assumption that the gramophone record was still a toy which was not to be taken very seriously. Such conductors could not, or would not, accept the difference between a literal transcription of musical notes onto a record and an imaginative approach to the same operation, through which one studies the score with a view to presenting the music in a way that will especially appeal to the listener at home. They resented what they thought was the intrusion of technology between themselves and their audiences, while forgetting that enlightened technology exists only to aid that communication. Certainly they would never have adapted themselves to today's studio requirements.

The problem no longer exists in any serious form. As a rule, artists today understand that the actual techniques of recording are best left to those who understand them; and those who understand such techniques best are those who seek to establish the closest contact with the artists in the studio, and so gain their confidence. And in any case the costs of recording have risen with such rapidity that an indulgence in whims and conceits can no longer be afforded.

Maurice Rosengarten, head of Decca's European operations, relaxes in Tel Aviv with his wife and daughter and producer John Culshaw. Rosengarten pushed Decca into recording complete operas in the early LP days, and his tenacity was a vital factor in making the first recorded "Ring" a reality.

The structure of any major gramophone company is like an iceberg: the part which shows, at least to the public, is only a fraction of the whole. Before the first notes of any recording reach the tape, the administration may have been at work for anything up to two years to coordinate the forces involved. Major artists are busy people and cannot be booked at short notice; orchestras are by no means available just when you want them; and if you are working on location it can happen that the hall you want is not free at a time to suit the artists.

The bulk of the *Ring* administration was effected from the headquarters of Decca Recordings (Europe), Ltd., which is in Zurich. At the head is the remarkable character of Mr. Maurice Rosengarten. He, and Mr. Leon Felder, who is one of his assistants, will appear and reappear as the story of the *Ring* recording emerges; and for those of us who worked on it, the presence of our somewhat mercurial Mr. Rosengarten was very much with us during those eight years. He is totally committed in his enthusiasm for the classical catalog, and there is nothing he does not know about the record business (except, possibly, what happens in the modern studio, and that he is happy to leave to others).

Without him, I do not think there would have been a *Ring* recording, or, if there had been, it would certainly have cost twice as much as it did. His tenacity when he believes he is right is as unbudgeable as Mont Blanc.

He signed a contract with Georg Solti in 1946, and I asked him to think back to that time and give me his impressions in the light of all that has happened since. He said:

"It was in 1945 that Max Lichtegg, the tenor, told me about a pianist called Georg Solti. He said he was a first-class musician and would certainly have a big future. Then, in 1946, I flew to London with Lichtegg, who was going to record some arias, and he mentioned Solti's name again, so when I got back to Zurich, I asked Solti to come and see me to discuss the possibility of making some piano recordings, perhaps as an accompanist. The first thing he said as he came in was that he wanted to conduct. I said 'Mr. Solti, have you ever conducted?' and his answer was no. What was I to think? Many people come to me and say they want to conduct or play an instrument or sing. I knew very well what Lichtegg had said to me about Solti, but he was talking about Solti the pianist, not Solti the conductor. All the same, there was something in Solti's personality that made me feel certain he would have a big future. . . .

Georg Solti in 1946. He was working in Switzerland as a pianist when Maurice Rosengarten signed him to his first contract with Decca.

"I invited him to play the piano for Georg Kulenkampff, the violinist, with whom we wanted to make some records, and he agreed, though he kept on saying that he really wanted to conduct. Anyway, I arranged for these violin and piano recordings to be set up in the Radio Zurich studios.

"Meanwhile, I had heard that Solti was going to conduct after all—he was about to become the musical director of the Munich Opera, so I thought I had better see him again to talk about a contract as a conductor. I found then what I now know very well—it's not easy to discuss programs and terms with him. He had never conducted before, but he discussed conditions as if he'd been a star conductor for years! He was so sure of himself that I decided he must have the makings of a great conductor. When we had finished our talk and agreed on the conditions, he promised that he would do his best, and he has kept that promise. I must say that his great success over the years has not changed him. . . .

"I never thought he would make the *Ring*. In those days, one thought first of Knappertsbusch in connection with the *Ring*. Of course in 1947 when I was setting up the classical recordings for Decca in Europe we were still dealing with the old 78-rpm records, but I already had in my mind the idea that complete opera recordings in the original languages must be a success. But we had to wait for LP. . . . Even so, the *Ring* is so much bigger than anything else. I think we had the courage to make it because all the right things came together—the right conductor, the best artists in the world, a superb technical setup, and of course the Vienna Philharmonic. I was never in doubt for a second that the *Ring* would be less than a great success. The biggest surprise for me was the way Solti emerged as a great Wagner conductor; I did not expect that at all, but you know how delighted I am about his success. . . ."

Solti's version of the story is very similar, but with a different emphasis. He said:

"During the second world war I was in Switzerland working as a pianist. I had a work permit for piano teaching, but not for what I wanted to do. I wanted to be a conductor, or at any rate a *répétiteur*. Well, I was doing some work with a very nice tenor called Max Lichtegg—he was Swiss, but really Polish by birth—and he told me that he had a friend in Zurich who represented Decca in Switzerland, and that he would recommend me to his friend.

"So Lichtegg recommended me—but as a pianist. It must have been a great surprise to Rosengarten that as soon as I met him I said, 'I don't want to play the piano, I want to be a conductor.' He must have thought I was absolutely mad. As it happened, I had just been playing the piano at concerts with Yehudi Menuhin, and Rosengarten had the idea of bringing me together with another great violinist, Georg Kulenkampff, who had just come out of Germany.

"You see what happened. I went to Rosengarten to ask to be a conductor, and this was his counter-proposition. He said, do this record with Kulenkampff first, and then we shall see. It must have been in the early months of 1947. I remember it very well because I had to come back to Switzerland from Munich and I had a breakdown in the car. I had a driver because I couldn't drive a car then. We broke down somewhere in the south of Bavaria and I had to wait a long time before I managed to get another car to pick me up—it cost two packets of black-market cigarettes, that's all! And so with this second car we reached the Swiss border where I was met by friends who took me to Zurich where I made my first record with Kulenkampff.

"I can't remember when I first met Mr. Rosengarten. It was in the office in the Badenerstrasse, but not the one he has now—it was the small one, near the post office. There was something strange which I remember very well. There was a smell of coffee and of some kind of electrical equipment somehow mixed together. Maybe I imagined it, but I can still remember what it was like, because I am very perceptive about that sort of thing and about noises. Things like that are not important, but they are what you remember when you are young. . . .

"I remember two people at the recording. One was Victor Olof, who kept saying, 'Take it easy, take it easy,' and the other was Rolf Liebermann. I know I was very excited, and so was Kulenkampff—understandably, because he had not worked in public for about two years. The very first session was the Brahms D minor Sonata, I think. I could be wrong, but I think that came first, then the Beethoven and then Mozart.

"When we had finished I asked Rosengarten again for a chance to conduct for records. He promised to arrange it, and he did. It was with the Tonhalle Orchestra in Zurich, and it was Beethoven's Leonore Overture No. 3. I'm sure it's a terrible record, because the orchestra was not very good at that time and I was so excited. It is horrible, surely horrible—but by now it has vanished.

"I don't know whose idea it was that I should come to London and record Haydn's Drum Roll Symphony with the London Philharmonic. It must have been in 1948. . . ."

Neither Solti nor I can remember when we first met, though it was certainly not before 1948. We were probably introduced in that year, for in 1949 I made a lecture tour of the American Zone of Germany which included an engagement in Munich on June 20. For some reason I was back in Munich on June 26 and went to a performance of *Rosenkavalier* which Solti conducted in the Prinzregent Theater. We spoke briefly in one of the intermissions, but my main memory is of the theater itself, which is a near copy of Bayreuth—and in 1949, Bayreuth was still in darkness.

A month or two later—on August 29 and 31 to be precise—we worked together for the first time. Solti had come to London to record Haydn's Symphony No. 103, the Drum Roll, with the London Philharmonic in Kingsway Hall, and I was given the sessions because Victor Olof was recording on the continent. There remains only a vague recollection of Solti's vitality and enthusiasm and cooperation—a realization on my part that making a record could be more than the routine business of putting so many notes of music into a groove. Apart from anything else, the sound that Solti was able to produce from the orchestra was exciting, and I longed to work with him again on something which, in that particular sense, offered more scope than Haydn. He was at the farthest possible extreme from the only other conductor with whom I had worked that year—the enchanting but very aged Oscar Straus, who had been lured to London to record orchestral selections from his Viennese operettas.

In the following year, 1950, I went again to Germany on another lecture tour. These tours, to judge from my diary, were really an excuse to attend as many Wagner performances as possible, and this one included a *Tristan* in East Berlin on May 14 and a *Walküre* under Solti in Munich on May 21. I like to think of the latter as the real beginning of our association, for it affected me more than any other Wagner performance I had ever heard. It was not the best I had heard, but it was the most unified; it was a conception; and it was theater. Above all, it came at just the right time, for the *Tristan* in East Berlin had been a dismal affair, and I was bored by the task of delivering the same lecture night after night and answering the same, slightly embarrassing questions from tolerant audiences who deserved a better advocate than I to convince them that a new musical tradition was emerging outside Germany.

There had been no lecture on May 21, and it was a stifling hot day. I took a train to Starnberg, hired a rowing boat and, so to speak, dropped anchor in the middle of the lake. The swimming was so good and the sun so hot that it would have been easy not to go back to Munich and the possibility of a disappointing *Walküre*; but back I went, to emerge five hours later from the Prinzregent Theater drunk with enthusiasm and conviction about a performance which vocally did not compare with those I had heard at Covent Garden since the end of the war. But I had never heard an opera orchestra play with the sort of power and nobility that Solti drew from his Munich forces. In my experience, it

Georg Solti (center) takes a bow with stage director Heinz Arnold and cast members Ferdinand Frantz, Maud Cunitz and Helena Braun following a performance of "Die Walküre" at Munich's Prinzregent Theater in the early 1950s.

connected only with the memory of the Beecham/Marjorie Lawrence *Tristan* which the BBC had presented after the war, the Vienna State Opera performance of *Salome* under Clemens Krauss at Covent Garden in 1947, and Richard Strauss conducting at the Albert Hall on October 19, 1947. But whereas all those had exciting contributory factors, the Solti performance in Munich was strictly repertoire, with no big stars (the Wotan was Ferdinand Frantz, and Brünnhilde was his wife, Helena Braun) and was achieved with an orchestra of good but not exceptional quality.

Yet *Walküre* emerged triumphantly. The music and the drama made sense in a way that had escaped the postwar Covent Garden performances, despite the excellence of the casts in London. (For example: on March 23, 1948, at Covent Garden, there was a performance in English with Flagstad, Hotter, and Carron.) What really hit me on that evening in 1950 was the overriding importance of the conductor in Wagner, and if this now sounds naïve it is worth remembering that in 1950 any young Englishman's experience of Wagner was restricted to Covent Garden, with a glimpse now and then of better things when Furtwängler or de Sabata conducted concert performances—but concert performances, however good, simply cannot add up to the totality of opera. And there were no records of substantial quality or quantity, by which I mean that no complete performance of Wagner's music-dramas existed on records.

The Munich performance of *Walküre* brought me face-to-face with what I think is the essential truth about any Wagner production: you can get away, in the opera house at any rate, with a modestly talented cast if you have a brilliant conductor at the helm; but the most brilliant cast in the world will not save the performance if the conductor is a dullhead. Of course, the ideal is to have a great cast and a great conductor in a great production; but if for any reason there has to be a weak link in the chain, then the one that can least afford to be weak is the musical director. (I happen to think this rule applies not only to Wagner, but to the whole of opera, which is really to say that inferior operas survive only to provide employment for inferior conductors: can you think of one *real* conductor who has shown an atom of passion for Bellini?)

I remember the sword coming out of the tree on that evening in May; the terror of Sieglinde's mad scene in Act Two, when she thinks she hears the barking dogs and Hunding's horn; the strings in the first appearance of the so-called Redemption theme; and, above all, Solti's handling of the E major orchestral passage in the final scene when Wotan becomes a human father instead of an unforgiving god. I know that the brass crescendo at the summit of that passage is not, in fact, written; I know that a few conductors, Erich Leinsdorf for one, refuse therefore to make it; and I suspect that Georg Solti learnt it from Hans Knappertsbusch, who knew more about Wagner as *theater* than any man of his time. I shall never forget that moment, musically or dramatically; and as I went home from the concert hall that night there was born, dimly, the idea of recording *Walküre* with Georg Solti. It was, of course, utterly impossible, and I would have been laughed at if I had even mentioned it.

The next day, May 22, I went to see Solti at his flat in Munich. Although we had worked together on the Haydn recording we were still virtually strangers, and I must have appeared like an overgrown adolescent in my admiration for the *Walküre* performance. After all, he was building a repertoire in Munich, and putting as much intensity into one piece as another: why should *Walküre* have appeared so extraordinary to a visiting Englishman? We talked mostly about what he was to record next, and I became aware of what had, for quite a time, been implicit in his relationship with Decca: he did not get on with Victor Olof, who was in charge of the artistic aspects of the classical catalog. With Rosengarten, who had after all discovered him and given him his first opportunity as a pianist, he had no differences; but Olof had serious reservations about what he thought was an uncontrollable brashness in Solti's approach to music. Indeed, it was his disinclination to work with Solti that gave me my first chance on orchestral sessions, for Victor organized the program in such a way that he could always be available for sessions with artists for whom he had musical sympathies—and as this applied to most of them, it left very little opportunity for anyone else. He had decided that Solti should not be let loose on any more Haydn symphonies; he felt that Suppé overtures would be more in keeping with Solti's abilities, and this was the news I had to break the day after that shattering *Walküre*.

Actually, I think Suppé overtures are splendid pieces, and I had a hunch Solti would make them with tremendous brio. At the same time, the prospect was a bit of a comedown after Haydn, and Solti rightly felt that as *Generalmusikdirektor* of the Munich State Opera it was Decca's duty to give him something more substantial. At that time I was very much on the periphery of things, and I am sure that whatever arguments I produced in favor of Suppé did not convince him. At a guess, the deed was done by Zurich, and the next thing I knew was that the sessions were fixed, again with the London Philharmonic, for April 6 and 10, 1951.

Sadly, the first session coincided with the funeral of the man who had been in charge of the Artists' Department at Decca for many years. His name was Harry Sarton, and he too had been convinced of Solti's eventual potential as a conductor. Among the mourners that day was a young man called Christopher Jennings, who worked as a pop record producer but whose heart was really with the classics. Eighteen months later he, too, was to die; but had he lived I am sure he would have played a major part in our *Ring* recording.

Christopher Jennings had three passions in life: his family—he had two children—and Wagner and Johann Strauss. In 1949 and 1950 we went together to just about every Wagner performance at Covent Garden, and it seemed absurd that a man of such knowledge should be wasting his time on pop music for which he had no special affection. He was also a very talented writer, and ironically it was this which finally prevented his transfer to the classical staff, and also taught me my first lesson about certain aspects of the Viennese character which I was unlikely to forget in later years.

Certain remarks or actions stay with one for life, like bruises which never heal; and if, in later life, I was never completely at ease in Vienna I am sure it was partly because of an incident concerning Christopher and a Viennese conductor who had given a concert in London. Christopher had published an article about the concert—a splendid piece, full of love for the music and fervent in its praise for the conductor. Along with it appeared an "action" picture to which the conductor took exception, though it was hard to see why, for to most people it conveyed the intensity the conductor was putting into his work in order to achieve the brilliant results which Jennings described.

The conductor made it known to Sarton that Jennings should be kept out of his sight; he was disinclined even to visit the Decca offices unless he could be assured that Jennings was elsewhere. In vain, we tried to explain that Jennings had not been responsible for the photograph, but it made no difference. My friend's chances of coming over to the classical staff were just about eliminated by this affair; and I, as a junior member of the department, could do nothing to help. As for Christopher, his bewilderment was extreme, since the conductor was one of his idols.

On August 4, 1952, Christopher Jennings died very suddenly of polio. He was not then thirty. In the last months of his life one of his great joys had been the *Parsifal* recording we had made in Bayreuth the year before, and he had spent evening after evening with me at the Hampstead studios helping to choose the passages which went into the master. To the end, he could never understand how he had upset the Viennese

Although Christopher Jennings produced pop records for Decca until his untimely death from polio in 1952, Wagner was one of his passions. A friend of Culshaw, he helped edit tapes of the Bayreuth "Parsifal" recording.

conductor. We were both too young and too inexperienced to understand that an ability to conduct and to make beautiful music does not necessarily imply any nobility of character, or indeed any character at all. A week or two after Christopher's death I had to visit the conductor in his London hotel, and as soon as I entered the room he started to bombard me with questions. Was Jennings still with Decca? Had he *still* not been fired? I told him Jennings was dead. His big eyes lit up. "God has punished him," he said, "and his family, for what he did to me."

The Suppé overtures with Solti were a revelation of what can happen when music of modest invention is played for all it is worth. It is precisely this sort of music which needs strict rhythmic control and tight ensemble, and Solti's intensity came close to exhausting the London Philharmonic. We went all out for brilliance and power, because subtlety is a quality not conspicuously present in Suppé, and inevitably some people found the result vulgar. But it was a big success, and was perhaps the first step towards establishing Solti as a conductor capable of producing an individual "sound" from an orchestra. This has always been one of the hallmarks of the real conductor: Toscanini, Bruno Walter, Furtwängler, Ansermet, Stokowski, Szell, Kleiber, Beecham, de Sabata, and von Karajan are among those whose sound is immediately recognizable because of the individual ways in which they balance and control the dynamics; and the sound produced has more to do with them than with any innate tonal qualities of the orchestras they conduct. Ormandy has said recently that the so-called Philadelphia sound is a myth, and indeed Stokowski has proved the point time and time again by recreating something very like it wherever he has worked. Leonard Bernstein, rightly or wrongly, made the Vienna Philharmonic produce a completely different sound for *Falstaff* from that which von Karajan created when he was in charge of the Vienna Opera; and no one present will ever forget the transformation in the Covent Garden pit when, in the early nineteen-fifties, Erich Kleiber plunged into the *Carmen* prelude. Kleiber had not imported the Philharmonia for the occasion, nor had he filled the orchestra with specialist deputies; he had simply made the orchestra play precisely, rhythmically, and with a strict dynamic gradation. The effect of this, after years of sloppy, routine performances of *Carmen*, was a revelation.

In 1951, Solti was a relatively unknown figure. Much of his time was spent in his own theater in Munich, and the recording companies were rightly concentrating on the older, established figures like Clemens Krauss or Furtwängler who, a year later, made the Flagstad *Tristan* for

EMI in London. Decca's Wagner activity at that time, apart from Bayreuth, was a recording of *Meistersinger*, Act Three, under Knappertsbusch in Vienna, to which Acts One and Two were later added. Despite Knappertsbusch's supremacy as a Wagner conductor in the theater, about which I shall write later on, his talents never took well to recording-studio conditions, and he was not helped by a recorded balance which favored the voices to the virtual elimination of the orchestra. Of course in those days it made no difference what the opera was: one used the same setup for everything, and the prevailing philosophy merely required that one transcribed the notes more or less accurately and in sequence. Confronted with such a disappointing *Meistersinger*, the memory of Solti's Munich *Walküre* began to nag again; but six years were to pass before it became a possibility, and even then we were restricted to a single act.

In the summer of 1951, I was sent with my technical colleague Kenneth Wilkinson to Bayreuth where we were to record at the first postwar festival. We had a rather vague brief, but as we were both vehemently keen to get to Bayreuth whether we recorded anything or not, we felt it wiser not to ask too many questions before leaving London. The equipment and assistant engineers were being provided by our German company, Teldec, and the business negotiations were in the hands of Teldec's artists' manager, who was rushing around in full sail when we arrived.

The sense of actually being *there*, in Wagner's own town, was too much for me on the first day; I went off duty and spent it wandering from the Festspielhaus to Wahnfried and Wagner's grave. Then there was the Margrave theater, the most beautifully preserved, if not also the most beautiful auditorium of its size in the world. The town of Bayreuth, on the other hand, was a disappointment: it had little beauty of its own, and I could not help wishing that Wagner had wandered a few miles west and established his festival at Bamberg which has the charm, the architecture, and the setting which Bayreuth almost entirely lacks.

Meanwhile the sort of confusion attending the reopening of an international festival six years after the end of a war was evident wherever you looked, despite the trappings of German efficiency. Accommodations were nonexistent, which doubtless upset those who had not made reservations, but was even worse for those who had. We were lucky, because our bookings were honored; hundreds were not, and the daily screamings and yellings at the reception desk, with useless letters of confirmation being brandished on high, became so commonplace that

Besides its Festspielhaus, Bayreuth boasts a magnificently preserved Baroque opera house built for the Margraves by Giuseppe Galli-Bibiena in 1748. Its immense stage was what first led Wagner to consider Bayreuth as a festival site, but the auditorium's small size and lack of a modern orchestra pit forced him to build his own theater.

one ceased to take any notice at all. In the middle of all this, a recording crew arrived from EMI, our British rivals, headed by Walter Legge, and we spent the next two or three days avoiding one another, since nobody really seemed to know what anyone else was doing.

Eventually it turned out that we were supposed to record *Parsifal*, and EMI was to concentrate on *Meistersinger*. As soon as he saw the EMI crew arrive, Kenneth Wilkinson had indulged in a shrewd bit of one-upmanship and fixed with the Festspielhaus that Decca should have the better of the two available recording control rooms in the theater, the sole advantage of which was that it had a trap door through which one could overlook the orchestra and part of the auditorium, but not the stage itself. EMI had no visibility at all, except over the Festspielhaus restaurant; and ours was of no practical use whatsoever, except that it made us feel better. As our rooms adjoined, it was necessary to pass through theirs to get into ours; and of course it was no time at all before the two rival engineering teams got on friendly terms, effected through the usual tribal approach of "Do you think I could possibly borrow your screwdriver?" I cannot say the same for Walter Legge, for whose work I had the greatest respect; we inhabited adjoining rooms for almost a month without exchanging a single word.

To get an idea of the Bayreuth sound we attended a *Siegfried* rehearsal in the theater on July 19, and began to make recorded tests with microphones during a *Walküre* rehearsal on the 20th. EMI were, of course, doing the same, but they were baffled by a very noticeable difference of sound quality which was strongly in Decca's favor. Wilkie, my technical colleague, continued to find this quite inexplicable and indeed expressed a lot of sympathy; but he knew and I knew that he had been down to the theater in the dead of night and installed a favorite microphone of his in a particularly unlikely and undetectable position. It made all the difference; and although our friends next door found out and tried to get a similar microphone, they were vetoed by their chiefs in London.

I was bitterly disappointed that Decca had not decided to make the *Ring*, and incensed when the news broke that EMI intended not only to make *Meistersinger*, but Act Three of *Walküre* as well. I asked Decca to let us record the Knappertsbusch *Ring*. (The other cycle was conducted by Herbert von Karajan, and we knew we could not touch that, as he was then an exclusive EMI artist.) I called Mr. Rosengarten, to whom I had only spoken twice before in my life, and implored him to let us record the cycle and sort out the financial problems afterwards. He must have thought I was mad, but to my amazement he agreed. Thus *almost* began the story of the Decca *Ring*.

A tremendous tension was developing in Bayreuth; it permeated everything. Out of respect, and to avoid the disillusion of a dream that does not come true, we would not at this stage admit to ourselves that events seemed unlikely to match expectations. Bayreuth, viewed from a distance, had always appeared as Mecca for a devoted Wagnerian; and now, on the brink of the first festival, we were busily and privately persuading ourselves that our gnawing sense of disillusion was caused by nothing more than the tribulations involved in starting anything so ambitious after so many dormant years. We were like children at a long anticipated party: the more disappointing it became, the more we sought to convince ourselves that it was as wonderful as anything we could ever have imagined.

The first disappointment came on July 21, during a *Götterdämmerung* rehearsal. During the last days of 1950, and up to my departure for Bayreuth in 1951, I had been to every performance of Wagner at Covent Garden that I could possibly afford, and this amounted to three complete *Ring* cycles (one cycle was in December/January, and the other two in May). Wilkie had never seen the *Ring*, though he enjoyed the music and liked the technical challenge it presented, even in the limited circumstances of a live recording off the stage. Despite our peephole in the recording control room at Bayreuth, it was still impossible to see even a square foot of the stage, and when it came to the *Götterdämmerung* rehearsal my enthusiasm for what I supposed to be happening on the stage of Wagner's own theater got the better of me. For days before I had given Wilkie vivid descriptions of the cataclysm with which the *Ring* ends; I had told him of its shattering musical and *theatrical* impact at Covent Garden—which, by definition, was said to be miles inferior to Bayreuth. On that day in July 1951, when Astrid Varnay was halfway through the Immolation scene, my patience refused to be confined any longer to that dim control room. I told Wilkie to leave the tape machine to run itself, and come with me into the auditorium to watch the spectacle: for once the performances proper had started, we would never have a chance to see it.

We crept into the darkened theatre. The brightest light was on the producer's stand in the middle of the auditorium. When our eyes had adjusted from the dim, bare bulb of the recording room to the even

Conductor Hans Knappertsbusch shows a postcard to Wagner grandsons Wolfgang (left) and Wieland. The Wagner brothers revived the annual Bayreuth Festival in 1951 and ran it jointly until Wieland's death in 1966.

dimmer lighting of the stage, we were just able to perceive Astrid Varnay, singing like an angel and dressed in what appeared to be an old sack. Of anything recognizable as the Gibichung Hall there was no sign. Needless to say, there was no horse. The great moment—when Brünnhilde, with her final words, rides into the funeral pyre and the Rhine bursts its banks and overflows and the great hall collapses in ruins—came; and went. Nothing happened, except some magnificent orchestral playing. Or, to be more accurate, the portrayal of these tumultuous happenings was as if an enthusiastic amateur with very limited funds at his disposal had tried to create them with a few drapes and a spotlight. This, so far as the funds were concerned, may be very near the truth, for there was not very much money available to the Wagner brothers when they courageously reopened Bayreuth in 1951, and I have a feeling that financial considerations had more influence on the creation of the "new" Bayreuth style of production than is usually admitted.

What we saw was more than a disappointment: it was a shock. I would concede the possibility of an abstract or symbolical approach to the production of the *Ring*—a setting by Henry Moore might or might not work, but it would at least be serious and technically secure in its aim. I failed to see how Wagner's grandson could stage a production of the end of *Götterdämmerung* which struggled every inch of the way against the music. It was not even challenging. To describe it accurately in English, one word alone would suffice: it was tacky. And perhaps the only consolation was the knowledge that Hans Knappertsbusch, who conducted the first cycle, thought likewise, though his comments on it were firm, private—and utterly unprintable. Later on I shall return to the question of Bayreuth and the story of its influence on productions of the *Ring* over the following fifteen years; but it was the realization that we were in for a period of hopeless inadequacy in terms of staging that made me more than ever determined to try to compensate for this by creating an *aural* production of the *Ring* whose values could not be negated or distorted by perversity on the stage.

Tension by now was at an extreme. Those who had seen the dress rehearsals formed a select and utterly bewildered group; those who had not, caught a sniff of the prevailing wind and knew that something highly controversial was happening inside the sacred confines of the Festspielhaus. There were divisions, too. The dress rehearsal of *Meistersinger*, conducted by Herbert von Karajan in an enchanting traditional production by Rudolf Hartmann, almost did not start because, according to the rumors, Wilhelm Furtwängler had taken a seat in the theater and von Karajan was not inclined to begin until he was removed. (When, years later, I worked a lot with von Karajan, I never bothered to check whether this story was true or not, but in the atmosphere of Bayreuth in 1951 anything was possible. All I learned in that long, long wait for *Meistersinger* was how damned uncomfortable the seats are. But then, it's not a theater, it's a shrine.)

Furtwängler opened the festival on July 29 with Beethoven's Ninth Symphony. On the next day we recorded the first *Parsifal.* Before it started we stood at our peephole and watched the audience fill that part of the auditorium we could see. The greatest English writer on Wagner, Ernest Newman, came in with one of the Wagner brothers. The story may or may not be true, but it is said that Newman took one long glance at the immaculately dressed audience and said to whichever Wagner he was with: "Your grandfather would never have approved of *this!*"—referring to the fact that the composer had wanted Bayreuth to be anything except a fashionable place in which to see and be seen, and had gone out of his way to provide seats at reasonable prices for students who wanted to get to know his music.

Parsifal was a profound experience. This time, Wieland Wagner's production—which we had seen in the dress rehearsal—was a masterpiece. The cast was excellent, and introduced Wolfgang Windgassen (as Parsifal) and George London (as Amfortas) to an international audience, and confirmed without any doubt that Ludwig Weber was the great Gurnemanz of his generation. Above all, there was Knappertsbusch in the pit. He loved the Bayreuth cowl, which renders the conductor and orchestra invisible to the audience. Down there he could work without the distraction of people ranged out in rows behind him; and since *Parsifal* relieved him of the problem of curtain calls—which he loathed—he was able to work in shirt sleeves and braces, and to hurl praise and abuse at the orchestra as often as he wished. In fact I had to speak to him cautiously about this the next day, for two of our microphones were close enough to catch not only his grunts and snorts (which are evident on the published recording) but several of his comments as well (which mercifully are not).

What in those green days I thought might become the Decca *Ring* began on July 31 with *Rheingold.* One of the main difficulties was that we would have so little material with which to cross-edit, and so eliminate bad mistakes: for the *Ring* was being conducted only once by Knappertsbusch, which meant we would have at our disposal one public performance of each opera, and one general rehearsal. (For *Parsifal,* on the other hand, we had two general rehearsals on tape, plus four or five public performances, and this gave ample cover to enable most mistakes

Conductor Knappertsbusch (above)
loved Bayreuth's invisible pit (right)
where he could work in shirtsleeves
undistracted by the audience. The
unhurried grandeur of his "Parsifal," a
highlight of postwar festivals until his
death in 1965, was complemented by
the production of Wieland Wagner,
whose simple, soaring set
for Act I, Scene 1, is shown below.

to be removed.) By the end of *Rheingold* that evening I knew that, quite apart from any other considerations, there would be no Decca *Ring* from Bayreuth that year: the performance was one of those unlucky occasions when everything goes wrong, and whatever cover we had in the rehearsal tape was certainly inadequate to put things even half right. *Walküre*, on August 1, fared a bit better, though it failed as a performance because of a poor Wotan, and as a recording because all sorts of devils somehow got into our machines. By the time we came to *Siegfried* we had rather lost heart in the proceedings, but *Götterdämmerung* on August 4 was another matter: it was as good as the rest had been mediocre. Varnay sang a superb Brünnhilde and Ludwig Weber was a devilishly black Hagen; and as if he had realized that the preceding parts of his *Ring* cycle had been less than magnificent, Knappertsbusch suddenly came to life and conducted with colossal power and intensity. (The Funeral March in that performance was the talk of Bayreuth for the rest of the festival: I doubt if Knappertsbusch himself ever brought off such a shattering experience again.) This time our machines behaved themselves, and even the gods seemed to be playing a part: a thunderstorm which had been threatening all day hovered in the distance throughout the first two acts, came perilously close at the start of the third (which would have ruined it from our point of view), and finally burst just when it was needed at the end of the opera.

We thought we had a masterpiece by the tail, and planned to release *Götterdämmerung* and forget the rest of the 1951 *Ring*. Our German colleagues assured us that they would negotiate immediately for the rights, and we resumed our work on *Parsifal*, of which there were several further performances to be recorded. A few weeks later, when I was editing the *Götterdämmerung* tapes in London, word came through that in no circumstances could the recording be released, though from that day to this I have never discovered exactly why. There was one factor which may or may not have determined the issue. The tiny part of Woglinde was sung by the distinguished soprano Elisabeth Schwarzkopf, who was the wife of Walter Legge of EMI, and I do not suppose he was anxious to see her name on a rival label.

In retrospect, our inability to issue the 1951 *Götterdämmerung* does not seem to matter as much as it did at the time. Before the embargo was imposed, about eight of the anticipated fourteen sides had been cut on disk, and over the years since 1951 a few copies of these test pressings appear to have leaked through Decca's usually stringent security precautions. Like anything with scarcity value, the reputation of this set has soared out of all proportion to its artistic worth. I can vouch for this, having heard the complete tape version again during the last twelve months. It would have been a worthwhile addition to the catalog in 1952, but it is of little more than curiosity value today. Knappertsbusch *is* magnificent—but the mistakes in playing and ensemble are pretty intolerable, and the audience and the prompter contribute a great deal of unwanted intrusion. Astrid Varnay sings splendidly, and her scene with Elisabeth Höngen as Waltraute is on the highest possible level. When it turned out that we could not issue the set, my own thoughts were really with Varnay, for she has long seemed to me to be the most unjustly neglected artist of her generation. (When Flagstad sang her only Sieglinde at Covent Garden, it was opposite Varnay's Brünnhilde, who seemed at that time to be Flagstad's logical and worthy successor; but the critics never seemed to take to Varnay.) The remainder of the cast of that 1951 *Götterdämmerung* left much to be desired.

There is a lesson in all this, for my impression at the time was of a performance of stupendous quality, and I would certainly have retained and defended that impression if I had not, in later life, had access to the tapes. Memory is fallible, and judgment is subject to environment and occasion. When the climate is right, when there is some special electricity in the house, a sort of communal unanimity can overtake an audience and in so doing numb the finer critical faculties. This is the stuff of which memories are made, and is a good and rewarding thing—except that, as with the 1951 *Götterdämmerung*, it cannot be preserved and repeated, for sentiment is no substitute for quality.

My last recording encounter with Bayreuth was in 1953 when we went to make *Lohengrin*. Little need be said except that the cast was only of moderate quality and we had access to far too few performances to make up anything really worthwhile. It was still felt that this was the only economic way to record Wagner, for the expense involved in taking his major works to the studio did not seem to be justified by the sales potential. But after the *Lohengrin* experience I found myself fervently hoping that I would never return to Bayreuth, at least in a recording capacity.

In the middle of 1953, I was approached by Alan Livingston of Capitol Records, Inc., who had been given my name by their classical chief, Richard Jones. He wanted me to join Capitol with a view to setting up a classical recording program in Europe; and I did so because, although I did not think Capitol stood much of a chance against the European giants, I was at that time getting nowhere in Decca. Victor Olof, who was musically in charge of Decca, was in his prime and was a very

Astrid Varnay as Brünnhilde, which she sang under Knappertsbusch in 1951. Varnay appeared in leading roles at Bayreuth throughout the 1950s.

Culshaw, Solti and his first wife Hedi Oechsli are among those enjoying a good laugh during playbacks for a Brahms "Requiem" recorded by Capitol Records in Frankfurt in 1955.

active man, with a firm disinclination to share the program with anyone else. Also, the offer came immediately after the very depressing *Lohengrin* episode at Bayreuth, so I was in the mood for a change. Almost as soon as I had done it, I knew it was a mistake, but by then it was too late.

The Capitol incident is relevant to the *Ring* recording only in the sense that it did much to consolidate my relationship with Georg Solti. It was an unenviable task to search around Europe for good artists with which to start a serious recording venture, since anyone with even moderate talent was already under contract to one company or another.

Added to this, Capitol, though full of charming people, was to a large extent inexperienced in the economics of classical music, and had a president who seemed uncertain, to say the least, of the benefits of an expansion in that direction. Unlike Decca, where it was not, and is not, difficult to get a decision on something even though it may not be the one you want, Capitol had an extraordinary hierarchy—you would suddenly find that a project which you had reason to believe had been approved had been blocked by a total stranger in a Hollywood department of which, until that moment, you had not even heard. However, I managed to set up a modest program in London and Paris, and one day I met Georg Solti by chance.

He was not happy with the way his recording career was progressing with Decca. He had still not been allowed to record an opera, and his most recent work had been an accompaniment for a concerto the soloist of which could not possibly have been less in accord with his own style and approach. It was a perverse piece of miscasting, and it had upset him. Now, one of the works I had proposed to Capitol was the Brahms *Requiem*, largely because it was inadequately represented on LP. By chance, Solti was preparing the same work for two performances in Frankfurt during 1955, and I told him I would write to Mr. Rosengarten in Zurich to see if Decca would give a release to Solti to record the *Requiem* for Capitol.

The permission was given, and we made the recording in the Frankfurt theater. The result was no masterpiece from any point of view, but the conditions of battle under which it took place were not dissimilar to those which, in totally different surroundings, were to face us again when we came to the *Ring*. In Frankfurt, I came to understand what an extraordinarily adaptable and professional man Solti had become through his years of theatrical experience. Nothing on earth would persuade him to accept an artistic result lower than the best he could get within the time available and with the forces at his disposal; but unlike so many other conductors, he was also aware that others in the studio had different and, to them, equally serious problems, and with such matters he never attempted to interfere.

The problems in Frankfurt that year included a theater which had never before been used for commercial recording; a pair of soloists who just could not see eye to eye with the Capitol business representative; a brand-new set of very beautiful portable recording equipment which had been built in Germany, the operating instructions for which were printed in the most baffling sort of technical German; and a young engineer who had been flown specially from Hollywood to operate the equipment, although he knew not a word of German and was inclined to put his personal interests ahead of Capitol's. After two disastrous sessions I had a council of war with Solti, and we decided it was a waste of his time and Capitol's money to proceed unless we could find another competent engineer locally.

Through all this mess Solti, who on the podium is one of the most dynamic conductors alive, remained calm and poised. A failure in Frankfurt would have been serious for him, for he was now the *Generalmusikdirektor* there, and not surprisingly the arrival of a major American recording company in the city had not escaped the attention of the press. In the end we found another engineer, and the *Requiem* was finished more or less on time, thanks to the sort of emergency schedule which circumstances had forced upon us, and which turned out to be a useful dress rehearsal for the far more serious emergencies which in a few years were going to face us when we embarked on the *Ring*—though with one huge difference. With the Capitol operation as it was, we were working in isolation, with no local administration to help: the nearest point of contact was New York, but the real headquarters was in Hollywood, and it was a special quirk of fate that whenever something very serious happened of the sort requiring a policy decision at director level, telephonic communication could be relied upon to break down, or become subject to the sort of delay which involved one party or the other in a meaningless conversation at four-thirty in the morning.

Wagner scarcely entered the picture during my period with Capitol, except for one ill-fated venture. I put forward the idea that a single LP containing fine performances of the closing scenes from *Rheingold* and *Walküre* would be a potential success, and a few people liked the idea. Glenn Wallichs, the president of Capitol, did not; he had an aversion to opera which nobody could change. I remember that one day when we were walking in Paris together I told him that the best French orchestra available to work for Capitol was that of the Paris Opera, though we intended to use it for French symphonic music. We were near the Opera itself at the time, and he suddenly spotted the large plaque inscribed *Académie Nationale de Musique*. "Can't we call it the Paris Academy Orchestra?" he said. "Nobody ever pays money for opera, or anything with the name opera on it."

Alan Livingston, who was then vice-president of Capitol, liked the Wagner idea and agreed we should do it with Solti or Knappertsbusch. The trouble was that having obtained one release for Solti from Decca, I thought the chances for another were slight. The whole situation was more perilous than I knew, for Capitol Records was about to terminate the arrangement through which British Decca distributed the Capitol catalog, and was deep in negotiation with EMI. Of this I had no knowledge at all. On the face of things, Capitol was going ahead with its European classical venture, and the only cause for suspicion was the farce surrounding the factory which Capitol sought to establish in Germany. No sooner had Ernest Krebs, their European business manager, found a suitable location at the agreed price than Hollywood abruptly suspended his operation and sent him off to investigate a similar site in another city. Poor Ernest spent the best part of a year scuttling from one German city to another, leaving behind a trail of deals which had been called off at the last second without any clear reason. It was, of course, merely a stalling operation to give Capitol time for its negotiations with EMI, to which company Wallichs eventually sold out.

None of this concerned me, but in May 1954 I went to Munich and had dinner with Hans Knappertsbusch, who liked the idea of recording the closing scenes of *Rheingold* and *Walküre*, but felt, as I did, that the real future lay in recording the works complete. We agreed provisionally to set up the extracts for the summer of 1955, and he felt they should be done in Munich.

It was not to happen. Early in 1955, EMI bought Capitol and immediately closed down the European classical venture. Because I had not the slightest idea that this was on the horizon, and because I had said as much to Mr. (later Sir) Edward Lewis only a week earlier, I felt obliged to call him and confirm my innocence, for it was clear that Decca would quickly lose the distribution of Capitol. He said: "When are you coming back to us?" and I returned to Decca in the autumn of that year.

It was marvelous to be back in the Hampstead studio. The place was buzzing with talk about stereo, and when Victor Olof, who had clearly opposed my return, pointed out how difficult it would be to fit me into the program because of commitments of his two new assistants, I proposed that he let me work solely on the artistic development of stereo in general, and stereo opera in particular. As he seemed to consider neither of any importance at all, he was quite happy to agree. There was no prospect of any Wagner, however, even on the most distant horizon.

Among the changes and additions to the staff when I returned to Decca was one which was to prove of vital importance to the *Ring* project. While I had been away, the studio chief, Arthur Haddy, had been driven mad by persistent applications from someone called Gordon Parry, who wanted to be a recording engineer. In the end, by dint of the tenacity which was later to prove to be one of his most remarkable

Gordon Parry, chief assistant to John Culshaw for the "Ring" recordings, adjusts a microphone boom in Vienna's Sofiensaal Studio.

qualities, he got himself an interview and a job, though by training he was a chemist. He was on recording location in Yugoslavia when I returned to the studios, but he was very much a topic of conversation. Everyone seemed to agree that he was very likable, several people thought he was mad, and nobody had any doubt about his passion for Wagner.

While still an undergraduate at Durham University he had hitchhiked to Bayreuth for the 1953 festival, and did so again in 1954, shortly before joining Decca in September of that year. Somehow, he managed to get himself on the recording team which was scheduled for Bayreuth in 1955 to make *Fliegende Holländer*, and once there he managed to persuade the Decca authorities to record both *Ring* cycles complete and all the rehearsals. Thus, for a second time, did Decca embark on a Bayreuth *Ring*, and this time there was the additional advantage of stereo equipment. (Keilberth was the conductor.) Again, conflicting contracts prevented the commercial release of the recordings, but the experience was invaluable for Gordon Parry. He came to know every aspect of the famous Bayreuth sound; and by recording the *Ring* twice in stereo, even in the course of a stage production which made no allowance for recording considerations, he gained the experience which was to prove so invaluable a few years later in Vienna. He also, I suspect, gained his first experience of something which had nothing to do with his work as a balance engineer, but which constantly obstructs the work of anyone who is single-minded in his approach to an artistic venture—the squabbling and bitterness and pettiness which some artists bring to bear when anything is likely to prove advantageous to a rival.

I first met Gordon Parry in the late autumn of 1955. He came bounding into Kingsway Hall one night, direct from Belgrade, just as I was finishing an orchestral session. With the possible exceptions of Georg Solti and Leonard Bernstein, I have never met anyone with such limitless sources of energy. Gordon was then in his middle twenties, relatively inexperienced as a recording engineer, large and, as someone aptly put it, bouncy. When it came to Wagner, he was a carbon copy of my late colleague Christopher Jennings, for he had the same enthusiasm coupled with a genuine knowledge of the music and the drama. There are plenty of people in and out of the music profession who wear enthusiasms as other people wear shirts, and change them just as often; but Gordon's knowledge of Wagner was based on years of enjoyment and study, and his feeling for music was, and is, instinctive. There are some people who find that the maltreatment of music in any way affects them painfully; and over the years he and I have walked out of more ill-prepared, ill-conducted, or ill-sung operas than either of us would care to count. If this is considered too idealistic, so be it; for in the course of an average year, one has to put up with enough suffering in the course of duty in the studio without smiling through it on social occasions.

The elements which were soon to fuse into the material for the *Ring* recording were now unwittingly coming together. I still believed that in Georg Solti we had the great Wagner conductor of our time. Decca had the Vienna Philharmonic securely under contract, and for Wagner it remains the greatest orchestra in the world. Stereo was about to be launched on an unwilling world; and by good chance we had an engineer who not only fervently believed in Wagner, but who agreed with me that the proper use of stereo would transform the world of recorded opera. There were still some major obstacles, including the expense, the understandable commercial uncertainty about whether the public would respond to stereo, the absence of a major Wagnerian soprano on our otherwise unrivaled list of singers, and the fact that Victor Olof did not really care for Wagner. The *Ring*, if it was ever to happen, needed another stroke of luck; and it came in 1956 with the re-emergence from retirement of Kirsten Flagstad.

At the end of the war, Kirsten Flagstad was already a legend to thousands who had never heard her in the flesh. In fact it was a generation that had heard virtually no Wagner at all, except in the form of concert excerpts and 78-rpm recordings of "detachable" pieces like the *Liebestod*. I know that I was taken to a performance of *Meistersinger* at the Empire Theatre, Liverpool, either just before or just after the outbreak of war—and that, until 1946, was that. But among the records that were carried around to various parts of the globe during the war by the lunatic fringe of aircrew/music-lovers in my particular Swordfish squadron were those of Backhaus, Toscanini, Schnabel, Heifetz—and Kirsten Flagstad.

By the summer of 1946 there was already some Wagner activity for those who felt starved or who merely wanted to gain experience of the music. Marjorie Lawrence and Sir Thomas Beecham gave the new generation its first taste of *Tristan*, and in December of that year Decca brought over Paul Schöffler from Vienna to sing the closing scene of *Walküre* at the Albert Hall and to record the same excerpt a day or two later. I heard Flagstad for the first time in the flesh on February 7, 1947, and again in what I think was a concert performance of *Walküre*, Act Three, on May 29. The sheer sonority of the voice surpassed every expectation, and those of us who were hearing her for the first time had little patience with the older generation who were inclined to grumble about her inflexibility and compare her unfavorably with Frida Leider and Florence Austral. To us, for better or worse, Flagstad was *the* Brünnhilde and *the* Isolde, and nobody else, alive or dead, came within miles of her. It was with the deepest envy that I had to accept her contractual status as an exclusive artist with a major competitor, as a result of which it seemed unlikely that there would ever be a chance of working with her.

Although in the end she was to play so small a part in our *Ring*, I cannot help feeling that without Kirsten Flagstad the project might not have happened at all. She was a remarkable and very lovable woman, and I doubt if she ever realized how much she helped and inspired everyone around her during the last years of her life.

Before she came to us she had had an unhappy recording career. From the mid-thirties she had been the great Brünnhilde of the age; but the 78-rpm record was a clumsy medium for Wagner, and Flagstad had to be content with extracts from the *Ring*. She did not help matters by insisting, whenever she could, on a particular conductor of her own choice, who was not—to be charitable—among the great podium talents of the century. Still, there are a few RCA and EMI records which manage to give us some idea of what her voice was like in its absolute prime. Then came the war, and her decision to return to her home and family in Norway, despite the German occupation and the rumor that her husband had collaborated with the invaders. I do not know the facts about this; but I do know that whatever did happen delayed her return to the stage after the war, and marked her for the rest of her life. She was in many ways a simple woman, in that she followed her instincts. I am sure she returned to Norway because she wanted to be with her family, and I think she suffered terribly when, after the war, some sections of the press attributed her motives to politics and money. When I first met her in Norway, ten years after the war, it was hard at first to grasp that she was not a popular public figure in her own country . . . yet her patriotism was unbounded. Probably the happiest moment of her professional life was when she was appointed director of the Norwegian Opera, though it coincided with the first attack of the disease which was eventually to kill her.

She came to Decca by a strange and circuitous route. In the early nineteen-fifties, when she was still active at Covent Garden and elsewhere, EMI finally embarked on a complete recording of *Tristan und Isolde* with Wilhelm Furtwängler conducting. It was, and is, a very

Kirsten Flagstad works at her desk during her tenure as head of the Norwegian Opera in the late 1950s. She generously devoted her energies to raising the company's standards.

great performance. It seems that Flagstad was afraid of, or even incapable of, the lightning high C's which occur when the lovers first meet in Act Two, and therefore they were sung for her by Elisabeth Schwarzkopf, who was presumably persuaded partly by her friendship with Flagstad, and partly because she is the wife of EMI's recording director, Walter Legge. It was, in my opinion, a justifiable and well-executed trick. You cannot do the scene at all without the top C's in place; and I doubt if anyone but the participants would ever have known or cared had not someone, about a year later, opened his mouth to the press and revealed the whole story. (Oddly enough, at the time of the recording I was living in the same house as a violinist in the Philharmonia Orchestra, and I remember being very puzzled one day when he returned from a *Tristan* session and said that the sequence they had just recorded involved *three* women. No such scene exists in the piece, and despite his insistence I assumed he had made a mistake—after all, the Philharmonia was a new orchestra with no operatic experience at all. In fact he was right: the women were Flagstad as Isolde, Blanche Thebom as Brangäne, and Elisabeth Schwarzkopf to provide the top C's.)

The newspaper uproar which followed the revelation embittered Flagstad for the rest of her life. When we came to know her there were only a few things that were sure to upset her: she hated to be called Flag*stadt*, as if pronounced in German; she hated all photographers except Hans Wild, and even he had a struggle; and she hated any mention of the EMI *Tristan* affair. In retrospect, I suppose it was foolish of EMI to imagine that the matter could be kept quiet. Somehow, somewhere, it would have leaked out, and a plain, dignified announcement of the facts at the time of the original release would never had become an issue for the front pages of the national press, nor an excuse for the silliest outburst of moral indignation on the part of a few opera critics that it has ever been my misfortune to read. This time, they screamed at the top of their little voices, technical license had gone too far in its ability to assist artistic endeavor. (It was neither the first nor the last of such outbursts, as we shall see.) Flagstad, at home in Norway, replied bluntly that she would never record, or sing in public, again.

About a year later, when I was working in Paris, the American pianist Julius Katchen surprised me by saying that he and Flagstad had a mutual friend whose firm impression it was that she might be persuaded to make a few more records, though certainly not for EMI. Katchen had heard that her voice was in marvelous condition, and that she had maintained her vocal exercises throughout the years of retirement. All this turned out to be true, for at about the same time, in London, Flagstad's actor friend Bernard Miles had been in touch with Decca and had offered his services for the tricky assignment of a go-between in an attempt to persuade the reluctant Flagstad to make a trial recording in our studios. Without his efforts, and those of Frank Lee who was at that time the artists' manager of Decca, I am sure she would have stayed in retirement for the rest of her life.

The negotiations with Flagstad began in 1955, and a provisional contract was drawn up covering some *Lieder* recitals and an LP of Wagner to be made in Vienna. Early in 1956, shortly after I rejoined Decca, Bernard Miles let us know that Flagstad had recently given her farewell performance of *Götterdämmerung* on the Norwegian radio, and had expressed a strong wish to see the performance released on commercial gramophone records. He suggested—and I am sure he was right—that this might prove something of a test case for our goodwill: there were plenty of other companies interested in the tapes, but Flagstad, who at that time had not recorded a note for us, would consider our acquisition of them as a confirmation that her "marriage" to Decca was serious.

The trouble was that nobody in Decca had heard the tapes, and there was little information available about them except that the Siegfried was Set Svanholm and the conductor Oivin Fjeldstad, who was musical director of the Norwegian Radio. The policy of Decca has always, and rightly, been against the issue of radio tapes except in very special circumstances, but this time we felt obliged to investigate. I was sent to Oslo on March 8, 1956, and rang Flagstad at her home in Kristiansand the next morning. She answered the phone herself, and I had a shock: her speaking voice was identical to Kathleen Ferrier's—the same richness and warmth, the same laugh, the same hesitation. In that brief conversation, Flagstad suggested that I should go to the radio station and hear the *Götterdämmerung* tapes, and meet her on March 12, when she would be coming to Oslo on business.

Further shocks were in store at the radio station the next day. I had been told that her "farewell" performance was complete, but it was far from that: the Norn scene with which *Götterdämmerung* opens was missing, and so was the scene between Alberich and Hagen at the start of Act Two. Even less explicable was the omission of the entire orchestral interlude in Act One which separates the passage known as Hagen's Watch and the Brünnhilde/Waltraute scene. In all, something like forty minutes were missing from this "complete" performance. The rest of it was, to put it gently, a very mixed bag. On the one hand, Flagstad and Svanholm sang well, and the sound was acceptable within the limits of a radio transcription; on the other, the rest of the cast left very much to be desired, and the conductor, though an excellent musician, was fathoms out of depth in a work of such dimensions. I could not possibly be enthusiastic about what I had heard, and advised London accordingly. I said the thing could only be considered for issue as a gesture towards Flagstad, and with a view to preserving her performance in the part of the *Götterdämmerung* Brünnhilde; and I recommended that if we decided to go ahead on that basis, we should at the same time take steps to restore the missing scenes, without which the performance was a travesty.

London quoted a figure for the acquisition of the tapes, and said that the missing scenes could be recorded in not more than two three-hour sessions. Then began a nightmare. The Norwegian Musicians' Union saw the chance of a lifetime to make a lot of trouble and possibly a lot of money. Apart from that, the only day on which we could have the hall where *Götterdämmerung* had been recorded was the 14th—four days away, and we had no Alberich and no Norns. And before we could go ahead, contracts had to be negotiated with every other artist who had appeared in the cast, plus the conductor, orchestra, chorus, and the radio company itself. Never has so much effort been expended on something which was, frankly, inadequate from all standpoints but one—the preservation for posterity of Flagstad's performance. (And even then there were reservations—her Immolation scene, for instance, did not compare with the earlier versions she had recorded.)

On March 12, I went to see Flagstad at her Oslo hotel. Walking there, I was full of apprehension and excitement. I had known her voice for fifteen years on records, and had admired her on the stage for nine years. I could not imagine what she would be like as a person, though I had a suspicion she could be a handful. (Bernard Miles had said repeatedly that she was the nicest person under the sun; on the other hand, most people in the record industry had read Charles O'Connell's *The Other Side of the Record*, which contained unflattering portraits of several major artists, including Kirsten Flagstad.) Years later, when we were having dinner at the Stadtkrug in Vienna, Kirsten suddenly turned to me and said, "You were always a bit frightened of me when we first met, weren't you?" I readily admitted it. "I'd seen you too often in the second act of *Götterdämmerung*," I told her, and she burst out laughing. But it was true: she projected such intensity in her fury about her betrayal by Siegfried that it was impossible to believe that the same tempestuous quality was not part of her own character.

She let me into her hotel room in Oslo. She was a striking, beautiful woman in jet black and diamonds, and on the table was a bottle of champagne and two glasses. I think I was struck dumb for a while, but as soon as we had settled down she asked what I had thought of the *Götterdämmerung* tapes, and I told her, as gently as I could, that we were prepared to go ahead unless she would like to consider remaking the work under proper conditions in Vienna, with an international cast and a Wagner conductor around her. (I had no authority for this, but I knew that Decca could do so much better and felt reasonably confident that my superiors would agree.) She would not hear of it. The point for her was that in the radio performance she was appearing with a cast of Norwegians; and this, because of her intense patriotism, meant more to her than the musical or dramatic qualities which might have been obtained with an international cast. At the same time, there was no trace of blackmail in her views: she was certainly going to honor her new contract with Decca; but if Decca turned down the *Götterdämmerung* tapes, she would do everything in her power to make them available to any other company that might care to bid.

I tried again to indicate the virtues of recording in Vienna (a city which at that time I had never visited), but she was not to be persuaded. One of the problems was that she was not exactly in love with Decca's musical director, Victor Olof, because she considered his manner pompous, whereas she was very fond of Frank Lee, who was then head of the artists' department but did not direct classical sessions. I think she had made an unfair snap judgment about Victor, but there was no changing her views. Flagstad had put him into a pigeonhole and that was that.

I tried another avenue. We could only have the hall on the 14th and we had no Alberich and no Norns. This was a tactical mistake, for she immediately produced names (Norwegians again, of course), and pointed out that all of them happened to be free on the 14th—she had checked to make sure. She then added that there were a few parts of her own performance with which she was dissatisfied, and which she wanted to remake during the two sessions Decca had allocated. I got the message very clearly: the Decca/Flagstad relationship—quite apart from contracts—turned entirely on our willingness to go ahead with this *Götterdämmerung*. And while I did not agree with her about its virtues, I could see her point: she was campaigning for something in which, rightly or wrongly, she believed most fervently—the creation of a Norwegian National Opera, which she thought might be launched by the release of a *Götterdämmerung* recording in which she and Set Svanholm appeared in the principal roles.   *Continued on page 48*

Flagstad: A first lady

When Kirsten Flagstad agreed to sing the role of Fricka in the Solti recording of *Das Rheingold*, she was 63 and had been singing professionally for 45 years. No less amazing than the span of her career was its unhurried, ungrasping nature. "I believe in gradually growing into things," she once said; and with the steady patience of the Norwegian country folk she slowly built her initially small soprano into the uniquely lustrous and powerful voice that critics often were to compare with a force of nature. Only in

Flagstad, at age nine, poses demurely for the camera with a flower in her hair and the dress she wore to her first dance.

Nuri in "Tiefland" was the rol in which the 18-year-old Flag stad made her debut in 191

# of opera

Flagstad wore harem pants for "Her Excellency," a musical comedy she sang in Finland in 1928.

Flagstad's serene beauty is strikingly shown in this early Norwegian portrait.

The team of Flagstad and Melchior in "Tristan und Isolde" guaranteed sold-out houses for the Depression-starved Metropolitan in 1930s. During her career she sang 182 Isoldes.

Flagstad in full voice as Kundry in "Parsifal." She learned the role in 11 days during her first Met season.

1929, after years of singing operetta and the lighter operatic soprano parts, did she tackle her first Wagnerian role, and, aside from two engagements at Bayreuth, she appeared only in Scandinavian theaters until the age of 40. She was on the verge of retiring when her unheralded debut at the Metropolitan Opera in 1935 thrust her into the international spotlight. After seven seasons as the Met's brightest star, she went home in 1941 to Nazi-occupied Norway to be with her husband, a prosperous businessman, and only resumed her career in 1947. At Rudolf Bing's invitation she returned to the Met for two more seasons in 1951 and 1952 and then gradually stopped singing in public. But with her indestructible voice she continued to record prolifically until her final, fatal illness.

Flagstad knits calmly in her dressing room at Covent Garden, where she made her London debut in May 1936.

Paramount lured Flagstad to Hollywood to sing Brünnhilde's War Cry atop a plaster crag in "The Big Broadcast of 1938."

Clutching a loving cup, Flagstad bows with Met manager Bing after her farewell "Alcestis" in 1952.

The Lord Mayor of Oslo whirls Flagstad around the dance floor during a Norwegian Opera Ball in 1959.

On March 14 we held our two sessions in the University Hall, agreement somehow having been reached with the various artists and organizations involved. The same radio technicians who had worked on the broadcast did their best to match the sound for the inserts, but the artists were grotesquely underrehearsed and there was hardly time for retakes (not that I think they would have brought much improvement, for most of the artists were sight-reading). It was all very depressing. Although she was only involved in two tiny corrections, each running for a matter of seconds, Flagstad turned up at the beginning and stayed all day. She presented a sight I and my colleagues were soon to find very familiar—that of an ample, placid woman, simply dressed and wearing rimless glasses, apparently intent on her knitting to the exclusion of everything else while in fact keeping a very close ear on the music and doing what she could, quietly, to help her colleagues with music which she knew far more intimately than they. At the end of the second session we ran out of time, and the orchestral interlude between the first and second scenes of Act One was never recorded. My gloomy feelings about the whole affair were not relieved by the conductor's well-meant but naïve assurance that the interlude was really of no importance at all, and had been inserted by Wagner to provide adequate time for the scene change required at that point. At the end of a day like that, I did not even try to put him right.

Decca had been very shrewd in pursuing this radio *Götterdämmerung*, despite its considerable failings. The fact that we had done it utterly convinced Flagstad of two things: first, that she had signed with a company that would keep its promises and take risks on her behalf; and second, that there was a huge potential for the sort of Norwegian State Opera in which she passionately believed. She was wrong on the second point; but the basis for the happy and fruitful relationship which existed between Decca and Flagstad until her death was the company's willingness to pay rather a lot of money for a Norwegian broadcast of *Götterdämmerung* in 1956. Had we turned it down, I am convinced she would have gone back into her shell. On the other hand, though the topic never arose between us, I am equally sure she knew how inadequate it was. A stubborn *prima donna* may or may not respond to persuasion; but a stubborn *prima donna* on a patriotic campaign is simply not to be budged.

There was not much anyone could do with the Norwegian *Götterdämmerung*. We spliced in the additional sequences, which matched the rest of the work surprisingly well; and we shed a tear for the missing orchestral interlude. The whole effort was nothing to be very proud of, but when Flagstad came over to make some song recitals in March 1956, we played the result to her, and she seemed pleased.

In addition to the many songs she recorded on that visit, she had agreed to sing Gluck's *Alceste* for the BBC; and Decca had decided to make a recording of the entire opera immediately after the broadcast. This was to be her first major undertaking on records since the EMI *Tristan* in 1952, and it was an ill-fated venture from the start. I went to the BBC studio on the evening of April 22 to find Flagstad battling with a terrible cold. There was no nonsense about this—she was ill, and should have been in bed, but her innate professionalism and concern for the rest of the cast had led her to come to the studio on time. Somehow, she got through that evening, though by the end she was on the point of collapse. We were scheduled to start *Alceste* in Walthamstow Town Hall on April 25, and it was clear to me that she would be in no condition to sing on that day. We quickly rearranged the schedule to enable Flagstad to start later, but, as was to happen to us many times during the *Ring* recording, this turned out to be a mixed blessing. An intelligent operatic schedule should try at all costs to spread the strain, so that the principals do not have too much tiring music to sing on any one session; and the effects of rescheduling *Alceste* to let Flagstad get over her cold meant that the other singers had to work much harder during her absence, and that she became obliged to record her part in considerably fewer sessions than had been originally allocated. One always dreams of extending the recording period indefinitely, and thus making life easy for everyone—but it never works. In the case of *Alceste*, the tenor, Raoul Jobin, had to leave for engagements in Paris by a certain day, and the hall in which we were working was not available after May 2. We told Flagstad that she would have to start on April 28, three days later than originally planned, for otherwise we would stand no chance of completing her part.

On April 27 she called me at home and said she felt much better— indeed, she was going to a theater that evening. On the 28th she sang two magnificent sessions, and everyone felt certain that *Alceste* was, so to speak, back on the rails again. There was no session on the 29th, but on the morning of the 30th she called to say that she had a bad throat and feared she had caught another chill. We were exactly four sessions from the end of *Alceste*, and with no time in reserve. I asked her to come to the studio, and promised that we would do everything possible to make the recording easy for her.

I feel some reticence in describing the next two days. If I had had more experience or more authority I have no doubt that I would have stopped the sessions. Poor Flagstad was considerably worse than she had been on the Sunday of the broadcast, but she was determined to go through with the recording. I was also disinclined to persuade her to stop, because I could see no chance of reassembling the cast for at least a year, and it was evident that Flagstad herself set great store by the completion, on schedule, of her first commercial recording in five years. She fought a tremendous physical battle with herself, and I am afraid the result is evident on the record. In retrospect, I blame myself. The world was not exactly panting for the release of *Alceste*, and it would have been wiser to have waited until the cast could be reassembled. Yet there was the anxiety that Flagstad would assume responsibility for the whole breakdown and take herself off into retirement forever. So we finished *Alceste*, and wished, at the end, that we had never started.

On May 4, I went to Paris, where we were to have a month of sessions with the Conservatoire Orchestra under Knappertsbusch and Solti, among others. I spent a lot of time with Knappertsbusch on that trip, and in addition to recording he conducted a magnificent *Tristan* at the Paris Opera with Astrid Varnay in even better voice than in 1951. (For her A and A flat cries of *"Rache! Tod!"* at the end of the Act One narration she dared to go right to the back of the vast stage, which is often a trick to cover up some vocal deficiency, though this time it was anything but that. I have never heard the passage sung by anyone with such penetration and intensity. Knappertsbusch blew her a kiss.)

When Solti arried in Paris, Knappertsbusch left for recordings in Vienna where, with Kirsten Flagstad, he was to make a beautiful record of Wagner's *Wesendonck* songs. As usual, Victor Olof was in charge in Vienna, but there had been some changes which were soon to erupt into a crisis. With the idea of injecting some new blood into Vienna, Arthur Haddy had sent Gordon Parry and James Brown to take over the technical responsibilities in that city; and to add to the problems, Decca had just moved to a new recording location called the Sofiensaal which, though an unknown factor then, was soon to become the base for the *Ring* recording.

My final session in Paris was scheduled for May 31, and I had booked a flight to London on June 2. On the morning of June 1, I had a telephone call from Decca in London to say that Victor Olof had resigned. He had accepted a post as artists' manager for His Master's Voice, but had suggested that he might be allowed to conclude the current series of Decca sessions in Vienna. Decca, however, thought otherwise, and I was told to go to Vienna and be prepared to take over immediately. In this job you get used to playing the airline schedules, and I was not particularly worried to find that all direct flights from Paris were full and had closed waiting lists. I asked Air France to route me through Zurich or Frankfurt or indeed any city in Europe which had a connection to Vienna. It proved impossible. While all this was going on, Mr. Rosengarten rang from Zurich to ask why I wasn't already *in* Vienna; but not even by flying back to London was there any means of getting to Vienna faster than the train which left Paris that evening. It was the only time in my life when I have been told to go somewhere quickly and have had to admit defeat.

I arrived in Vienna by train on June 3. Like most foreigners arriving there I was unprepared for the drabness of the city. True, it had been occupied until 1954; but it had not suffered like Berlin or Hamburg or Cologne during the war, and was it not in any case the legendary city of wine, women, and song? My orders were to go straight to my hotel and remain there; in no circumstances was I to go to the Sofiensaal where, by a strange irony, Knappertsbusch was recording the funeral march from *Götterdämmerung* as a fill-up for a Bruckner symphony. I had no idea of the turmoil that had been created by Olof's resignation, for at that stage I had no experience of the Austrian mind. Some years earlier I had taken over the bulk of the Decca program with the Amsterdam Concertgebouw Orchestra, and the transition had been smooth and friendly; the same had happened in Paris, when Olof found himself unable to handle all the Conservatoire sessions. Naïvely, I imagined that a similar transition might take place in Vienna.

The Viennese thrive on situations. Indeed, one can safely say that if at any moment no situation exists it becomes immediately necessary to invent one. Over the preceding five or six years Victor Olof had become a sort of father figure to the Vienna Philharmonic, and the effect of his resignation, plus the threatened appearance on the scene of an unknown and much younger man, created an atmosphere of tension and suspicion that was unbearable. Matters were not helped by two other radical changes which happened to coincide with this event: for Decca had just changed its recording hall from the famous Musikvereinssaal (a great concert hall but a disappointing recording studio) to the Sofiensaal in the third district of Vienna, and a new team of engineers headed by Gordon Parry and James Brown had taken over from those who had worked in Vienna over the past five years. The Philharmonic does not like change of any sort; it was suspicious of these new faces, and objected strenuously to moving to the Sofiensaal. It was a dance hall, and a

The Sofiensaal, scene of the recording sessions, stands on a drab, undistinguished street in Vienna's third district.

place where conventions were held; at one time it had even been a swimming pool; and the fact that Johann Strauss had conducted there during its era as a concert hall made little difference to the Philharmonic, whose members found it undignified as a setting and inconvenient as a location.

It takes a long time to get to know the qualities of the Vienna Philharmonic, and in the weeks that followed Olof's departure for London I know I would have lost my nerve completely had it not been for the constant support and the streams of advice I received from Mr. Rosengarten in Zurich. He had no particular reason to have confidence in me, for he scarcely knew me; but he was not going to let anything get the

When the Sofiensaal is not being used as a recording studio, it reverts to its traditional role as a dance hall. This 19th century sketch shows a masquerade ball attended by composers Liszt (left, in cassock), Offenbach (center, in pince-nez) and Wagner (right, in beret).

upper hand over Decca. He could see the situation in perspective; I could not. One night, during my third and most miserable week, I became convinced that I would never make a personal contact with the orchestra. Over the years I had learned a lot about orchestral psychology, but my experience got me nowhere in Vienna. As bad luck had it, the sessions I was handling were with a very elderly conductor who was on the verge of senility. He could not make up his mind about the tempo for the first movement of the symphony we were recording, and at the end of the second session he had played the piece no less than eleven times with eleven different tempi. I could do nothing to alter his indecision. The orchestra, understandably bored by all this, assumed that it was my fault and sent complaints to Zurich and London about the way in which sessions were being mishandled. I decided that the only decent thing to do was to resign, and I told Gordon Parry. "Don't do anything rash," he said. "Give it a few more months. One day we might make a *Ring* here. . . ."

I know now what was wrong with my approach to the Vienna Philharmonic. "They're all professors," a colleague had told me before I went to Vienna, "and you have to treat them with kid gloves." I had taken that advice, and that was my mistake: for the particular quality you need in order to work in Vienna, apart from musicianship, is the ability to lead and take decisions. By being deferential, and by openly showing humility to an orchestra of such fame and distinction, I had chosen a hopelessly wrong course. Years later, long after the Vienna Philharmonic had presented us, as a recording team, with its coveted Nicolai Medal, much wiser words were spoken, again by Gordon, who said: "There's only one way to work in Vienna—you have to *organize* the Viennese." Far from being said with contempt, it was said with love and understanding.

Vienna is a village in more senses than one. Its people do not behave like the inhabitants of a great capital city, and there is generally a remarkable unawareness of the rest of the world. No city with such a history could be entirely without architectural distinction, yet Vienna has surprisingly little and what it has is frequently obscured by some of the dreariest, least imaginative modern building on the continent of Europe. The city as such lacks the one thing you expect it to have, which is charm—the very quality which is the essence of Viennese music and Viennese musicianship. Vienna still lives in its past, with what I suspect to be highly colored memories of the days of the Habsburg Empire and dear old Franz Josef. (That same Viennese conductor who had commented so piggishly after the death of Christopher Jennings burst into tears one day as we passed a statue of Franz Josef in a Vienna park. His

Cartoonist's view of Herbert von Karajan's delicate balancing act during the period when he ran the Vienna State Opera, the Salzburg Festival and the Berlin Philharmonic simultaneously. Karajan was constant headline news in Vienna until he quit the opera in 1964.

sentimental stories about Franz Josef's kindliness, tolerance, and goodwill to all men were interspersed with positively murderous reflections about Herbert von Karajan's career and intentions.)

The famous Viennese coffeehouse tradition of gossip and scandal—another village trait—has shown no sign of waning in the second half of the twentieth century, and has no parallel that I know of elsewhere, largely because in other big cities most people are too busy or too taciturn or too ambitious to indulge in sustained malice with such abandon. Minding one's own business is strictly unknown to the Viennese. It takes a while to become accustomed to this, and to learn not to take offense—to accept, in fact, that the English approach to life is as far removed from the Viennese as can be imagined. During the era of Herbert von Karajan at the State Opera there happened, in the rest of the world, several events of some international importance; but in Vienna, the topic of conversation was von Karajan. It was carried on not just by people involved in the musical world, but by people who, like the majority of Viennese, have never been inside either the opera or the concert hall. He was headline news almost every day, and when he was not people wanted to know why he was not. His clothes, his cars, his aeroplane, his domestic life—these and a lot of other things would keep coffeehouse conversation going for hours. When, as a foreigner who happened to be working a lot with von Karajan at the time, I made it clear that I found such talk exceedingly boring, I was regarded as a fool.

The compensating factor is that the Viennese capacity for talk and intrigue is so great that it leaves very little time for action, and the inevitable result of so many conflicting opinions is a sort of organizational paralysis. A large enough crisis in the government or the opera will eventually produce a summit meeting at which those who really hold the authority will spend many hours deciding that the wisest decision is to agree amicably not to take a decision. This endearing national attribute must of course produce its opposite now and again, and an efficient Viennese is probably the most efficient person on earth. He has to be.

All the same, there is a flexibility in Austrian life that is both precious and pleasant. People have not lost the art of relaxation, and the countryside around the city is of surpassing loveliness. The old joke is really very apt: a situation in the rest of the world may be serious but not hopeless, whereas in Vienna any situation is hopeless but not serious. And the personal charm inevitably comes in. Throughout the *Ring* recording we have from time to time needed to use a part of the Sofiensaal which is bounded by a main road, which makes recording impossible unless the road can be closed to traffic. The police have never failed to help us, no matter what the inconvenience to them (to say nothing of the diverted motorists). When, as it happened, we did not need to ask for the road to be closed for a period of almost eighteen months, the

Viennese, young and old, gather in one of the city's many coffeehouses to read, relax—and gossip. Behind-the-scenes intrigue at the State Opera is a favorite topic of conversation over "Kaffee mit Schlag" (coffee with whipped cream).

police turned up one day to ask us if they had displeased us in any way, and to offer their road-closing service at a moment's notice. This is, I think, enchanting; it is the more agreeable side of the village mentality.

Out of this strange social structure has emerged a musical tradition and a style of musicianship which is unique and, I believe, unrivaled. Any professional can name orchestras in Europe and America whose standards of technical proficiency leave the Vienna Philharmonic at the post; but no other orchestra in the world can approach the Vienna Philharmonic when it comes to what an orchestra is *about*—the sense or instinct through which suddenly a hundred men become a single musical instrument of infinite flexibility, the sense through which those men unanimously and instantly feel the contour of a phrase, the hush of a diminuendo or the buildup of a crescendo. It is achieved by knowing what your neighbor is doing, and doing it with him. It is an unspoken tradition handed from generation to generation. Tone is the secret of the Vienna Philharmonic: the rich, unforced tone which makes it the perfect instrument for Mozart and Schubert on the one hand, and for Wagner and Richard Strauss on the other.

It is not an easy orchestra to come to know or to work with. Its special qualities cannot be produced merely by raising a baton, and when the orchestra is bored or depressed or overworked the results can be disappointing. This is the whole point: the tradition is not something material. It cannot be analyzed, except in the most superficial terms, and therefore cannot be copied. It is the most precious jewel in the heritage of orchestral performance in Europe, and it deserves, and should receive, every form of protection to ensure its survival into the future. For me, and for my colleagues, Vienna *is* the Vienna Philharmonic. It has been more than an education to get to know and understand its qualities: it has been an honor.

By the end of 1956 the new recording crew was beginning to settle down in Vienna, and we were at last getting the measure of the Sofiensaal. The neatest way to place an orchestra in an empty hall will not necessarily produce the best sound, and for months we had experimented with the orchestra in all sorts of different positions before finally choosing the precise situation it has occupied ever since. (It would surprise the layman to know what a difference a matter of a few feet one way or the other can make.) After six months my colleagues and I were learning to understand the qualities of the Vienna Philharmonic, for despite a bewildering inconsistency it was as clear as day that under the right conductor the orchestra was in a class of its own. (Some sessions under Fritz Reiner in September of that year had been a revelation.) Gordon and I talked a lot about Wagner, and he was surprised by my enthusiasm for Solti, with whose work he was not very familiar. Memories of the Solti *Walküre* in Munich began to stir again, and at the international repertoire meeting in November, I put forward the idea that we should record the work complete in 1957. To my great joy, it was approved.

Almost at once we ran into trouble. The whole venture depended on Flagstad's willingness to sing Brünnhilde, and I had a suspicion that, still suffering from the memory of those interpolated top C's in the EMI *Tristan*, she might refuse to attempt the opening of Act Two. So it was—and nothing would induce her to try. Furthermore, she wanted to sing the Act One Sieglinde, and hinted that her willingness to record Act Three would depend on our agreement to that proposal. Our dream of a complete *Walküre* vanished overnight.

There seemed to be only one solution, which was to set up two completely separate recordings of Act One (with Flagstad as Sieglinde) and Act Three (with Flagstad as Brünnhilde). To make it clear that these were not intended to be sections of a complete *Walküre*, we decided to use different conductors, and engaged Knappertsbusch for Act One (to be made in the autumn) and Solti for Act Three (scheduled for the spring). It was an uneasy compromise, but the best we could do in the circumstances. As it happened, it was the ideal solution from the long-term viewpoint, for we were not at that stage really experienced enough to tackle anything so difficult as a complete *Walküre*, and Solti had never before worked with the Vienna Philharmonic. Through our experiments in 1957 we were able to learn what mistakes to avoid when it came to *Rheingold* in 1958, and in several senses the Solti/Flagstad recording of *Walküre*, Act Three, turned out to be a sort of "pilot" scheme for the Decca *Ring*.

The arrangements pleased Flagstad. On January 21, 1957, she wrote to me from San Francisco:

Thank you for your letters of December 17th, 28th and January 15th. There really were no answers needed for the first ones and you don't know how difficult it is to find time to write letters when I am with my dear ones.

I have the different dates for the recordings, and I keep my fingers crossed that the beginning of May will be for *Walküre*, Act Three. I plan to go from London to Zurich to study the Brahms-Mahler suggestions with someone who knows. I cannot make up my mind whether to choose *Kindertotenlieder* or *Lieder eines fahrenden Gesellen*. When do you need that decision? The *Alto Rhapsody* is fine for me, I think. . . .

Surrounding and indeed enclosing the world of professional opera is an international community of gossips and intentional troublemakers. These people are certainly not musicians, and do not come within any sensible definition of music-lover. They are interested only in playing off one singer against another; and since, as a race, singers are fairly simpleminded, it is not surprising that time and time again they fall victim to the irresponsible chatter of the sycophants. Flagstad was no exception, for on her way back from San Francisco she called at New York and got involved with some fans who evidently thought they knew more about Decca's intentions than the company itself. Flagstad evidently believed them, and wrote to me at once:

> Some musical friends in New York talked a lot and touched a lot of different matters. First, I heard that the Italian tenor di Stefano (or was it del Monaco—I can never tell the difference?) was going to record *Walküre* Act One with me. I was very disappointed. He is, I am sure, an excellent singer, but he is studying the role *now*, and Wagner is not that easy to sing or, rather interpret, and should be sung by someone who has done the role on the stage many times. If you want my suggestion, I can think of only one: Set Svanholm. . . .

I wrote back at once and reassured her that we had already engaged Svanholm, and implored her not to get so disturbed about the gossips. (It made no difference, for we were to have a worse example of the same kind of thing when we were trying to schedule *Rheingold* in 1958.) Evidently the incident was still on her mind, for in her next letter she started to have doubts about recording the whole of Act Three. What had started as a complete *Walküre* and had then been reduced to two separate acts was now about to disintegrate entirely. "I would much prefer," she wrote,

> to do only the second part of Act Three, from "*War es so schmählich*" to the end. If we do not have the Walkyries and Sieglinde for the third act it might be easier to find a better time than the end of May and the beginning of June. To be very frank, I am scared of the heat, and am afraid it will hurt my singing, too. . . .
> I have changed my mind about the *Alto Rhapsody*, I don't think it suits me well enough. We have lovely cold weather with lots of snow and it is just beautiful. I wonder why I don't stay at home in Norway all the time. I love it here. . . .

The danger signs were unmistakable. I rang her in Kristiansand, and she admitted that the talk about an Italian tenor had worried her so much that she had gone off the whole *Walküre* project. I told her that we were in a terrible fix, because contracts had already been made with

the other artists and I could see no way of getting out of them. She thought for a while, then agreed to record the whole of Act Three.

Meanwhile, I was talking to Georg Solti and Gordon Parry about how to tackle this technically challenging piece. We wanted to take the first steps towards making a proper production for stereo, and the first requirement was a stage on which to work. (There is a stage with a proscenium arch in the Sofiensaal, but it is very small, and in common with all such areas it is acoustically "dead," which means that unlike the rest of the hall it lacks reverberation.) Gordon and Jimmy Brown made up a plan for an extension which would grow out from the stage into the hall, thus giving us the space we required while taking advantage of

Flagstad and bass-baritone Otto Edelmann stand in the center of a specially constructed extension of the Sofiensaal stage as they record Act III of "Die Walküre" with Solti and the Vienna Philharmonic in 1957. Note how stage is marked off into squares to help plot dramatic movements for stereo.

the acoustical qualities of the main hall itself. In retrospect, what seemed at the time a very adventurous and daring thing was in fact extremely modest compared with the stage requirements we later found necessary for *Rheingold* and the rest of the *Ring*. We were cutting our teeth.

Flagstad wrote to confirm the dates, and added a note that was typical of her generosity, not common in the world of opera, towards other singers:

> Ingrid Bjoner made a sensation as Donna Anna in Oslo. I heard the performance on the radio and was very much impressed, she was excellent. Nothing was too difficult for her in this very difficult role. I am so happy for her. . . .

By the time we assembled in Vienna at the beginning of May we had worked out the somewhat primitive stereo production that was required for the first thirty minutes of Act Three. Still, primitive though it may now seem, it went a great deal further than anything previously attempted in any recording studio. We had marked out the extended stage in a pattern of squares, and devised moves for each of the Valkyrie maidens through which the listener equipped with stereo would, we hoped, get a clear idea of the comings and goings which play an important part in the scene. Some of the voices are required to be heard first from offstage, and for these we used the simple expedient of placing the artists involved in one of the upper boxes which line the sides of the Sofiensaal. (At this stage we had not devised the multistudio technique which was to play a big part in the *Ring* recording.)

Among the points we had overlooked was the fact that our healthy and indeed heavy young ladies made a lot of noise in bounding from one side of the stage to the other—so much noise that after the first session we got them to remove their shoes and replace them with several layers of army socks. Flagstad, hard at work on her knitting, watched all this with a sort of benign amusement, for in common with many other artists at that time she had not yet grasped what stereo was about. (A little later she was to become one of its strongest advocates.)

The biggest innovation that we devised for *Walküre*, Act Three, was the "long take." In the past it had been the general practice to break every work, whatever it was, into short sections of four or five minutes, and to work on each of these pieces until satisfied that the result was good enough to justify moving on to the next. (This was a carry-over from the days of 78-rpm records.) Old habits are hard to break, and artists the world over had become thoroughly accustomed to working within these limits, for which there remained no justification what-

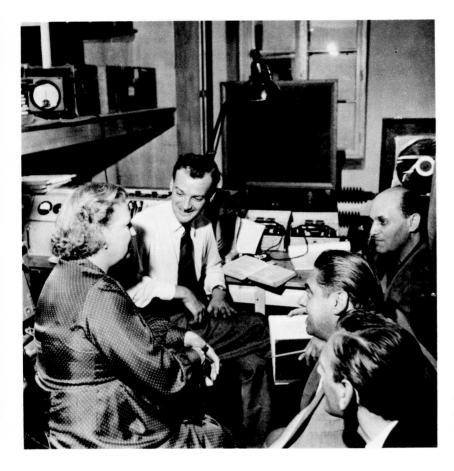

Culshaw, Solti, Edelmann and
unidentified observer listen as Flagstad
makes a point during playbacks for the
"Walküre" recording of Act III.

soever. We decided to change the system, and with Solti's complete
agreement we scheduled *Walküre*, Act Three, in sections of which the
shortest was seventeen minutes, and the longest twenty-four. We developed a routine which, with a few small modifications, has applied ever
since.

First, the conductor rehearses the orchestra in the section to be recorded. In the case of a sixteen- or eighteen-minute sequence this rehearsal—in which the singers do not take part—can require anything up
to fifty minutes. The first recording is then made with the singers,
though we often tell them to "mark" (that is, not to sing with full
voice) during any particularly difficult or tiring passages. During the
intermission we listen to the first recording and decide what is wrong,
and after the intermission it is usually possible to make the entire section
twice, though without any further playback.

In the second half of the session it is essential for the recording producer to be able to spot any mistake or accident which might require a separate correction "tag," which can usually be made in the last remaining minutes of the session. (Some record producers prefer to stop a "take" whenever anything goes wrong, and so cover each error as it happens. I dislike this system because, by constantly interrupting, you are bound to destroy whatever dramatic intensity is being generated. Besides, it makes the artists nervous to have someone forever screaming at them over a loudspeaker. It is important not to forget that most artists are genuinely nervous in the recording studio, no matter how much they may try to disguise the fact, and can only give of their best when they are able to relax and feel that the people in the control room are giving them encouragement. This is why you should never leave the studio "cold" at the end of a take, i.e., leave it in silence. It does not matter how good or bad the performance has been, and it matters still less whether you have anything sensible to say—the important thing is to say *something*, and not leave the artists in a terrible, silent isolation.)

One thing cost us more time than anything else in 1957, and that was the problem of mistakes in the musical material used by the orchestra. It was handwritten material, and presumably dated from the time when *Walküre* was first played in Vienna. The mistakes which we had to remove had, of course, been a part of every public performance for years, but that gave us no excuse for committing them to record. The most baffling occurred just before Wotan's entrance when, on the first attempt, Solti and I had noted an apparent lack of ensemble in the bass strings which we both assumed to be an accident. On the second take it happened again, and Solti warned the basses to watch him carefully at that particular point. When it happened a third time I had to stop the take (we were running out of time), and Solti rehearsed the basses separately—to find that they were still not together. On looking at the parts, it turned out that the basses had an extra note in one of the bars, so that while the cellos were playing *alla breve*, the basses were in some sort of nightmare 5/4. In all the years in the theater this had passed unnoticed.

The third act of *Walküre* divides comfortably over three LP sides, and so we were left with the problem of what to put on the fourth side. We settled eventually for what is called the *Todesverkündigung* scene from Act Two, and we engaged Set Svanholm to sing Siegmund against Flagstad's Brünnhilde. For a number of reasons this twenty-five-minute sequence gave us more trouble than the whole of the third act, and almost came to grief on the day of the session. Fortunately, I had had

Set Svanholm offstage and on: At right he wears glasses to study a score during the 1958 recording of "Das Rheingold"; below, he appears in makeup and costume as Siegfried, the role of his 1946 Metropolitan Opera debut.

the chance to meet Svanholm on one or two earlier occasions when he had visited Vienna to give song recitals, and it was comforting to know that he shared Flagstad's calm, stoic temperament. Indeed, it was hard to reconcile the quiet, balding, and immensely polite Svanholm with the athletic, arrogant Siegfried he had portrayed at Covent Garden for season after season.

Between the end of the recording of the third act and the date we had set for the *Todesverkündigung* scene, Solti had to go to Paris for a concert, and this was the cause of the trouble. On the morning of the session he called from Paris to say that his plane had been delayed by technical troubles, and that there was no other connection that would get him to Vienna on time. He asked us to postpone the session by one hour—to start at 1530 instead 1430—to give him a chance to arrive. As bad luck had it, this would not work, for the opera performance that evening began at 1830, and the Vienna Philharmonic always, and rightly, insists on a clear break of one hour between the end of a recording session and the start of the opera. I tried to move the whole project to the next day, but that would not work either: Svanholm had to go to Germany for a performance the next evening.

There are things you can do in Vienna which could not possibly happen in any other western European capital. As was to happen innumerable times in the future, we consulted a man called Adolf Krypl, who is the superintendent of the Sofiensaal. I have reason to think that over the years our friend Adolf, who has a very sanguine temperament, has quietly reached the conclusion that most artists and all recording personnel are insane. With chaos all around him, Adolf Krypl has struggled in silence to preserve his own sanity and his impeccable, self-effacing manners. He is probably unique in Austria in that when you ask him for something, and question whether it may or may not be possible, his immediate reply is: "*Anything* is possible!" Among the things he has never understood is the English sense of humor, and we have learned not to try it on him. It is quite inconceivable to Adolf Krypl that anyone with the exalted position of recording engineer or recording producer could possibly be frivolous about anything. When, in a light moment, we hinted that we might need an elephant or two when we were about to record the Triumphal scene from *Aïda*, he took the idea with great solemnity and said that he had *already* had elephants in the Sofiensaal. "*Zwei stück*'," he added, which means two pieces, and I am sure that he thought we were very rude for laughing.

We took him our Solti/Air France problem. He knew the director of Air France in Vienna (he knows the director of *everything* in Vienna), but not even he could repair an aeroplane that had broken down in Paris. We had discovered that the estimated time of arrival of the flight in Vienna was 1515—forty-five minutes after the start of the session. By the time Solti had been through customs and immigration and found his way to the car, we reckoned we would lose at least another twenty minutes; and even by the fastest route, the journey from the airport to

Christopher Raeburn (right), a member of Decca's recording team, discusses a problem with Sofiensaal superintendent Adolf Krypl.

the Sofiensaal takes twenty-five minutes. With luck, then, we could expect our conductor at 1600, around the middle of the three-hour session, breathless, tense, and having had no rehearsal for a difficult scene which runs for almost twenty-five minutes.

Adolf Krypl went into action. He called his friend the Chief of Police in Vienna. He called customs and immigration at the airport. And I am sure he made Air France feel responsible for everything. When the orchestra assembled at 1430, I explained what had happened, and asked Professor Sedlak, who was then one of the leaders of the orchestra, to conduct until Solti arrived, for this would at least give Flagstad and Svanholm a chance to "sing in" and give us the opportunity to test the balance. Adolf Krypl appeared triumphantly just as Professor Sedlak started to rehearse: the Air France pilot had been told of the emergency and was flying flat out—with good luck he might knock fifteen minutes off the flight time and land at 1500. Further, customs and immigration had been waived, and a police car with escort would be waiting on the tarmac to take Solti straight off the plane. Just to make sure there were no delays on the journey to the Sofiensaal, all traffic lights would be manually operated by the police to ensure a steady green wave.

Solti was in the hall and conducting by 1520. We congratulated Adolf on his miracle of organization and influence. He looked mildly shocked. "For Decca and the Vienna Philharmonic," he said, "*everything* is possible."

Some months after making *Walküre*, Act Three, we reassembled in Vienna to make Act One, with Flagstad in the part of Sieglinde and with Knappertsbusch as the conductor. (As I have explained, we sought in this way to make it quite clear to the public that the two acts were not intended to be parts of a complete *Walküre*.) Nothing could possibly have been further from the tension of Act Three. For one thing, although it was interesting and moving to have Flagstad sing a part which she had performed infrequently on the stage, the truth was that she was altogether too matronly and mature to be a dramatically convincing Sieglinde; for another, there was our dear, enchanting, irresponsible friend, Knappertsbusch.

He received a huge round of applause from the Vienna Philharmonic when he walked out for the first session. Ten minutes earlier, in his dressing room, he had doused himself and me and anyone else in range with eau de cologne, while demanding: "How much have I to do?" I had shown him the scheduled sixteen minutes. "In three hours?" said Kna, looking incredulous. "What do we do for the rest of the time?" I said we could go on if we had time, if the singers did not get tired. "Tired?" he said. "She won't get tired, she's built like a battleship!"

Very reluctantly, he rehearsed for a few minutes, on the pretext that we needed to check out microphones. Then we did a take which was pretty chaotic, but which was worth hearing back for analysis. Kirsten and Set and Arnold van Mill trooped into the control room. Kna sat outside smoking a cigarette. "Tell me what's wrong when you've heard it again," he said. Then he grinned: "Of course, you'll say it's too slow—everyone says I'm too slow."

In vain did I try to get him into the control room to listen to points of balance and intonation which needed his attention. He would take every possible suggestion any recording director cared to make, and would faithfully do his best to carry out what he had been told—but, personally, he was not involved. The truth was that Knappertsbusch took very badly to recording conditions, and, no matter what we did, the genius which he so certainly revealed in the theater refused to come alive in the studio. He never complained. He told the funniest obscene stories I

Knappertsbusch and the Vienna Philharmonic pause between takes during the recording of Act I of "Die Walküre" with Flagstad in 1957. Knappertsbusch responded poorly to recording conditions and rarely produced studio performances the equal of those he conducted in the theater.

have ever heard. Everybody loved him. But the essence of Knapperts-busch simply refused to show itself. He needed the smell of greasepaint, and the waft of air from backstage. He needed the uncertainty of the theater, and the comfortable feeling that in the theater you can, as a conductor, take huge risks in the knowledge that if something ends in disaster only a minority of the audience will realize it at all, while the orchestra will know what it was about and will be forgiving. None of this applies to recording, and the resulting inhibitions were too much for him. (A year later, there was a moment when he was recording a Strauss waltz, as usual without rehearsal, and at one of the many repeats half of the orchestra went on, while the other half went back. The resultant mess lasted only four bars, after which the piece was on the rails again. At the end he called out, "Can you use that? We don't need it again, do we?" I told him what had happened. He said, "*Scheisse*—do you think anyone else will know?")

It is easy to give a facile account of this strange and immensely gifted man. He was the kindest, most modest conductor I have ever worked with. He was unfailingly generous to his colleagues. He would never join the rat race for fame and honor. In the theater I believe that he was a Wagner conductor of supreme ability. But on records he was a total failure. It is hard work to try and make a good record with someone with whom you do not have a personal or musical contact. It is heartbreaking to make a poor record of a performance by someone you respect and admire as we respected and admired Kna. We tried to drag him, kicking and screaming, into the twentieth century of the gramophone record, the era of the listener-at-home who hears without any visual aid and without the community of the theater. It was an alien world for him. He was a nineteenth-century professional, and to the end of his life the gramophone was a newfangled toy. We could not do him justice.

I know why orchestras loved him. I know why we loved him. The bitterest professional recommendation of my life was when I had to tell my directors that we should not record *Tristan* with Knappertsbusch, because I knew by then that he could not produce in the studio the remotest ghost of what had been the greatest theatrical experience of my life. Nobody can blame him for refusing to try to understand a new medium: it is enough that his extraordinary talents made such an impression on those few who heard him under the right conditions.

Vienna, city of music: Backdrop of the recordings

The emblem atop the 18th century wing of Vienna's royal palace features, appropriately, two trumpeting angels. No city in the world has so illustrious a musical tradition. Of the many memorial rooms, houses and monuments honoring the greats of Viennese history, roughly half are devoted to musicians and composers.

Rome enjoyed one Golden Age; musical Vienna keeps coming up with new ones. The first occurred in the late Renaissance, when Hapsburg Emperor Maximilian I formed one of the earliest court chamber orchestras and conducted it personally. Then there was a Golden Age in the Baroque period, when Ferdinand III—himself a composer of sacred music—introduced opera to Vienna with Bonacossi's *Ariadna abbandonata* in 1641 and Cavalli's *Egisto* in 1643. Perhaps the period from 1760 to 1828 should be known as Vienna's Diamond Age: at one time or another during this period Gluck, Haydn, Mozart, Beethoven and Schubert made

An overflow crowd listens to an amplified relay of "Fidelio," the work chosen to open the rebuilt Vienna State Opera House in 1955.

Vineyards are found within Vienna's city limits in village-like sections such as Grinzing, which lies on edge of the Vienna Woods. A nearby valley inspired Beethoven's "Pastoral Symphony."

the imperial city their home. Traces of these giants' footsteps are reverently preserved: their statues grace the parks and squares; streets are named for them; plaques mark their haunts and houses, which are often open to the public.

After such a siege of greatness, any other city might have rested on its laurels. Not Vienna. Close on Schubert's heels followed the waltzing Strauss dynasty, whose music has become synonymous with Vienna. The second half of the 19th

St. Stephen's spire dominates Vienna skyline. In foreground: Burgtheater, where classical drama is performed, was designed by Semper, who planned a Wagner theater in Munich.

century brought in another crop of geniuses: Bruckner, Brahms, Wolf, Mahler —and, for a brief period, Richard Wagner. A decade or so later came Richard Strauss, Max Reger and Franz Schmidt. The last of the great periods was that of Schoenberg, Berg and Webern.

World War II seems to have put an end to Vienna's Golden Ages, but great composers are in short supply everywhere nowadays. If Vienna lacks a current musical Messiah, she is far from lacking music. The Austrian government spends $5 per capita annually to subsidize musical performances. There are two busy opera houses and two famous orchestras; the recital halls are alive with chamber music; and the many churches perform the masses of Mozart, Haydn, Beethoven and Schubert. Each spring the Vienna Festival Weeks attract visitors from all over the globe. And, of course, the city is a center of recording activity. In matters musical, Vienna still has few peers.

Street signs and statuary recall

Everywhere the pedestrian turns in Vienna he finds memorials to music and musicians. Johann Strauss plays a lilting violin in the Stadtpark, Brahms contemplates the burdens of greatness in the Resselpark, and Mozart soars from a high pedestal in the gardens of the royal palace.

a great heritage of music

Beethovenplatz is dominated by an effigy of the "Mighty Thunderer" (left above). Schubert (left) and Anton Bruckner (above) grace corners of Stadtpark, while Tamino plays his "Magic Flute" to Pamina in Mozartplatz.

The dwelling places of genius

As a teen-ager, Joseph Haydn occupied the garret of the Altes Michaelerhaus, seen at left above, framed by the ornate wrought-iron grill-work of the entrance to the royal palace of the Hapsburgs.

At the foot of the narrow Blutgasse (right) is the so-called Figaro House, where Mozart lived from 1784 to 1787 and where he composed, among other great works, "The Marriage of Figaro."

Most of the great Viennese composers were born elsewhere, but true "Wiener Blut" (Vienna blood) flowed in the veins of Franz Schubert. His birth house is now a museum.

A commemorative plaque and banners mark the house in Heiligenstadt, near Vienna, where Beethoven resided during the summer of 1817. In the romantic courtyard of this 17th century building visitors can drink the new wine, or "Heuriger," which is one of the city's specialties.

In 1863 Wagner rented the upper story of this imposing house in Penzing, a Vienna suburb, but debts forced him to flee the city less than a year later. Plaque tells us that here "during the darkest days of his life, Richard Wagner worked on his sunniest opera, 'Die Meistersinger.'"

CHAPTER TWO

1958 Das Rheingold

THE IDEA of a complete *Ring* recording was taking form in our minds. I was still, I admit, haunted by the thought of a complete *Walküre*, and frustrated by our bits-and-pieces compromise of 1957. Two people kept up a constant barrage of suggestions to try and convince me that *Rheingold* was the work with which we should start: they were Gordon Parry, and a man called Robert Boas who at that time worked in the department of Decca concerned with album design and written commentaries. Of the two, Gordon was by far the more persistent, but Bob would lose no opportunity to tell me how much the world needed the first recording of *Rheingold*.

I was skeptical, not because I disliked the work—on the contrary—because I was far from convinced that it could be any sort of commercial success, no matter how well it might be done. My doubtful attitude was confirmed by those in high places in the operatic world: for nobody ever puts *Rheingold* on the stage except as a prelude to the *Ring*. It is not, and should not be, an ordinary repertoire piece. It has no real "star" parts, at least not of the kind that bring the public in. Foremost (and quite wrongly) in my mind was the cautionary thought that if we had a bad flop with *Rheingold* there would be no chance of any money for the rest of the *Ring;* whereas if we started with a complete *Walküre, Siegfried,* or *Götterdämmerung,* we would stand a chance of creating an audience for which *Rheingold* would have no terrors.

Fortunately, as it happened, there was a big casting problem to which I could offer no solution. So far as we knew, Birgit Nilsson was under contract to Columbia, Ltd., and therefore we had no Brünnhilde. (True, there were other Brünnhildes in the world, and for one of them—Astrid Varnay—I had a deep admiration; but the sales people believed that any *Ring* opera involving Brünnhilde would not get off the ground without Nilsson.) *Rheingold*, therefore, was the only *Ring* opera we could possibly consider for 1958, and it was with considerable apprehension that I put it forward to our international repertoire committee in the autumn of 1957. Points in its favor were that it is, by Wagnerian standards, a short work (three LP's, against six required for *Walküre* or *Siegfried*, and six for *Götterdämmerung*). *Rheingold* had never been recorded at all, and therefore would have whatever market there was to itself. Finally, I could point out that it would give us a perfect opportunity to show what a difference the proper use of stereo could bring to the world of recorded opera.

This last point was not considered of much importance, and one can see why. It was only a few years earlier that the record business had been plunged into turmoil by the advent of LP. The demise of the old 78-rpm format, in which hundreds of thousands of pounds and millions of dollars had been invested, was sudden and final. By 1957 the LP was well established, and a huge amount of money had again been spent on recording all the standard classics for the new form of disk, together with an impressive range of complete operas. Now, suddenly, another technical development seemed likely to require another re-recording of all this material—but would the public invest in stereo, so soon after the change from 78-rpm to LP? It seemed likely to be a costly investment, too, for stereo doubles every playback requirement except the turn-table. One can sympathize with any management when faced with a technical innovation which cannot be resisted or ignored, but which is still an unknown quantity in terms of public appeal. Indeed, there were some who felt that the launching of stereo so soon after the LP revolution might be too much for the record public altogether, and cause a lapse of interest in records as such.

Thus my technical arguments in favor of *Rheingold* did not make much effect. A clearer indication that a public existed for Wagner on records was the success of our various recital disks and excerpts with Kirsten Flagstad. If we could get Flagstad into the cast of *Rheingold*, we might at least stand a chance. . . . But there was no part that Flagstad had ever sung, and none that she was likely to sing. There are only three really substantial parts in *Rheingold*, and they are all for men: Wotan, Alberich, and Loge. The rest of the characters tend to stand about and put in a line or two here and there. Neither Fricka nor Erda, which were the only possibilities for Flagstad, seemed likely to be of any interest to a woman who had commanded the international Wagner stage for over twenty years in such huge parts as Brünnhilde and Isolde. I said I would try to persuade her to sing Fricka for us, but warned that we should make a safe "reserve" casting in case she just laughed at me. There was an even more disagreeable prospect, which was that she would be offended.

I had two arguments with which to approach her. One was to point out that we *had* offered her a complete *Walküre* to be recorded in 1957, which she herself had turned down because she did not want to sing Act Two. She had been very direct about it in one of her letters:

I am so happy that you have abandoned the thought of the second act. I have been thinking and worrying all the time about your proposal, but my intuition tells me NO! I am wonderfully lazy these days and staying all by myself, reading, embroidering, and playing solitaire by the hour. Wasn't I fortunate to miss the heat wave? . . .

The move I had to take seemed obvious. As long ago as 1956 she had turned down my unofficial proposal for a complete *Götterdämmerung* in Vienna. She had then turned down a complete *Walküre*. In effect, she had conceded that if we, or any other company, embarked on a complete *Ring* it could not be with herself as Brünnhilde. It was simply too late. I therefore wrote her a long letter in late December 1957 to tell her that we hoped to record *Rheingold* in 1958, and that there were some of us who hoped that it might be the foundation of the first complete recorded *Ring*. It was necessary to tread cautiously, for I had a suspicion that she had never heard or seen *Rheingold*, but I went on to say that the part of Fricka might suit her very well and begged her to have a look at it.

There was no reply for a while, and when it came it was a blunt inquiry: could we supply a set of tapes of any stage performance of *Rheingold?* A set of 1955 Bayreuth tapes was quickly duplicated and sent off to her in Norway, but by that time she had left for Phoenix, Arizona, where she went to stay with her daughter. She wrote from Phoenix on March 14:

Thank you for the letter from Vienna and the greetings from Max Lorenz. I have had a score of *Rheingold* sent to me here and have been working on Fricka. The part is very easy for me, but I cannot make up my mind and will wait for the tapes. . . .

By this time the rest of the cast was secure, and the starting date in September had been fixed. I was being pressed by Zurich either to get a confirmation from Flagstad or to propose an alternative casting. Several further letters from me, written on different pretexts but always managing to get in a reference to *Rheingold*, produced no response from Flagstad; and then what seemed to be a further stroke of bad luck suddenly turned to our favor. The singer who had been engaged to sing Flosshilde wrote in to say that she had become pregnant and therefore wished to be released from her contract. Leon Felder called me from Zurich and asked me to name a suitable replacement, and I suggested he should try Ira Malaniuk, who had just the right sort of voice for Flosshilde. She replied at once to say that *her* part was Fricka, which she had sung many times on the stage—and one could sympathize with her desire not to appear as a lesser character on a recording. We then took a chance, and told her that Flagstad was still considering Fricka. Would Malaniuk therefore take a sporting risk? If Flagstad turned up and sang Fricka for the first time ever, would Malaniuk sing Flosshilde for us? But if Flagstad turned down Fricka, we would guarantee the part to Malaniuk. We have always had a soft spot for Ira Malaniuk, and her immediate reply was to the effect that if indeed we could persuade Flagstad to sing, then it would be an honor to appear in the same cast, no matter how humble the part.

By this time, the end of April was approaching and there was still no news from Flagstad. Schedules had been prepared and distributed to the rest of the cast, but with no name shown against the character of Fricka. Then an acquaintance of mine who had been in New York, who was the sort of person who likes to hang around the periphery of the musical world although not connected with it professionally, tipped me off that Flagstad, who was also in New York at that time, had made it clear that *something* had displeased her very much. Whether it was the persistence of my letters or not he didn't know, but he thought our chances of getting her into *Rheingold* in September were extremely slender. I passed on this gloomy news, for what it was worth, to Zurich, and went off to Vienna. Gordon Parry put his finger on the trouble immediately. He guessed, rightly, that someone had been talking, and that we had on our hands a repetition of the situation which had earlier led Flagstad to believe that we were casting an Italian tenor opposite her in *Walküre*, Act One. But without more information, and without a single word from her, there was not much I or anyone else could do.

Then, at the beginning of May, I received a classic letter from her. I am sure she had not pondered over it for a moment, yet its construction was masterly. Writing from the Grand Hotel, Oslo, she said:

I have listened to the *Rheingold* tapes and would like to send them back. Will you, please, tell me to whom and where I shall return them ?

When I was in New York I was told that Mr. George London was going to record *Rheingold* as Wotan with me as Fricka. How can they make public such things before I have consented? Is it a way to try to force me to say yes?

The part is very small but quite good for me, I believe, but hardly worth the long journey to Vienna. But, as I like so much to work with you and your friends, I will consent to do Fricka for you. I will be quite busy in September, but will take the time off. Kindest greetings to you all. . . .

We cabled back at once: "Terribly sorry about American indiscretion but overjoyed by your decision." In retrospect, it may seem that we paid an inordinate amount of attention to the idea of persuading Flagstad to sing what is, after all, a small role. There were two main reasons, and the first was commercial. In 1958 the name Flagstad was still a very powerful draw for the Wagner audience, and nobody at that stage could possibly predict whether *Rheingold* was going to be an expensive success or an expensive flop. Anything which might contribute to its sales potential was of importance to those who were investing money in such an unknown starter. Had she refused, we would have gone ahead without her because by then it was too late to withdraw. The other reason was that those of us who dreamed that *Rheingold* might be the beginning of the first recorded *Ring* wanted above all that Flagstad should be a part of it, no matter how modest, for we sensed that time was running out for her. When her letter came with the acceptance of the *Rheingold* Fricka, we thought about what she might do in the rest of the cycle—*if* the cycle went ahead in the near future. There was the *Walküre* Fricka, and Waltraute in *Götterdämmerung* and possibly Erda in *Siegfried*. But there was no point in mentioning such things at this stage. We had to know the fate of *Rheingold* first.

Zurich had coordinated the rest of the cast for the dates we wanted. We had split the piece into two sections, the first of which, between September 24 and 30, concentrated on the second and fourth scenes, while the second stretch, between October 2 and 8, was for the recording of scenes three and one, in that order. The idea of recording an opera in its proper sequence is the dream of any opera conductor or producer, but it very rarely happens. If you hold strong views about a particular cast you have to be prepared to accommodate the artists when you can get them; the alternative is to start downgrading the cast until you find a set of replacements whose availability will enable you to record the work in the correct sequence. But by the time you have got down to that sort of cast, the job is not worth doing anyway.

We were lucky in having George London (as Wotan) throughout the entire period, and Set Svanholm (as Loge) for all but two days. The rest of the schedule was governed by the fact that Flagstad would not stay after October 1, while Gustav Neidlinger (as Alberich) could not be with us until that day. (Fortunately, they have nothing to sing together in *Rheingold*.) Oddly enough, *Rheingold* was one of those blessed occasions when the comings-and-goings of artists did not make for more than the expected number of anxious moments, but one such moment landed me in an inextricable situation.

There had been some confusion about the arrival of Ira Malaniuk, our Flosshilde, and though she is normally extremely punctual and correct, I began to worry when she had not arrived by the early evening of the day before her first session. I tried calling her in Munich, but there was no reply. I tried her agent, and there was no reply. Finally I spoke to our Munich office, who said they would try to trace her and ring me back. By that time it was ten o'clock, and we had a rehearsal scheduled for her in the morning. I went into the bar of the Hotel Imperial to have a drink while waiting for Munich to call back. Set Svanholm was there, externally as sober as the president of a temperance society, despite having consumed an enormous amount of whisky. (One must envy the majority of Scandinavians their ability to drink five times as much as other people and keep three times as sober.) Set greeted me and asked me what the trouble was—over another drink. I was genuinely worried, and told him about Malaniuk. He didn't seem to know her; and so, with my mind on other things, I made a ghastly mistake.

I said he would probably recognize her even if he didn't know her name, as she frequently sang one or another of the *Walküre* girls in Act Three in opera houses all over Europe, and must have been in several productions in which he had sung Siegmund. I knew my mistake as soon as I'd said it, but he pounced. Didn't I know that Siegmund got killed at the end of *Walküre*, Act Two? Therefore, he would be in no position to meet the girls in Act Three. Siegmund always took his curtain call at the end of Act Two, got changed and went out to supper. "I think," Svanholm said solemnly, "I had better tell you the story of the *Ring*. We shall have some more drinks...." And tell it he did, right from the beginning, and there was no stopping him.

Somewhere in the first act of *Siegfried*, the porter came to say that Munich was on the line. I excused myself, and got the good news that Malaniuk had been traced and was on her way. She would not be late for the rehearsal. Greatly relieved, I went back to the bar, by which time Set, with another round of drinks lined up, had reached the second act of *Götterdämmerung*. I enjoyed the rest of his account. He was an enchanting man, and he really thought he was helping.

As September 24 approached, there was a feeling of tension unlike anything I had experienced. We were going flat out for something new and untried, and a lot of money was about to be spent. There was the usual nagging feeling that something might go hopelessly wrong and put us two sessions off schedule; there was also the feeling that whatever we did, *Rheingold* might be a failure. There is always the serious possibility with a recording (or a film or a play) that no matter how much heart everyone puts into it, there may simply not be enough people in the world sufficiently interested in the result to justify the expense.

The artists began to arrive. We went out to Schwechat (Vienna) Airport to meet Flagstad on September 21 and took her to dinner. She seemed very happy and relaxed, but determined not to stay a minute longer than October 1. Solti flew in the next morning and had his first piano rehearsal with Flagstad in the afternoon of that day. She sounded fabulous and had obviously studied Fricka with a lot of care. George London arrived, and somehow all of us ceased to feel nervous any longer. The artists were rolling in, the rehearsals had started, and we had to get out of the clouds and on with a job of work.

George London, who sings Wotan in the recording of "Das Rheingold," is shown as he appeared in the role at the Metropolitan Opera in 1961.

It may seem strange now, but up to that time piano rehearsals were not considered an essential part of making an operatic recording. It was generally assumed by those in charge that since the majority of artists likely to be engaged for a recording would be those who had won renown on the operatic stages of the world for performances of the parts they were engaged to record, it was somehow unnecessary and even insulting to suggest they should re-rehearse at the piano. Most artists certainly agree with this; the small, select company of those who like to rethink and restudy their own interpretations, whether for the theater or for records, is certainly a minority. We had insisted, however, on more than adequate piano rehearsal for *Rheingold*, especially as it is a sort of ensemble opera and requires strict dramatic discipline if it is not to become boring. Some indication of the care that went into proper rehearsal planning may be gathered from this schedule, which shows the rehearsals in relation to the sessions:

Sept. 22	1500	Piano rehearsal.	(Flagstad)
Sept. 23	2015	Piano rehearsal.	(Flagstad, London, Watson, Kreppl, Böhme)
Sept. 24	1500	First session.	
Sept. 25	1115	Piano rehearsal.	(as above, plus Svanholm, Wächter, and Kmentt)
	1530	Second session.	
	2030	Piano rehearsal.	(Svanholm, London)
Sept. 26	0945	Piano rehearsal.	(All artists)
	1500	Third session.	
Sept. 27	1130	Piano rehearsal.	(All artists)
	1730	Piano rehearsal.	(All artists)
Sept. 28	1600	Piano rehearsal.	(Children)
Sept. 29	1400	Piano rehearsal.	(Six harps)
Sept. 29	1530	Fourth session.	
Sept. 30	1200	Piano rehearsal.	(Madeira, London)
	1500	Fifth session.	
Oct. 1	0900	Piano rehearsal.	(18 anvils)
	1130	Piano rehearsal.	(Neidlinger, Kuen, London, Svanholm)
	1500	Sixth session.	
	2100	Piano rehearsal.	(as for morning)
Oct. 2	1400	Piano rehearsal.	(Children)
	1530	Seventh session.	
	2100	Piano rehearsal.	(Neidlinger, Kuen) (18 anvils)
	1015	Eighth session.	
Oct. 4	0830	Piano rehearsal.	(Solo anvil and thunder machine)
Oct. 5	1800	Piano rehearsal.	(London, Svanholm)

Oct. 6	1500	Ninth session.	
Oct. 7	0900	Piano rehearsal.	(Six harps)
	1000	Tenth session.	
	1700	Piano rehearsal.	(Perspective test for Rhinemaidens in closing scene)
	1800	Piano rehearsal.	(Plumacher, Balsborg, Malaniuk)
Oct. 8	0930	Eleventh session.	
	1530	Twelfth session.	

A copy of this schedule, or something very like it, was given to each artist on arrival. There were the usual grumbles that it was unnecessary and a waste of time—*"Why should we have to rehearse just because Flagstad's never sung her part before?"*—but we managed to be firm and the objections subsided.

It was clear from the beginning that Solti had a very great affection for *Rheingold*. He saw it as we saw it—not as a mere prelude or exposition for the great trilogy to follow, but as a masterpiece in its own right. Years ago, he had chosen *Rheingold* for his farewell performance at the Munich opera before taking over the directorship at Frankfurt; and he knew that nothing in the world of opera can be more tedious than an ill-prepared, uncommitted performance of *Rheingold*. It is an opera which will not, as the saying goes, play itself, and its gloomy reputation in some quarters is the fault of conductors who try to make it do so. The night before we started the recording I had dinner with Solti in the Hotel Imperial, where we were both staying. He could hardly wait for the first session, and although he said nothing directly about it I knew that we were sharing at least one thought: if, by hard work or good luck or any other means, we could make a success of *Rheingold*, there was a fair chance that Decca would let us carry on with a complete *Ring* in Vienna. As you leave the restaurant in the Hotel Imperial you have to pass through the bar, and in doing so we bumped into a very distinguished colleague who did my sort of job for one of our main competitors. He greeted us and asked what we were about to record. As it was an open secret in Vienna anyway (and nothing on earth can be more open than an open secret in Vienna), we told him. "Very nice," he said, "very interesting. But of course you won't *sell* any."

The next day the artists assembled for the first session. Flagstad was keeping very much to herself, and I think she was a bit nervous. We knew she would feel better when her old partner, Set Svanholm, arrived. As we wanted to get the right sound from the orchestra before we started working on the voices, we had asked the singers to come thirty minutes late for the first session. But they arrived thirty minutes early, which meant they had to hang about, getting more nervous, for almost an hour.

The orchestral test was essential. I am convinced, and so are my colleagues, that the basis of any successful operatic recording is the orchestra. This may sound paradoxical or even perverse, but it is true. One should approach each opera on its own terms and try to imagine what sort of sound the composer had in mind, assuming he had the acoustic facilities in which to create what he wanted. Just because nineteenth-century theater design imposes a generally invariable pattern on orchestral layout is no reason for a similar inflexibility in the recording studio. The sound you should seek for *Otello* is not the same as the sound for *Aïda; Rosenkavalier* is not the same as *Elektra;* and *Pelléas* stands all by itself—or should do so, instead of being forced into the same deployment as *Cavalleria*. To vary the approach is not a gimmick: it is simply the application of imagination to the business of making operatic recordings. For *Rheingold* we wanted above all to have a great richness of sound for the big climaxes, while at the same time retaining a proper clarity. The texture is symphonic, and the motives *must* be clear, for this is their first appearance. To use a crude and somewhat debased word, we wanted the result to have impact—a sumptuous kind of impact. This is what we were looking for in the orchestral test.

We chose the interlude known as the descent into Nibelheim (without the anvils) as our test passage, plus the opening E flat pedal and the first horn phrases. After a time we got the sound we wanted, and Solti seemed pleased. The singers stopped pacing up and down, and Solti introduced them to the orchestra. At about 1620 that afternoon we made our first test of the opening of the second scene, and when Flagstad sang her first line—"*Wotan Gemahl! erwache!*"—the entire orchestra turned round to gape in amazement, so extraordinary was the authority and power of her voice. We got fifteen minutes or so of master material recorded on that first session, but it was far too soon to celebrate. The artists had quickly responded to the optimistic mood; Flagstad, indeed, suddenly revealed an unsuspected enthusiasm for what can be conveyed by movement on the stage as heard on a stereo recording, and made a couple of suggestions for additional moves which we happily accepted.

For the next day or two the work went splendidly, but there was a tense moment when two of the younger Viennese members of the cast turned up for their first session and were overheard making uncharitable comments about Flagstad, more or less to the effect that old women should retire, and who did she think she was kidding if she thought she

George London apostrophizes newly built Valhalla as Kirsten Flagstad follows with her score during take of opening of second scene of "Rheingold."

still had a voice at her age? I don't think Flagstad heard any of this, but I happened to be out on the stage when she sang her first line on that particular session, and the look of utter bewilderment on the faces of the two Viennese was a joy to see. One of them later tried to make amends in the control room, but with disastrous effect. He breezed up to Flagstad and said, "How are things in Sweden?" She looked him up and down and replied, "I come from Norway, young man." He looked straight back at her and said, "Same thing, isn't it?" I left the room at that point, because there are times in life when it is necessary to be somewhere else.

Looking back to the *Rheingold* schedule, I see that I provided what was called a "Minimum effects list" which contained only ten words:

> Subterranean anvils.
> Children for Nibelungen's screams.
> Hammer striking rock.
> Thunderclap.

This was a far cry from the four closely typed foolscap pages which a few years later were to cover the technical requirements for *Götterdämmerung*, Act One, alone. But in the days of *Rheingold* we had beginner's luck and beginner's cheek: for although we did a mighty amount of preparation, it was all compressed into a few days; and while we were recording the opera in the afternoons, we were also recording Beethoven symphonies in the mornings—which was inexperienced planning, in that it left us very little time for the elaborate effects we were dreaming about.

All this time Zurich had been watching the mounting costs with understandable horror; but there was worse to come. The cast for *Rheingold* was excellent, but very expensive; and now we were about to add to the costs by requesting all sorts of extra facilities of a kind never before seen in a recording studio. We were about to *produce* an opera for records in a way never attempted before, except for our own fumbling efforts with *Walküre*, Act Three, one year previously.

First, we needed anvils—eighteen of them in various sizes, and eighteen percussionists to play them. The rhythmic hammering of Nibelheim

Some of the 18 extra percussionists hired for the "Rheingold" sessions bang away at the various-sized anvils Wagner calls for in his score to represent the hammering of Alberich's slaves.

slaves is heard twice in *Rheingold:* first in the interlude when Wotan and Loge descend to Nibelheim, and again when they depart with Alberich as their captive. The rhythms are precisely notated by Wagner, and you would think that anyone with the slightest dramatic or musical perception would grasp, simply by looking at the score, what he was after. Yet I have never seen a theater production which attempted to meet his wishes. Sometimes you get fobbed off with a sort of electronic compromise; sometimes you get a tinkling sound made by a few people beating metal bars together; but you never get the firm, frightening sound of eighteen anvils hit with rhythmical precision and building into a deafening assault on the nerves which, to quote Newman from a different context, should "approach the threshold of pain." Of course it *could* be done in the theater; I imagine the reason for its absence is that although Wagner made it quite clear that he wanted a primitive *noise* for dramatic reasons, most conductors cannot abide noise of any sort. Their instincts tell them that it is unmusical, and so they skirt the problem by making it as inconspicuous, and as inoffensive, as possible. (They cannot, however, omit it altogether, for the anvils have quite a lengthy solo during the first of the two interludes.)

Once again we called upon our friend Adolf Krypl for help. We required eighteen anvils and a few spares, and lots of different hammers to bang them with. We then called Professor Wobisch of the Vienna Philharmonic and said that we needed at least eighteen percussionists for two long rehearsals and a session. It is not easy to find as many capable percussionists in any city in the world, and probably least of all in Vienna, but Wobisch eventually rounded up enough players, though many of them were not percussionists at all, but harpists, trumpeters, and other instrumentalists who were willing, as the saying goes, to have a bash. Adolf Krypl announced that he had discovered something called an anvil school from which we could obtain any number of anvils in all sorts of shapes and sizes. To this day I have failed to discover what goes on at the anvil school, or what career you adopt once you have graduated there, but we were grateful for its existence. Zurich was very worried, for not only were the anvils expensive to hire and insure (we damaged three of them) but there was also the cost of eighteen extra players for two rehearsals and a session, which brought the complement of the Vienna Philharmonic to over one hundred and twenty-five.

The anvil sound on the first rehearsal was a sensation, but there were problems. Solti rightly had to convince the players that the effectiveness of the passage depended entirely on absolute rhythmical precision; but the noise was so enormous that the players could not hear themselves, and could therefore not tell when they got out of rhythm. (The little ones had the worst of it, and we had to solve the problem by experiments in deployment.) When it came to the session itself, the rest of the Vienna Philharmonic was aghast when the anvils came in with such relentless, unswerving precision. (It is an interesting point that Wagner wrote for nine small anvils, six larger anvils, and three very large ones, and indicated precisely how he wanted them placed, almost as if he had been designing the most effective possible stereo layout. He also wrote for them to sound the note F, although in any serious sense an anvil is a pitchless instrument, like a triangle. Yet somehow the sound of our eighteen anvils *does* seem to maintain an F tonality. This is probably an aural illusion, in the sense that the human ear, when suddenly confronted with a loud pitchless or tonally ambiguous sound, imparts to that sound the pitch of its context. I can think of no other explanation.)

The sound we were trying to get was meant to engulf the listener (in the stereo sense it would enclose him, for it would come from all directions), and we were determined to get the crescendo just right, so that the passage would build to a point where the listener could hardly bear the hammering a moment longer—at which instant it would start to decrescendo. It is true that the passage sounds comical if it is not rhythmically precise; but when the anvils are really playing together, and playing the rhythm that Wagner wrote, the effect comes out as a dramatic masterstroke. And by taking it seriously, we were unconsciously adding a strong selling point to the recording, for within a year those anvils were clanging out all over Europe and America in living rooms, in record shops, and in large and small halls where records are demonstrated. The anvil passage and the thunderclap at the end of *Rheingold* became a sort of international standard by which you judged the quality of your gramophone: if it could play them, it was fine. If it could not, you were all set to buy yourself new equipment, for there was nothing wrong with the records.

For a long time we had been dissatisfied with the timpani used by the Vienna Philharmonic. What happened in concerts and in the opera house was not our business, but the sound produced in the Sofiensaal was soggy in the extreme: it carried no impact. It was unthinkable to use them for *Rheingold;* we wanted a very loud but very *firm* sound for the entry of the Giants, and for the passage where Fafner kills Fasolt. We knew we would never get that sound from the existing instruments, so we imported a special set of timpani from London, plus an enormous single-sided bass drum which had been built by our old friend L. G. Hunt. The improvement was so vast that in the following year the Vienna Philharmonic equipped itself with an entirely new set of timpani from Chicago, reserved specifically for our use. They also fell in love with the big bass drum, the likes of which they had never seen. When, after *Rheingold*, I was returning to London, Professor Wobisch suggested I should get a price from Hunt, as the orchestra might be interested in keeping the monster in Vienna. A week or two later I cabled the price to Wobisch, and several weeks after that I received a very enigmatic telegram which had started its journey from the Vienna post office, bearing the following complete text: BUY DRUM WOBISCH. On the way to London it became garbled, so that on arrival it contained only two words: BIDRUM VABISH. I got the message, and immediately adopted the two words as a splendid pseudonym, above which several ostensibly serious letters have since appeared in various magazines and newspapers. (The revised text for Prokofiev's *Peter and the Wolf* as recorded for Decca by Beatrice Lillie was written, as the label indicates, by that distinguished Persian, Bidrum Vabish.)

We needed forty children to shuffle and scream as the tormented Nibelungen, and again Adolf Krypl came to our aid. It would come as no surprise to a theater producer to be told how difficult it is to get any person or group of persons to scream convincingly. No matter what the nationality, all sorts of special inhibitions seem to take over at the very moment that the scream is required. We had great trouble with the screams in *Rheingold;* we had trouble a few years later with *Carmen* (the women in Act One); we had trouble in *Götterdämmerung* (Brünnhilde, Gutrune, and Hagen), and trouble in *Walküre* (Sieglinde). Most singers prefer to do their own screams, and are very good at it until the microphone goes live, at which point they freeze. The only way is to try and catch them when they are practicing screams, which is how we got most of ours. The *Rheingold* children, however, were not so much inhibited as intimidated by the presence of a dear old Austrian professor of music who was acting as our *répétiteur*—in other words, he played the piano at rehearsals. We had explained to him that it was necessary for the children to hear the music a few times at the piano to get an idea of how the passage built up, so that they would know, even without a cue, where to begin their slow, shuffling entrance and where to emit the scream of terror. All children have remarkably good memories for this sort of thing and prefer to do it spontaneously. But we reckoned without our Austrian professor. With all the children assembled on the stage, the professor made a solemn, slow entrance to the piano, where he sat himself down. The children froze. He took off his glasses and wiped them carefully. He replaced them, opened the

As the Austrian "répétiteur" looks on at left, Solti works to loosen up the 40 awe-struck schoolchildren and get them to scream like tormented Nibelungen.

vocal score he was using and peered at it closely. Only then did he look up at the children and say: "Richard Wagner. *Das Rheingold....*"

It took us two hours thereafter to undo the damage: to say, in effect, that they were all supposed to be tiny trembling dwarfs carrying huge lumps of gold and scared stiff of a hideous man with a long whip. If you simply tell children to scream they immediately make the sort of sound you hear in a school playground, whereas we wanted a scream of terror. Our professor really couldn't see what it was all about, but Solti was marvelous with the children, and by the time we came to the session they performed splendidly, simply because the *idea* had been made clear to them. Nobody particularly likes children in the studio because they get into everything and have a talent for removing vital microphones when you are not looking and placing them anywhere but where you want them. But if you take them into your confidence and explain *just* what it is you want, they will always oblige. Benjamin Britten knows more about dealing with children in the studio than anyone I know, and he is at the farthest remove from our Austrian professor. During the recording of the *War Requiem*, when he did not like the way in which the Highgate boys were singing a particular passage, Britten looked up at them and said: "Boys, the trouble is you're singing it much too beautifully. Think about the words. Just remember you're about to go through that door and have your little throats cut."

While all this was going on, our Swiss engineer Karl Brugger had taken himself off to Linz to talk to the manager of a large steel foundry. We had worked out how we wanted to handle the moment, towards the end of *Rheingold*, when Donner swings his hammer, strikes the rock, and causes the mists to vanish and the rainbow bridge to appear. Immediately after the hammer strikes the rock there has to be a huge thunderclap, and, after experiments, we did not think that Mr. Hunt's big drum, even when reinforced with timpani and another bass drum, would provide the sound we wanted. It was not a question of loudness, but of quality; we wanted a sound which would linger, and *from* which the music of the strings and six harps would emerge logically. The bass end of the sound was right, but there was nothing at the top, which was why we sent Brugger off to Linz in search of a steel sheet, some twenty feet by five feet, which we eventually suspended in the center of the Sofiensaal. It took two men to shake it, and two more men to wallop the bass drums which lay at the foot of the sheet. And it worked. It, and the immediately preceding sound of the largest of the anvils being struck by the largest of the hammers as wielded by the toughest of the percussion players, are the two loudest things in the recording and, I have been told, break all the golden rules of what one should and should not do, technically speaking, on a gramophone record. Perhaps because of that, they provided another sensation.

The final extravagance concerned the scene where the two giants have to check that the lumps of gold they have accepted in payment for the return of Freia are sufficient to conceal her figure when piled one above the other. This scene is always tricky on the stage, for no matter how much the giants may stumble about it is clear to the audience that the gold blocks are as light as the painted cardboard from which they are built. Apart from that, they make very little sound when dropped into place, which would certainly not be the case with chunks of solid gold. We therefore could not see how we could produce an adequate sound effect without.... "Blocks of solid gold," Gordon Parry said.

"The banks must have some. Isn't this place on the gold standard?" We called on Adolf Krypl once again, who seemed to think that this time we had gone too far.

We had. Nothing would induce any Viennese bank to part with an ounce of gold, but the Creditanstalt was at least sympathetic. There were other valuable metals, it was suggested, which might be placed at our disposal, on condition that we could persuade the police to cover the entire operation (and the session) with armed guards. We knew that the police would cooperate, and the metal turned out to be tin, in the form of long and exceedingly heavy bars. I happen to think that this effect does not work particularly well, possibly because one has become accustomed to the comic cardboard bumpings as heard in the theater. The sound of heavy metal blocks being moved around fails somehow to create the right image; yet it would have been inconsistent to have omitted this effect and left in all the others. It is the one sequence in *Rheingold* which all of us would have liked to have done again, if time had permitted. That, and the instant when Wotan tosses the ring upon the hoard of gold, which one critic kindly likened to the sound of a pebble thrown into a chamber pot. It struck us later that if we *had* thrown a pebble into a chamber pot it might have turned out better.

As if we had not enough problems with *Rheingold* sessions, *Rheingold* rehearsals, and Beethoven symphonies all going on at the same time, the Decca international promotion people chose that very same period for a big stereo demonstration to be held in the banquet hall of the Hotel Imperial. The technical installation was in the hands of Cyril Windebank, who had been a member of the original Vienna crew in the early nineteen-fifties, but whose main work was now devoted to research and development, though he was soon to find himself very much involved with the problems of transferring *Rheingold* from tape to disk. To ensure the success of the Vienna demonstration, I was asked to invite as many artists as possible, not only from the *Rheingold* cast but from those who had contracts with Decca and were appearing at the Vienna State Opera at that time. We decided to run three "houses," as the room was not big enough to accommodate more than a hundred people in comfort at one time. The first was at six, and was expecially for the Vienna Philharmonic, which turned up in force not only to hear itself in the glories of stereo but to take full advantage of the free bar. (Afterwards, the orchestra staggered over to play in the State Opera across the road, and the performance must have been something to hear.) My colleague, Erik Smith, speaks perfect German and so we got

Unable to borrow real gold, Culshaw and his crew had to use these heavy tin bars to produce the sound effect needed for the scene in "Rheingold" where the gold is piled up in front of Freia.

It took two men to shake the 20-ft. steel sheet at the right, and two more to beat the enormous, single-sided bass drum behind it to produce the great thunderclap in the last scene of "Rheingold." The shimmering Rainbow Bridge music that emerges from this calls for a complement of six harps, a requirement seldom able to be met in the theater but provided in the Decca recording by the four ladies and two gentlemen above.

him to introduce the program and explain what the demonstration was all about; but during the first house he appeared to be nervous, so in the interval before the second house, which was for the press and record dealers and therefore by far the most important of the three, we filled him with about four strong dry martinis. The result was a huge success, and the promotion people were delighted. The final house was much more informal, and was for those artists who cared to appear. Most of the *Rheingold* cast turned up, along with Giuseppe di Stefano, Giulietta Simionato, and Ettore Bastianini, plus a number of the resident stars in Vienna. At about ten thirty Flagstad made her entrance and proceeded to her place in the middle, where we had placed a small table with an ice bucket and a bottle of her favorite champagne. Unlike her colleagues, who had been demanding to hear only their own records, she refused to let us play any of hers, which meant that the others had to listen to their own efforts a second time round. Finally, towards the end of the bottle, she relented and we played some of the *Walküre*, Act Three, she had recorded the year before. In a room full of strong and even overdeveloped personalities, her domination was absolute. I have never met anyone else who could exude, at one and the same time, such warmth *and* reserve.

The party went on a long time and got boisterous. At about twelve-thirty, Flagstad got up to go. She was certainly not drunk, but she was definitely unsteady on her feet (as was everyone after a day like that). I said I would take her to her room, which was on the second floor, whereas the banquet room was on the mezzanine between ground level and the second. She made for the elevator and we got in together. The elevators in the Hotel Imperial are very modern, very silent, and very small. Flagstad peered at the panel and pressed the mezzanine button. We stayed where we were.

After a moment, I said: "It's the second we want."

She said, "But we are going up . . ." which we certainly were not. "Of course we are going up," she repeated.

I reached around behind her to press the second-floor button just a fraction too late—for somebody on the ground floor pressed the recall button, and down we went.

"Now you've done it," she said. "Now we are going *down*. But before we were going up." We got to the ground floor, and she grasped the inner handle of the door firmly to prevent it from being opened on the outside. She waited a second or two, and then to my amazement pressed the mezzanine button again. Up we shot, and out she sailed to our precise point of departure several minutes earlier. I gave up and

walked her to her room. She said she would be at the early piano rehearsal the next morning, and she was.

Flagstad finished her part on time and left for Norway; and on the
day of her departure, Gustav Neidlinger arrived. I had not met him
before, but had long since admired his appearances as the *Rheingold*
Alberich on the stage. Crouching, cursing, and singing with a very individual sort of metal in the voice, he seemed the very embodiment of
evil, and I had not seen another Alberich anywhere who came within
miles of him. In reality, he turned out to be a completely disarming
person with a mania for collecting old books and a habit of addressing
everyone at first sight by the German familiar, *du*. "*Liebes, süsses
Fräulein Hotter*," he wrote to my secretary in reply to a formal business
letter some time later, and though he had never met her, he ended with
"*Vielen lieben Grüssen und Küssen*." It proved indeed quite impossible
to reconcile Neidlinger as we came to know him with the Alberich who
most certainly came to life on our tape. If Kirsten Flagstad and George
London dominated the first half of the *Rheingold* sessions, the second
series belonged without question to Neidlinger. I believe that in the
purely dramatic sense (that of conveying character in terms of sound
alone) his performance in *Rheingold* has rarely been equaled by any
male artist in any operatic recording anywhere. It is thought out; it is
acted out; and it is sung out. I cannot adequately describe the tension he
engendered in the fourth scene when Wotan has finally divested him
not only of the gold but of the ring itself, and Alberich pronounces the
curse that will fall upon all those who gain possession of the ring. We
had proceeded with the usual routine for that session. Solti had given
the orchestra a general rehearsal to prepare for a test of the sequence,
which we intended to play back during the interval and then remake
until it was satisfactory.

When Neidlinger started we all but froze in the control room. You
could touch the intensity. I know I forgot to give Gordon several cues
he had asked for. The venom in the man's voice, the way in which
words seemed to curl in his throat, his hysterical, animal laugh . . . we
had told him we wanted a performance and not a *lieder* recital, and we
were certainly getting one. When it was over, Solti came into the control room shaking his head. "Incredible," he said, "absolute incredible"
(his English gets modified when he is excited). We listened to what was
supposed to be a test, and when it was over I said to Solti that it was a
waste of time and money to think of doing it again: we would never in
a million years get such spontaneous intensity back again.

I have always been convinced that a successful *Rheingold* turns on three characters—Wotan, Loge, and Alberich—for if they are weak there is little the rest can do to compensate. In George London we had a healthy, young Wotan, which is what is required in the piece; he was in his vocal prime and the part caused him no strain. As Loge, we had the immensely experienced Svanholm. Even in earlier years he never had a particularly beautiful voice, but he had intelligence and technique. He could convey what was essential for the record, which was Loge's scheming nature, his confident manipulation of the other characters around him. And in Neidlinger we had our trump card, among the men.

Paul Kuen, as Mime, was the ideal partner for Neidlinger and for years they had been appearing together in *Rheingold* productions all over Europe. They had both recorded before for other companies and were intrigued by the new techniques we asked them to adopt on this occasion. Very soon after the start of scene three, Alberich puts on the Tarnhelm, which is a magic helmet, and disappears. Mime cowers in terror, until suddenly the invisible Alberich, armed with a whip, pursues him all around the cavern. No matter where Mime runs, the whip catches up with him, and Alberich's satanic voice confronts him whichever way he turns.

To bring this sequence over for stereo, we kept Mime very forward (close to the main microphones) so that one could catch his terrified

Svanholm (left) and Paul Kuen are seen through the glass panel of the telephone-boothlike box devised to isolate Neidlinger's voice for special effects in the scene where Alberich, made invisible by the Tarnhelm, pursues Mime about the caverns of Nibelheim.

whispers ("*Wo bist du?*"), and put Alberich in something rather like a telephone booth equipped with its own microphone and a glass panel through which he could see the conductor. This meant that while Mime was in the same acoustical conditions as the orchestra, Alberich, from the moment of his disappearance, was in a wholly separate acoustic which was under our control by means of the special microphone in the box. Therefore, while Mime remained himself, we were able to change and magnify Alberich's voice and make it move at our will to any part of the stereo arc and back again. (As soon as Alberich removes the Tarnhelm and becomes visible again, it was necessary only for him to step out of the box and resume his performance on the open stage and in the normal acoustic.)

All this was only a modern extension of what Wagner himself had in mind. Electrical amplification was unknown at the time of the first performance of *Rheingold*, and so Wagner used the only means at his disposal—a vast speaking tube through which Alberich was directed to sing during his invisible moments. Out of a misguided loyalty to tradition, many theaters still continue to use quite ineffective speaking tubes and megaphones, although a very simple system of a single offstage microphone linked to various speakers deployed around the stage area used by Mime, and with a switching facility to enable the sound of Alberich's voice to be moved from one speaker to another according to Mime's movements, would solve the problem effectively. (I have heard a modern Alberich sing through an electric "loud-hailer"—the sort of thing used by the police to control traffic—which works quite well, except that the voice remains in one place and so makes nonsense of the words and of Mime's movements.)

Gustav Neidlinger (above) made a menacing Alberich in the 1966 Bayreuth "Ring." Paul Kuen (below) played the cowering Mime in the 1951 festival.

By this time, we were approaching the end or, to be precise, the beginning, for our Rhinemaidens were the last of the artists to arrive. This left us with the Prelude and the entire opening scene, plus the end of the work when the Rhinemaidens are heard again offstage. The opening scene, detached from the Prelude, went well because we had very carefully plotted the movements of the girls as they flirt with Alberich, and Solti had been through the scene half a dozen times at the piano. I had an eye on the clock all the time, for we had only one session to go, in which we had to complete the opening scene, record the closing scene, and somehow get a master of the Prelude.

The Prelude of *Rheingold* is a terrifying piece to play. No matter how good the orchestra, it is always touch and go in the theater because the horns are so exposed and because, as they rise through the arpeggio of the opening motive, they tend to "crack." The eighth horn begins, followed by the seventh and the sixth and so on until the phrase reaches the first horn, by which time all eight are playing over the sustained E flat contrabass pedal. The danger is that if *one* horn is unfortunate enough to crack (or, as the Viennese put it, make a "fish"), the effect tends to demoralize the others. The conductor is also at their mercy: for forty-eight bars in slow 6/8 tempo he is really powerless to do anything except beat clearly, pray silently, and *count the bars*. From the moment where the cellos enter in bar 49 he can become a conductor again instead of being a human metronome, but heaven help him if he brings them in a bar too soon or too late.

The horn section of the Vienna Philharmonic is superb, but the players were apprehensive. On the one hand, they did not want to tackle the piece "cold"—that is, at the very start of a session. Equally, they did not want to have it tagged on to the end of a session when they would certainly be tired. From my point of view, although I sympathized with them, their request to make the Prelude in the *middle* of a session was all but impossible. I had to think of the singers and the fact that they were leaving and not coming back. If the worst came to the worst we could always remake the Prelude at some unspecified time in the future; but if we left a single line of the vocal music unrecorded we would have the problem of bringing back at least four singers from different parts of the globe. In recording opera, it is a general rule that you leave orchestral material on one side until the end of the schedule, or as a reserve for those occasions when a singer goes ill or loses his voice.

We had one shot at the Prelude during the penultimate session. It was not bad, but it was not good enough. To add to the difficulties, it is one of those pieces which refuse to be edited: which is to say that, at least until the cellos start the theme, you cannot intersplice between different takes and thus eliminate mistakes or noises. This is because the horn phrases overlap, and so wherever you cut you are breaking into a sustained horn note somewhere down the harmony, and ten to one this will give you an unbearable "bump" when the tapes are joined together. There is also a continuous bass pedal on E flat throughout the passage, and this too cannot be spliced unless, by a sheer fluke, it happens to be at *exactly* the same level (played with the same strength of tone) in the two performances. As players are human beings, there is always a slight discrepancy which the ear would not perceive in hearing the two performances consecutively—but join them together across the pedal, and the bump becomes instantly audible.

We had drawn up a plan for the last session. At all costs we had to finish the opera. We had to make the closing scene with the offstage Rhinemaidens. We had to make the Prelude. Having done those items

The eight horns and four Wagner tubas of the Vienna Philharmonic are seen during the recording of "Rheingold." To expand the range of tone colors available to him, Wagner greatly increased the number of brasses in his "Ring" orchestra. The so-called Wagner tubas, his invention, combine the agility of cornets with the mellow timbre of true tubas.

we could at least say that every *note* of *Rheingold* had been recorded. We then had a list of essential remakes, most of them very short indeed but necessary to correct a few errors here or there. We also had what has come to be known as the luxury list, which contains those remakes you would like to do if there is enough time, but which in a crisis can be ignored. I told Solti that we were all worried about the final scene because, although short, it was technically very tricky for us, and we couldn't afford a misfire in the last six minutes of the recording.

The final scene is tricky because of the perspective required for the offstage Rhinemaidens. They must be clear, but distant. There is one harp with them, and six in the orchestra. The voices of the girls have to sound on an entirely different *plane* from that of the voices on stage (Wotan, Loge) and, desirably, they have to sound *below* the stage voices, as they are supposed to be coming from the river. Technically, this is impossible. Stereo will do anything you want on the lateral sense, but it cannot give you a vertical perspective. But sometimes there are ways of compensating: there are ways, quite frankly, of cheating the ear into informing the brain that it has received an impression which it has not in fact received. We worked very hard to get a special acoustic on the girls' voices and then, in an article published just before *Rheingold* was released, I drew attention to the way in which the voices appeared to come from below. In fact they do nothing of the sort, but the suggestion worked. One critic after another commented on the remarkable illusion, and letters poured into the office asking how it had been done.

The physical position in which we placed the three Rhinemaidens in the Sofiensaal caused them no discomfort at all, but precipitated a major crisis with the lady harpist who was playing the offstage harp. One is always having a harp crisis in Vienna, and this was one of the worst. It was a perilous position we had placed her in, she announced, and perfectly ridiculous. Gordon explained to her what we were trying to do,

The three Rhinemaidens, Oda Balsborg, Hetty Plümacher and Ira Malaniuk, flirt with their Alberich, Gustav Neidlinger, during a break in "Rheingold" sessions.

but it made little difference. She was not worrying about her harp, but about herself. Suppose she fell off and broke her neck? (We had perched her in one of the upper boxes which surround the auditorium.) Even with the clock running against us, I don't think we gave her the obvious answer. Eventually, mumbling and grumbling, she was pacified when we managed to provide two strong men who held her, and her harp, firmly in position throughout the session. Thus we managed to get our final scene.

We also remade the Prelude. This time it was acceptable, except for a few studio noises caused by creaking chairs or carelessly handled instruments—the sort of noises which would not be heard during most music but which stuck out badly in this ultrapianissimo beginning. We made our correction tags and decided to abandon the luxury list.

With about fifteen minutes to go we had a council of war in the control room. We knew it was all there; we knew we had finished *Rheingold;* we knew we had spent much more money than the budget. At that stage none of us would admit openly to the feeling that we had something extraordinary on our hands; but it was precisely that feeling which brought us all together in those last few minutes. Should we say stop? It was all there, and all very good. And yet . . . the Prelude *could* be better, in an ideal world. And the closing bars of the whole work. . . . Were we deceiving ourselves, or could they also be somehow heavier and grander? And in the opening scene, there was one passage where two of the maidens had always been a bit out of tune.

I knew there was no chance of a session the next day, as the orchestra was not free. All the artists—that is, those who were still with us—were leaving the next morning. There was only one chance, and that was to ask the orchestra to give us an hour or so *after* the performance in the opera house that evening. I told Solti I would talk to the orchestra, but couldn't guarantee the result. He said, "Okay—they can decide it for us. If they won't come back, that's it. Do what you can."

They were restless, and sensed that something was up. I spoke to Professors Strasser and Wobisch and they suggested I should speak directly to the orchestra. One has always to remember that for the ordinary rank-and-file orchestral musician a recording session is like any other job—a means of earning money. He is not paid for idealism. You can rightly expect him to be professional, but you cannot hope he will be charitable, either with his time or his convenience. On that particular day the orchestra had played two full sessions for us, a total of five and a half hours, and now the players were going on to the opera house for a three-hour performance there. I was about to ask them to come back after the opera and record difficult music at eleven at night, and they would have been perfectly within their rights as professional musicians and as human beings to refuse.

I told them quite simply that on this occasion those of us behind the scenes had the impression that *Rheingold* was much more than just another operatic recording. We felt it was so remarkable that we could not bear the thought of any compromise at the last minute. Therefore, in these exceptional circumstances, would the orchestra come back for an hour, or an hour and a half at the most, after the opera? There was some shuffling and muttering; and then an immensely satisfying, gratifying yes.

The session actually began at 2300. We had spoken to Adolf Krypl and asked him to arrange sandwiches and a huge amount of white wine to keep the musicians going over the interval, which we reckoned would come shortly after midnight. I talked to Roland Berger, the first horn, and told him he could dictate exactly where he wanted the Prelude placed in the emergency session, because I knew what a day it had been for the horns. Roland looked at the rest of the remakes and opted, sensibly, for the period just before the interval. This meant that we would spend the first forty minutes or so remaking the opening scene, or parts of it, with the Rhinemaidens; then we would tackle the Prelude; and, after the interval, we would all try to do something exceptional with the orchestral coda of the whole work.

By the time the orchestra got back to the hall it was after 2300, and everyone was tired. It was the last gasp. But the Viennese respond well to this sort of tension, and they like a crisis. The remake of the opening scene went well, and was finished just before 2345. Solti looked at Roland Berger, who nodded his agreement to try the Prelude again. Solti told the orchestra there would be no rehearsal. He told them we already had an acceptable Prelude, so all that was necessary was to relax, stop worrying, and try to get a better one. I announced the take, and the red light went on: the E flat pedal sounded again from the depths. The eighth horn started. The seventh horn started. The eighth horn started again—and cracked at the top of his phrase. The orchestra stopped playing and I put the light out.

Solti said, "Come on—don't lose your nerve, we'll get it." They started again, and again it happened. The horns were tired, and were losing their "lip." This time, when they broke down, I didn't put the light off. There was an awful silence in the studio, but not a word was spoken. The E flat pedal started again. And this time it went. In the control room we were holding our breaths, and I was counting the bars to the point where the cellos enter: for I knew that we could join there if necessary, and anyway by then the danger was over. It seemed to go on forever, with a danger spot for the horns in every single bar. But they made it . . . and you could almost feel the relief when the cellos came in and the music began to move steadily forward with the flowing variant of the motive. We had, at last, a fabulous Prelude.

The orchestra went off to the canteen—it was about twenty past midnight—and Solti came to the control room. He looked utterly exhausted, but very pleased. We did not listen to the Prelude because we knew it was fine. Instead, we played the version of the end of the opera we had recorded that afternoon, and tried to find out what was wrong with it. (Not that it was bad, but there was still something wrong.) It is a short

Photographer Hans Wild climbed up under the roof of the Sofiensaal to get this overhead shot of Solti rehearsing the Vienna Philharmonic.

coda. After the final notes of the Rhinemaidens, the trumpets play the sword motive, and their crescendo leads into the final pages, which consist basically of a combination of the Valhalla motive on the trombones and trumpets and the Rainbow Bridge motive played by the Wagner tubas. What was wrong in the afternoon performance, we decided, was concerned with the balance between these two themes, plus the fact that the tempo was very slightly too fast. We spent quite a time analyzing all this, knowing that the orchestra would be consuming the buffet and drinking the wine in the canteen. What we forgot was that we had not given Adolf Krypl any limit to the amount of wine to be provided; worse still, the canteen staff had assumed that, since it was already so late, the session was over. The wine flowed merrily. We called the orchestra back at about a quarter to one, and five minutes later, returning to the studio with Solti, we were confronted with an alarming sight. The Vienna Philharmonic had taken us at our word, and most of the players were delightfully and obliviously merry. It did not auger too well for the coda, but nobody on earth could blame them after such a day.

They played like gods. We made only one take, and it was over. Solti made a small speech of thanks and so did I on behalf of the Company, and they staggered home. At 0102 on the morning of October 9, 1958, the first recording of *Rheingold* had come to an unbelievably sonorous conclusion.

In the days of *Rheingold* we did not have a permanent technical installation in the Sofiensaal, and so a backstage dressing room was used for the equipment and as a control room. When the hall was booked for a function other than recording, such as a dance or a convention, our control room was also required to revert to its original function. For several weeks after the conclusion of *Rheingold* we had no access either to the main hall or to our control room because of a whole series of festivities in the hall, but we were extremely anxious to begin the editing while the events of the sessions and our recollections of what was good and bad remained fresh. At first, the management of the hall did not seem to be able to help us; then, suddenly, someone remembered a suite of storerooms in a remote part of the hall where we would be unlikely to disturb anyone at any time. The rooms were in an incredible mess, for they had become a depository for anything which happened not to fit elsewhere in the Sofiensaal. There were bundles of carpets, and huge parcels which turned out to be full of paper; mirrors of all shapes and sizes, broken and unbroken; a bicycle; sacks full of corn; and a barber's chair. There were two or three splendid old ceramic stoves in working order, and these were tended by an elderly lady who, a year or two later, was to become our housekeeper when we eventually turned those same storerooms into an apartment. In 1958 we were glad enough to have the use of the rooms as they were. We installed our equipment among the corn and the mirrors and the barber's chair, and settled down to the business of editing *Rheingold*.

It has become a tradition in Decca, and a good one, to do your own editing: which is to say that the producers and technicians on any major work will not only make the choice of what material is used out of what has been recorded, but will actually join it up and sign off the complete performance when it has been assembled. There are many people in other companies who consider this a menial task. They consign the tapes, and a marked-up score showing where the joins are supposed to be made, to a separate editing department. This may sound efficient on the grounds that it is saving the time of senior staff, but I do not think it is more efficient in terms of the finished product. Tape joints do not always work in just the spots where you want them to work, and as soon as you come up against a stubborn example, a *musical* decision has to be taken about where to move the join—which involves comparative judgment between several alternative performances. Since there can be many such instances in the editing of a complete opera, I believe it is right that the decisions should be taken by one or another of the people who were in control of the recording, and not by someone else, however capable, who may be totally unaware of what actually went on during the sessions.

Editing can be very tedious. Remember that we had been immersed in *Rheingold* for weeks—not only in recording and rehearsal, but in playback out of session time. We must have heard the opera nine or ten times in that short period, though always in disconnected sections, long or short. Now it was necessary to sit down and piece it all together, selecting the best material and making sure that the continuity, both musical and dramatic, remained stable. Any fool can join together bits of tape, and we could have strung up a complete *Rheingold* in two days and left it at that. But careful editing pays dividends, largely because memory can play tricks on you; in the heat of a busy session, one's convictions about what is either very good or very bad can later turn out to be hopelessly wrong. All the same, I like to make up as quickly as possible what is known as a rough-edit of the opera, which consists basically of those takes which *seemed* the best at the time of recording. This usually takes three or four days in the case of a work running for about

Svanholm, as the crafty Loge, gives
some advice to George London, the
Wotan. Kirsten Flagstad sits at the back.

a hundred and forty minutes, and we do not worry unduly about any temperamental joins. When this rough-edit is complete we play the whole work through to ourselves. At this stage it is not even divided into record "sides," but is just a series of reels of tape of varying length. By using two tape machines for the performance, one is able to hear the work complete and without interruption. Each of us in his different capacity (and often with overlapping capacities) marks in his score what he likes and dislikes. Afterwards, a note is made of every objection, on whatever grounds, with special emphasis on those which have been noted by more than one person.

Armed with this very considerable battery of notes, one then goes to work in earnest and seeks to correct each flaw as it occurs. It may be a bad ensemble which has hitherto slipped by unnoticed; it may be a single note out of tune, vocally or instrumentally; it may be a disagreeable join; it may be a studio noise; or it may be an effect which sounded good out of its context, but now fails to merge with its environment. This is where the reserve material comes in. Although, superficially speaking, all the obvious best takes have been used for the rough-edit, they are only the best by virtue of their *over-all* excellence, and many tiny details may be better in other, generally less excellent takes. This sort of correction work takes a great deal of time and requires the most expert judgment. (We often wonder if the artists, who are by that time on the other side of the world, realize that it sometimes takes half a day to search out an in-tune F sharp and coax it, all by itself, into a musical phrase which is otherwise perfect. Immoral? Some people would say so, but I do not agree. A record is a record, not a theater performance.) When this correction work has been completed, the opera is then divided into sides: i.e., it is divided into the form in which it will eventually reach the public on records.

This can also be very tricky, because several factors impinge and sometimes come into conflict. It is desirable, so far as possible, to equalize the side timings: in other words, not to have, in one and the same opera, one side which runs for seventeen minutes and one for thirty-two. This is for technical reasons; but there are also musical factors involved. One wants to make the side changes as painless to the listener as possible: in other words, they should at least be logical. But in the case of a work like *Rheingold* which has not been recorded before, and for which you have only a general timing in advance, it is impossible to predict exactly where the side changes are likely to come. There is a further reason (not in fact applicable to *Rheingold*, whose general timing clearly indicated six sides, however divided), and that is the commercial consideration governing those works which *might* be squeezed on to four very long sides, or accommodated very comfortably on six average sides. By adopting the former, one might compromise the sound slightly, but the record public would save the price of one record per set. On the other hand, the public for opera on records usually shows emphatically that it does not want any compromise on quality, and prefers to pay a bit more for a first-class product.

The question of length of side is often misunderstood by the public. Record companies are not trying to shortchange them by dividing a work in a particular way. On the contrary, they are trying to provide a record which will not only play beautifully and so, on the right equipment, give a good representation of the original sound, but which can also be properly processed without the kind of technical troubles which can sometimes be caused either by very long playing times, or by very uneven playing times within a set. Sometimes there are special exceptions: Britten's *Curlew River* really belongs on three sides, but Decca managed to get it perfectly upon two because we felt that the sustained mood of the piece would be ruined by a second interruption. The playing time for each side is well over thirty minutes, and the total time is around sixty-nine minutes. But although *Curlew River* has its loud moments, a lot of it is very soft and its eight instrumentalists obviously cannot approach the level of sound provided by a Wagnerian orchestra.

With *Rheingold* divided into six sides, we arranged the penultimate playback. Again, notes were taken, but this time the number was considerably fewer. The remainder of the editing process is known to us as "beauty treatment": we consider what points have been raised at the penultimate playback and see if anything can be done about them. It is surprising what can emerge. Between the first and second playbacks the work has altered considerably in detail, and this can sometimes change the emphasis of a scene or sequence when heard in its context. The "beauty treatment" seeks to correct that sort of thing, plus any other objections which may be raised at the last minute. At that point the final playback is held, and it has been our practice to invite friends from the Philharmonic and their wives to hear what had emerged. But we do not admit further correction. One of the things you have to learn (and cannot be taught) is the danger of overediting: it is literally possible to edit the life out of a performance through an excess of zeal, too much fiddling about, and an inability to make up one's mind between two close alternatives. There comes a moment when you have to say Stop! Almost from that point, the recording on which you have lavished so much care is out of your hands forever.

I wrote "almost" because it is usually possible to be around when the dubbing engineer, back in London, transfers the sound from the tape to the disk which will then be processed and will generate the material from which the finished record is pressed. The dubbing engineer has a long and often thankless task, but he usually appreciates the interest of the producer and recording engineer in helping him to ensure that the sound he is putting on his disk is an exact replica of what is on the tape. This is mandatory, at least in Decca. The methods of some companies who put any old sound on the tape in the hope that it can be "adjusted" or "compensated" at the dubbing stage are not tolerated. The responsibility for the sound always lies with the people who made the tape, and not with some committee of experts who have probably never been near a recording location.

Immediately after the final *Rheingold* playback, I had to go to Paris for our international repertoire meeting. As I left the Sofiensaal the final bars still seemed to be ringing in my head—among other things that were ringing, because after the playback we drank several toasts to the artists, in their absence, for the magnificent work they had done; and we had not been exactly reticent about our own efforts, for all of us knew that *Rheingold* was better than anything we had ever done before. Erik Smith was running me out to the airport in his Anglia, via a back route we had recently discovered which enabled one to get to

Gordon Parry and John Culshaw (right foreground) follow a full score during a "Rheingold" playback. Other auditors include Christopher Raeburn, Solti (backs to camera), Gustav Neidlinger and George London.

Schwechat in little over half the time required on the main road. About two miles from the airport this minor road joins the main road by crossing some unguarded railway tracks, but on that particular morning there was no means of getting across: the Austrians were repairing the rail and had barricaded the end of the road. They had also gone off for coffee and were not to be seen. As I had barely ten minutes to the flight closure time, there was no question of going back to try and find another access to the main road. We decided that there must be another means of crossing the railway closer to the airport entrance, so Erik turned the Anglia left onto a pebble track which ran parallel with the railway. After a few yards the Anglia began to sink, and after a few more it stopped altogether, embedded up to its wheel hubs in soft gravel. We tried all the obvious ways to coax it out, but it merely dug itself in deeper. I grabbed my luggage, stumbled across the railway tracks and waved my Air France ticket like a hitchhiker. It was an Air France van that eventually picked me up, and I reached the airport just as the flight was being called. My last recollection of the *Rheingold* period was of looking down from a Caravelle window some twenty minutes later and seeing the Anglia being dragged out of the gravel by a team of oxen. The queue of cars on the barricaded road stretched back to the Danube Canal, but the Austrians were still at coffee.

When I returned to London from Paris there was an urgent message to call Gordon Parry, who was still in Vienna. When I got through he said: "You've left eight bars out of *Rheingold!*" It was a terrible moment. At the end of any opera you always have the sinking feeling that there may be one small, insignificant passage you have forgotten in the rush, though I could not see how it had happened this time. The trouble was that I had changed my mind several times about the turnovers, and had revised them once again after the final playback. One of the side changes at that time had been in the middle of the interlude before the fourth scene, and at the playback everyone had been so busy chatting about the virtues and defects of what they had just heard that nobody noticed that the penultimate side began with the Giant's theme in D major instead of C major. After the playback I had asked my colleagues to change the turnover to a later point, with the result that when they now tried to join the interlude sequence back to itself they produced a grotesquely horrible modulation. The eight bars in question had been omitted in the original editing; but because of the time taken to change from one reel of tape to another and because at the start of the new reel everyone was still thinking about what *had* been heard rather than what was *being* heard, the missing bars were not noticed. Fortunately, as it was a simple assembly mistake, it was rectified in minutes by sorting out the missing bars from the reserve tapes and splicing them into the master. But it gave me an anxious moment.

A week or two later the *Rheingold* tapes arrived in London and the transfer to disk began. Until then, no one except the members of the Vienna crew had heard the recording, and it took a long time for word to get around that something unusual was on the way. I still could not forget the words of our competitor the night before we started in Vienna: "Very nice, very interesting. But of course you won't *sell* any." Not many people came out with it quite so directly, but I soon found out that he was not alone in thinking that *Rheingold* might just be a costly way of buying some prestige, which Decca didn't need anyway. It was difficult to adjust from the enthusiasm of Vienna to the phlegmaticism of London. It was just another record, wasn't it? What was all the fuss about?

I wrote to Wobisch to thank him officially for the marvelous cooperation of the Vienna Philharmonic, and to suggest that as the borrowed timpani from London had been shown to be such an improvement, his committee should consider buying a new set of instruments from either Dresden or Chicago. I also wrote to Flagstad to say that *High Fidelity* wanted me to write an article about her recent studio work, and requested her permission to do so. I added:

> Before I left Vienna last week I heard a complete playback of *Rheingold* and must congratulate you for having given such a marvellous performance and for having made something so striking and impressive out of a part which frequently goes for nothing. Everyone is very good and I suspect that one day we shall be rather proud of this recording.

She replied at once to say how much she had enjoyed her visit to Vienna, and added: "*You ask if I object to you writing an article about me for* High Fidelity. *Of course not. Write what you like!*"

The problems of getting *Rheingold* onto disk were formidable. The machine which cuts the disk is a very delicate and sometimes temperamental apparatus, and our fear was that if *Rheingold* caused it to blow up we would have severely impaired the production of the rest of the stereo catalog for as long as it took to repair. Our colleague Cyril Windebank, who knows much more about cutting than any of us, worked with us night after night when the rest of the studio was closed to find out how to accommodate our anvils and thunderclaps and all the other dangerous passages on what had to be, after all, a practicable mass-produced commodity. (We had, on the sessions, taken the precaution of recording "safe" versions of all the danger points, which could have been spliced into the master tape in the event of serious trouble.) I don't remember how many nights it took, but in the end *Rheingold* found its way onto disk without any compromise and without blowing up the cutter. Craftsmanship and devotion made it possible.

I had asked the studios in West Hampstead to let me have an "acetate" (a sort of test disk which can only be played a few times) of the closing scene from *Rheingold*. When it arrived I played it to Terry McEwen who was at that time in charge of classical promotion in London. He is a large, exuberant Canadian with a vast knowledge of and enthusiasm for opera, though his tastes incline as heavily to the Italian repertoire as do mine to the German. When I played him the closing scene he went wild; he kept playing it over and over again until I thought there would be no groove left on the acetate. But it was the first real enthusiasm I had seen since I came back to London (except for a telephone call from Arthur Haddy, the chief of the studio, who had summoned Gordon and Jimmy to congratulate them on what he had heard of the recording, and then rang me and said: "You've got a winner there"). The next thing I knew, Terry McEwen was going the length and breadth of Head Office, playing the closing scene to everyone who might conceivably have anything to do with selling, promoting, exporting, or advertising the record. And it worked: the amazing thing was that a lot of people who do their jobs quite satisfactorily, but who are not particularly opera enthusiasts, became fascinated and thrilled by music they had never heard before. Of course, initially, the Donner call followed by the hammer on the rock and the thunderclap leading to the Rainbow Bridge music was what caught their ears. And why not? Many people eventually bought *Rheingold* for submusical reasons, I am sure; but when the novelty of the effects had worn off I am equally sure that those same people found a much more rewarding appeal in the music itself. When you are dealing with unfamiliar music of any sort, the problem is to catch people's interest, and it seemed that *Rheingold* had that ability. Had we made a solemn, "musicological" approach to the opera we might still have sold it to the converted, but not to the mass of people for whom the title *Rheingold* meant, until this record appeared, something heavy, long-winded, and boring.

The release date was set for May. Terry McEwen arranged for the album design to be photographed by Hans Wild because, apart from his capabilities as a photographer, he happens to be a Wagnerian. Gordon Parry, Hans Wild, and I had several meetings to work out an idea. We started with a very elaborate mock-up of the gods entering Valhalla, which we abandoned as impractical. Eventually we saw that there was

The percussionist grimaces as he strikes a blow on the anvil to simulate Donner's hammer hitting the rock. This sets off the tremendous thunderclap heard in the concluding scene of "Rheingold."

only one clear and relevant symbol for the whole work, and that was the gold itself. Hans produced an excellent picture of the gold shimmering in the waters of the Rhine, and although he went on to photograph all the later *Ring* covers I still think that the *Rheingold* one is the best.

Understandably, though, a mood of caution still prevailed. For one thing, the *Rheingold* accounts were coming in, and it was already clear that the costs were unprecedented for a three-record set. It was all very well for opera enthusiasts to run around saying how marvelous it all was, but the big question still remained: would enough people actually come forward and buy it? Nobody would know the answer until May.

Meanwhile, the rest of us got on with the recording program. Flagstad was in London in early January to make a solo LP, and our correspondence began again in February, when we were discussing some new ideas and reviving one or two old ones. She had changed her mind again about the *Alto Rhapsody*, and now felt inclined to make it. *Das Lied von der Erde* came up again, and went down. What I really wanted from her was the Fricka scene from Act Two of *Walküre*, for although at this stage we had not the slightest idea when, if ever, our complete *Walküre* would be made, it seemed imperative after her performance in

Rheingold that she should appear as the same character in the next sequence of the *Ring*. We even thought of recording the scene with her and putting it in cold storage, if necessary for years, until such time as we made *Walküre*. I wrote to her with this suggestion on February 18, 1959, and enclosed a copy of Sir Arthur Bliss's *The Enchantress* which I thought might interest her. It was a sad omen, for this brilliant dramatic "scene" for contralto and orchestra had been written for Kathleen Ferrier; and our next news of Flagstad gave the first indication of her illness, though we did not know then that it was cancer.

In March we had a cable abruptly canceling a group of sessions in London. This was followed, in April, by a letter from Flagstad:

> I hope you did not get worried when you had my wire. You may remember last year that I could not stand on my feet for very long. It has become much worse so that I have to stay in hospital and get X-ray treatments. It is very painful and I take pills to relieve the suffering. I do not know how long I have to stay here, but so far the whole of next week. . . .

Exactly a week later, she wrote again:

> Today my doctor told me I could come out of here on Thursday, April 30th, and that means I could do some recordings in June if you have not changed anything. I am not free from pain but am supposed to feel well in about two weeks. I must move again, and the first thing I must move is my voice, and really work hard to get it in shape. . . .

I replied with greetings from all her Decca friends, and sent her a list of possible recording dates in June.

At about this time, a week or two before the release of *Rheingold*, we had agreed to give it a semipublic premiere on behalf of the Wagner Society of London. None of us knew this organization, for, truth be told, most of us are not enthusiastic about Wagner enthusiasts, whether in London or anywhere else. We found out that the Society consisted of people whose devotion to Wagner was unquestionable, and so it seemed appropriate to launch *Rheingold* in such august company. The engineers proceeded to install equipment in a hall off the Strand where the Society held its meetings. They asked me to introduce the recording and be their guest for the performance, but I suddenly got cold feet. My colleagues were all back in Vienna, and suddenly I could not stand the thought of hearing *Rheingold* exposed for the first time to a large audience. I knew every bar and every inflection, and I knew I couldn't bear to watch the audience reaction, good or bad. I told the Society that I had a session that evening, but would come at the end of the playback and try to answer any questions the audience might ask.

From the other side of the street I watched the audience going into the hall: it was obviously a capacity crowd. When the last people had gone in, I crossed the road and waited until I heard the sound of the E flat pedal; two hours and twenty minutes later I went back, and the coda, our famous one-in-the-morning coda, was ringing out loud and clear. There was a lot of applause at the end, and when I went into the hall it was an amazing sight. It was packed. At the back and down the sides and in the center aisle were people who had stood through the performance, or sat on the floor, in order to hear the first recorded *Rheingold*. It was enormously gratifying, though what followed was less so.

As soon as I got on the platform a dozen hands shot up. I picked one at random: "When will Decca make a complete *Walküre?*" I said I didn't know and that all depended on the success of *Rheingold*. I pointed out that we had our separate Act One and Act Three of *Walküre* available already, as a sort of stopgap. Next question: "What about *Siegfried?* Never been recorded. Why not?" Next question: "What about *Götterdämmerung?* The Flagstad radio transcription isn't good enough. Could *Götterdämmerung* please be the next?" And so it went on. Not a word or a thought about *Rheingold*, but a demand for the rest of the *Ring* and a total lack of appreciation for the risk Decca had taken in making the work they had just heard. It was the typical insensibility of the enthusiast, and I felt rebellious. Instead of answering any more questions, I said I wanted to ask a question of the audience. I said that the ability of a record company to continue with expensive and untried repertoire depended on how many people came forward to buy such repertoire. The audience had just heard the first recorded *Rheingold*. How many of the Wagner Society in the hall intended to go to a record dealer and order a set? Would those who intended to buy *Rheingold* please raise their hands?

There were about a hundred and seventy people in the hall. I counted twelve very tentative hands. I said, "There's your answer about *Siegfried* and *Götterdämmerung*," though I thought: only if you represent the real public, which I doubt. But it was very depressing. I had no doubt that they had enjoyed *Rheingold*. I had no doubt that they would talk a lot about it, especially as they were the first to hear it. But to spend six pounds for three records of *Rheingold?* There was the rub.

On my way out I was accosted by an apparition in a black veil. (Wagner audiences consist mostly of the very old and the very young, and this one had been no exception.) "Young man," said the apparition, "I understand you had something to do with all this. Can you tell me the name of the tenor who sang Froh?"

I said it was Waldemar Kmentt.

"You should be thoroughly ashamed of yourself. I know Kmentt's voice very well and it doesn't sound anything like him." The apparition glared at me and added: "I shall *certainly* not buy the record—I always judge *Rheingold* by how the tenor sounds in 'Heda! Heda! Hedo!' " And with that she swept out.

"Heda! Heda! Hedo!" is of course sung by Donner, a baritone, but I was too disillusioned to go after her and explain.

When *Rheingold* appeared in May the reviews from all countries surpassed our wildest hopes. It would be possible, but boring, to quote pages of them; but Andrew Porter in *The Gramophone* really summed up what all of them said when he wrote, in the course of a very long and detailed review:

> Stereo, we are told, is an illusion. This recording gives one a very complete illusion of experiencing a performance. The recording is not exaggerated, not over-brilliant or over-defined; the triangle does not jump out at you, as if to show just how hi-fi it can get. The supreme virtue of the finest stereo recording—and this is the finest I have ever heard—is its naturalness. The engineers seem to have aimed at a spacious theatre acoustic; not exactly an embracing Bayreuth one, but more like an ideal old-style opera house, of the kind in which Richard Strauss (who believed that "many of the inexhaustible riches of the score are lost at Bayreuth") preferred to hear the *Ring*. . . .
>
> This *Rheingold* recording shows that the Decca team has somehow discovered the secret of preserving an opera alive on disc in a way that offers something new in musical experience. . . .

As the reviews flowed in from all over the world, a much more exciting development than acclaim came into view: *Rheingold* was beginning to sell very well, and overseas orders were coming in. In the United States it started rather slowly, but by the autumn, to everyone's amusement and astonishment, there it was in the *Billboard* charts of the best-selling LP albums, surrounded by Elvis Presley and Pat Boone, and without another classical recording in sight. And there it stayed for many weeks. (I wondered what our colleague from the competition thought now.)

The French, who have always been mad about Wagner, gave it their highest award—and Decca's first—of the *Grand Prix du Disque Mondiale*. So excited were they that the award was given *hors concours:* they couldn't even wait for the official date. The record collected prizes from just about every country that awards such things—and it went on selling. *Billboard* said it was the biggest-selling operatic set in record history. Donner swung his hammer in Austin, Texas; in Melbourne; in Buenos Aires; and in Leeds. Only Germany seemed nervous about Wagner, and the explanation for that must come from a social philosopher, not from me.

In the midst of our jubilations came another sad letter from Flagstad:

> I am terribly sorry but it is impossible for me to sing the sessions in June. In spite of treatments, medicines, massage and diet I believe that the pain has increased and it is impossible for me to stand on my feet for more than twenty or thirty seconds at a time. I am very disappointed and hope the inconvenience will not be too great for you.

Early in June, Bernard Miles told me he had heard that there had been a sudden improvement in her health, and that although she would certainly not be able to do the June sessions I should write at once and try to revive her interest in the *Walküre* Fricka. I wrote:

> As you know, we have had a big success with *Rheingold* and it is quite possible that over the next five or six years my Directors will sanction a complete recording of the *Ring*, of which—if it happens—last year's *Rheingold* will be the foundation. You can probably guess what is in my mind, and indeed I did mention it to you earlier this year—it is, of course, that you should record the Fricka-Wotan scene from *Walküre*. The real problem is that I imagine *Walküre* will be the last opera we shall record, so we shall not be going through the *Ring* in sequence, and quite frankly I haven't the least idea when it will be made. But there is nothing to stop us recording the Fricka scene in the autumn of this year and then keeping it safely in store until such time as we record the whole opera. Will you please think about it?

Evidently the improvement had not lasted, for on June 16 she replied:

> I have just finished another series of X rays and may hope for a result in a few weeks. I am so far not a bit better but can manage so long as I do not have to stand. It is therefore impossible for me to tell you now if I will be able to record by the end of September. I would certainly like to record the *Walküre* Fricka, and can see your point in wanting me to. When do you need to have the final answer?

I wrote to say we would reserve the sessions in Vienna anyway, but that she should not worry: if for any reason she did not feel like making the trip we could always substitute an orchestral work. I did not hear from her again for some time.

Meanwhile, Mr. Rosengarten was negotiating an exclusive contract with Birgit Nilsson, the great Brünnhilde and Isolde of our time. She was naturally keen to record as much as possible of her repertoire, and if there was to be any intention of going ahead with the *Ring*, it was essential to have Nilsson under contract. Then, at the very moment when the outlook for the Decca *Ring* was at its brightest (because of the continuing success of *Rheingold*), a series of arbitrary events and impulses suddenly pushed the venture completely out of sight. It was nobody's fault, directly; it was not a conspiracy; it was what Americans call happenstance.

The logical follow-up for *Rheingold* was, of course, *Walküre*. But from the Decca point of view, money had already been spent only two years before on recording both the first and third acts, and they were still reasonably good sellers. Whatever the success of *Rheingold*, it seemed inadvisable from an economic point of view to plunge immediately into a complete *Walküre*, though no firm decision was ever taken one way or the other, because events themselves forced the issue. First, Birgit Nilsson made it quite clear that she wanted to record *Tristan und Isolde* before anything else. (She had made a record for us with Knappertsbusch of passages from *Tristan*, including the Act One Narration and the Liebestod, but what she really wanted was a complete *Tristan*, and her whole contract turned on that point.) So Decca had to set up a *Tristan* recording before giving any further thought to the *Ring*. At about the time all this was happening, our colleagues in RCA, New York, whose records were being distributed in the United Kingdom and some other countries by Decca, decided that they would like to make a recording of *Walküre*. (They were not unaware of the success of *Rheingold* in the United States, of course.) For their *Walküre* they would need Nilsson, who was by that time under contract to Decca.

The outcome of all this was that Nilsson's insistence on a complete *Tristan und Isolde* as a first venture for Decca helped at least to open the door for her release to RCA for a *Walküre* to be made in London and conducted by Erich Leinsdorf. Quite apart from the important Decca/RCA relationship, it was highly unlikely that Decca would want to set up *Tristan* and *Walküre* at almost the same time, and only three years after the release of the Flagstad versions of Acts One and Three of *Walküre*. The Decca *Ring* seemed to vanish in the mists of that autumn in 1959, at the very time when *Rheingold*'s success was at its height.

CHAPTER THREE

1962: Siegfried

IT MAY HAVE gone out of sight, but it had not gone out of mind. Letters poured in from all over the world about *Rheingold*, and our distributors began to pester us for a successor—but which? *Walküre* was out of the question for several years; I did not think we could properly cast the title part of *Siegfried*; and the idea of *Götterdämmerung* at that stage was too enormous to contemplate. Furthermore, Solti had said that he would not record *Götterdämmerung* until he had gained much more experience with the work in the theater, which was a modest and eminently sensible approach. We seemed to be stuck.

Flagstad wrote again in the summer of 1959 from her home in Kristiansand:

> A friend in San Francisco sent me your *High Fidelity* article. It is very good, but *much* too nice! Thank you.
> With me there is nothing new. I still suffer but hope to get better soon. So nice of Decca to wait for me, but I hope you will not be disappointed. Bernard Miles is here for eight days, and it is nice to have him here, he is such a good guest and easy to please. The weather is wonderful, and I rest very well but still do a little work every day. . . .

I wrote again in early August to ask how she was, and on the 19th she replied:

> I am sorry that I am unable to send you good news. However, I am starting a new treatment tomorrow, and if I can wait another two weeks I might be able to make a decision. At present I have a lot of pain, worse than before I am sorry to say. I am terribly busy these days—it is too hot as well—but I live in hope of better days and of seeing you and the boys soon.

Mr. Rosengarten had approved the budget for Flagstad's recording of the Wotan/Fricka scene from *Walküre*, and we now intended to set it up for the autumn of 1960, either before or after the *Tristan* recording with Nilsson. We were still holding some dates for the autumn of 1959, but the tone of Flagstad's letters gave us little hope, and sure enough at the beginning of September she sent a cable canceling the Vienna dates. This was followed by another letter:

> I have been in hospital since September 1st and my housekeeper is on holiday, so I have only just received your letters. I have had more treatments but so far nothing has helped. The doctors keep telling me I cannot expect to get better so soon, but maybe in two months. It is very annoying. I can do my office work at the opera, but cannot do all the representation needed, or walk around looking after things. I can sit without pain, but have to take aspirin every five or six hours. Next week I am home from the hospital, and I am longing to sing again. I cannot tell you how sorry I am to have upset your plans. . . .

The cruelest effect of certain types of cancer is its pattern of severe illness followed by apparent recovery. It was so in the case of Kathleen Ferrier; it became so in the case of Kirsten Flagstad. On November 11, 1959, she wrote:

> I am now feeling very much better. I can stand on my feet without pain and I feel my condition is improving every day. On Sunday November 8th I sang a church concert so you see I am feeling all right.
>
> I plan to go to America on December 10th to stay for five weeks or so, but in the New Year I might be available for recording. I really am *longing* to!

I wrote back to say that we would record whenever she felt like it, and in whichever city she preferred. I reminded her about the Fricka scene from *Walküre* and several other projects we had discussed many times. She replied from Phoenix, Arizona, on December 20:

> I believe I will be back in Oslo around January 10th, maybe a little before. Thank you, by the way, for sending me *Peter Grimes*, which I could not listen to before I left, as I think it best to take a long, quiet time to listen.
>
> The Brahms *Alto Rhapsody* and the *Four Serious Songs* would be fine. I am working at them daily. And the Fricka scene from *Walküre* is well under way. I *love* to sing it. You also mentioned the Waltraute scene in *Götterdämmerung*, where Nilsson will sing the Brünnhilde—but where does it start and end? I love that one too, but have not really worked at it yet.

The news that she was so much better and able to write such an optimistic letter gave us all encouragement; for even if we were going to make bits and pieces of scenes, it meant that she would appear in two, and possibly three, of our *Ring* operas—if the works ever came back on the schedule again. And even if we never completed the *Ring*, the Fricka scene from *Walküre* and the Waltraute scene from *Götterdämmerung* would make an attractive single LP when coupled together.

The improvement in Flagstad's health was short-lived. As early as January 17, 1960, she wrote from Oslo:

> I am sorry to tell you that I am again in hospital and that I have resigned from the Norwegian Opera.
>
> I was ill all the time in Phoenix, and was glad I was home again a week ago. As you can understand, I do not know anything about the future but will let you know as soon as possible. I am very unhappy.

After some weeks she was allowed to go home to Kristiansand. I did not want to give her false hopes, but feared that any silence from our end might lead her to think we had lost interest. I wrote again, but she did not reply until April 3:

> I am back again in the hospital after five weeks at home. I am constantly getting worse in my hip and am always in pain. I talked to my doctors when I arrived and I am sorry to say they cannot promise anything in the way of getting well enough to record in September or later.
>
> This is a terrible blow to me, as I had been hoping all the time to be able to go on making records. I find your plan about the *Ring* excellent, and would have loved to sing all the parts you mentioned.
>
> To give up singing when the voice is still good is hard, and to write this letter to you is very difficult for me, too.

All of us now realized that her illness was far more serious than the arthritis it was supposed to be. The heartbreak of the last sentence of her letter of April 3 obviously required some serious move from our side, and again the parallel with Kathleen Ferrier was unavoidable. When Kathleen, still in full possession of her voice, was too weak to make the journey from Frognal to the Decca Studios in West Hampstead, Arthur Haddy, the chief engineer, proposed to send her favorite crew to her home so that she could record whatever she liked. She accepted, and I think it gave her great encouragement; but the fatal attack came even before the arrangements could be made.

At least when Kathleen was dying she was surrounded by loving friends, whose devotion and self-sacrifice had no limits. What was so appalling in the case of Flagstad is that I think she was terribly lonely. This woman, who not so very long ago had commanded the opera stages of the world and had known all the adulation that opera audiences can bestow upon their favorites, was passing her final years in a self-imposed isolation. And those who loved her could do little about it, for they were too far away.

I talked to Gordon and Jimmy about a plan which was modeled on the suggestion others had made to Kathleen Ferrier. At least I hoped it might give Flagstad something to look forward to. I wrote to her on April 8, 1960:

> Of course we share your disappointment about the recording plans, but I really feel that this is an occasion when *we* should be flexible enough to enable you to undertake the recording in the most comfortable circumstances. Will you think about the following proposal?
>
> In September of this year we could record all the *Ring* passages in terms of the *other* artists involved (and of course the orchestra), and we would simply omit your part. In other words, you would not need to be there. Then, on a suitable occasion when you are feeling better, we could superimpose your performance on top of the recording made in September. We could come to Norway for this purpose, or you could do it in comfort when you next come to London.
>
> This is a perfectly legitimate use of technical facilities and spares you the trouble of a journey. It will not be the first time such a technique has been used. I believe it is of enormous historical importance to have your performance of these parts for our complete *Ring*, and you know that Decca has a reputation for doing the impossible rather well. Please think about it.

Even though in the end it came to nothing, I think the mere suggestion gave her confidence. She replied by return of post from Oslo:

> Thank you so much for your letter. I am really touched by it. I think the suggestion is fine and would greatly save my strength, so if it is at all possible I will try my best and let you know as soon as I can manage. I hope to go home again around May 10th, and will study the parts I do not know, like Erda, and those I do not know well enough, like Waltraute. Wish me luck so we can go through with your plans.

At that time we were working hard to prepare *Tristan* for the autumn, though we were immediately involved in a recording of *Fledermaus* with Herbert von Karajan in Vienna. Knowing how much Flagstad loved the work, I wrote to her lawyer and adviser in Oslo to ask whether she would be well enough to consider a brief appearance in the Gala sequence we were planning for the second act:

> In the second act of our Gala *Fledermaus,* the artist playing Prince Orlovsky will introduce guest artists who will each sing a popular piece of

his or her choice—though we can also make suggestions, if that is preferred. Among those appearing will be Renata Tebaldi, Mario del Monaco, Birgit Nilsson, Ljuba Welitsch, Jussi Björling, Teresa Berganza, Joan Sutherland, Fernando Corena, Ettore Bastianini and Giulietta Simionato. Actually the various pieces are being recorded in Vienna, London, Rome and other locations according to the availability of the artists, and we would love to think that Kirsten Flagstad could be among them.

There are two possibilities, assuming she is well enough. One is that we send an engineer and some light recording equipment to Oslo where we could record a two or three minute song with piano; or, if this is out of the question, we could at least get her speaking voice into the sequence by the device of a telephone call ostensibly made by Orlovsky during the Gala. We would then record her words directly over the telephone.

I hope this doesn't sound too preposterous, but there has never been such a gathering of artists on one record. Do you think she is well enough to take part in either of the ways I have suggested?

The reply was gloomy. Mr. Leif Stake, who was Flagstad's close confidant over the years, wrote back at once:

I have read your idea with interest and also discussed it with Madame Flagstad. However, I am sorry to tell you that it is quite impossible for her to arrange anything in this connection. She is at the hospital again and I am afraid it will last a very long time before she will be able to leave.

By September, Flagstad wrote again herself, and seemed more cheerful:

Excuse this scribble! I should have written to you long ago but as I have not had any good news I have hesitated. I have been very ill and it seems that the doctors cannot find out what it is so I am in and out of the hospital for control and tests. I am much better now, but quite weak from staying in bed so much.

Bernard came one day to see me and I told him to tell you about me and keep you informed. And I wanted to write to you when I heard over the radio your recording of Grieg's Piano Concerto with Clifford Curzon and Fjeldstad conducting. I think it is by far the best I have ever heard: the clear playing by Curzon and the lovely sound of the orchestra which seemed to have caught the real Norwegian spirit. . . .

By this time, we had started to send her "surprise packages" of records—all sorts of things, from piano music to Gilbert and Sullivan—and I think they gave her a lot of pleasure. It seemed that she really was getting better, for when Bernard Miles returned from Norway he seemed convinced that a full recovery might be around the corner. Then, on October 12, I had another letter:

I was told by my doctors today that I must give up singing and also any other professional work. My health is much improved, but I will not be strong enough and there is the danger that I could become ill once more.

I am sure you know how sorry I am to have to give up the recordings with you. I always enjoyed the work with you all so much.

Please, remember me to the boys and if I ever come to London and you are recording there I would love to visit you all. . . .

This, then, was the end. We could no longer help her by postponing or altering our plans; all we could do was to maintain what had really developed into a friendship over the years by keeping in touch and by reminding her, for it was true, that she was always very much in our thoughts.

Kirsten Flagstad runs through some music at the piano in her home in Kristiansand, Norway. With her is her sister, Karen Marie, who also pursued a singing career.

When *Tristan* was finished I went to Zurich to see Mr. Rosengarten, and brought up the question of the Decca *Ring*. Nilsson had been in fabulous voice throughout *Tristan*, and I feared that if we did not begin to take steps fairly soon, the *Ring* idea might become the province of another company. Both Solti and Gordon Parry were convinced that *Siegfried* was the next work to tackle, but neither of them could make a really suitable suggestion for the casting of the title part. (Neither could I.) I told Mr. Rosengarten about the problem, and suggested that I should have a look round some of the smaller German opera houses where a potential Siegfried might be found before the international circuit of fame ruined his voice. It was a good idea, and if what emerged from it was a disaster, I can only say in defense that it looked more than hopeful at the time.

The *Siegfried* situation was the bane of opera houses all over the world, because there was only one Siegfried: Wolfgang Windgassen. He was an extremely capable, professional, and hard-working singer whose father had also been a famous tenor. Windgassen really emerged during the 1951 Bayreuth festival, where he sang a superb Parsifal, as can be heard on the Decca recording made during the festival. He was thereafter in huge demand. He added both Siegfried and Siegmund to his repertoire; he sang Tristan everywhere, and Tannhäuser, and Lohengrin. And he sang them all very competently in just about every opera house you could name, because he was the only one who could sing them all. In addition, he had a large repertoire of Italian opera in German; and to the best of my knowledge he still sings Otello in Germany today. He was, and is, an out-and-out professional.

But there are limits to the use of any human voice, and in the late nineteen-fifties Windgassen's was showing distinct signs of wear and tear. He had all the tricks up his sleeve, and knew exactly where and how to conserve his voice during performances of the really heavy parts like Siegfried and Tristan; and because he sang so much, and because the routine conductors he often worked with knew him and liked him, he was not required to overindulge himself in rehearsal, with the result that his rhythm got slack. (He had, and still has, a rather endearing habit—except for conductors—of "running" ahead of the beat. In our subsequent two big ventures together I only once remember him managing to get behind the beat, at which moment Solti warmly congratulated him!)

Windgassen was therefore the only candidate for our proposed *Siegfried;* and bearing in mind the standards we had set ourselves in *Rheingold*, I could not convince myself, admire him though I did, that he was good enough. Hence the idea that I should try to find a new or relatively unknown talent to undertake this strenuous part for us.

The first and obvious step was to go and talk to Set Svanholm, who was in charge of the opera house in Sweden. It was great to see him again, but I spent two depressing days listening to dismal tenors and came away with nothing. There was a glimmer of hope in Copenhagen, but that also came to nothing. We auditioned in London and Vienna and Budapest . . . a seemingly endless procession of applicants with no potential whatsoever. Then, suddenly, we had what seemed to be a stroke of luck. We remembered a tenor who had auditioned for us some time ago, and who had had the advantage of working from time to time with Solti. We asked him to come and sing again, and when he did, I for one was sure we had found our Siegfried, except for one thing: he did not know the part.

It will be kinder, in view of all that happened, to refer to him only as "our Siegfried"—for that was what, for several months, he was intended to be. At the first audition he sang Tannhäuser with a great heroic ringing voice. He had not thought too much about the words, but then, among tenors, he was not alone in that. Given reasonable willingness on his part, we imagined it would not have taken very long to drive some sort of expression into him. His voice was certainly right for Siegfried: it had the timbre, and it had the power. More than that, he seemed interested in the part and willing to study it hard if we were prepared to offer him the recording. As we had not heard him sing a note of *Siegfried*, we suggested he should study certain parts of the score and come back in a month to sing them for us. He agreed, and I told Mr. Rosengarten that I thought we had found our tenor.

One month later our Siegfried came back, protesting that in the interim he had been forced to take so many engagements that he had barely had time for study. I suppose I should have seen the red light then, and probably would have done so with any other sort of voice. But a real *Heldentenor* is such a rare bird nowadays—and that is precisely what he was, vocally speaking—that I felt he deserved encouragement. He sang some bits of *Siegfried* for us, and as far as they went, which admittedly was not very far, they were excellent. We could imagine this beefy voice striding over the orchestra in the Forging Song, and matching Nilsson voice for voice (for once) in the final duet.

Before going any further I had a long talk with Solti. He, too, had great faith in the voice as such, but was extremely skeptical about our Siegfried's ability to *learn*—or, to put it more specifically, his ability to take time off from tempting engagements in order to give himself time to learn. I said that I had pointed out to our Siegfried that if he could bring himself to make a first-class job of the recording, the world would be open to him, at least so far as the role of Siegfried was concerned, for he had only one competitor.

After the utterly exhausting experience of recording *Tristan und Isolde* in a single period of three weeks without break (it was a physical *and* mental *and* emotional exhaustion), Solti had declared that he would never again tackle a work of such length and content within one continuous period, and I was completely on his side. Leaving out personal considerations, it was a decision firmly in favor of better results. People who are exhausted, whether they be singers or conductors or producers or engineers, can produce work which reflects that exhaustion, and we were determined it would not happen if we were to proceed with the *Ring*. We therefore worked out a provisional plan to record the first act of *Siegfried* and half of the second in May 1962, and to complete the second act and record the third in October of that year. Having obtained approval from Zurich, I cabled the various artists involved and asked them to reconfirm their availabilities. For once, everything seemed in order and I prepared a provisional schedule. Two months later, after some bewildering correspondence, it turned out that Birgit Nilsson's cable reconfirming the dates had lost two vital words in transmission, and had conveyed the opposite of her intention. It was meant to say that she was *not* available in October, as she would be in Buenos Aires; but it read as if she would be available because she was *not going* to Buenos Aires. We had to start all over again.

On consideration, though, and bearing in mind the possibility of problems with our Siegfried, who was presumably at that time already hard at work on the part, the misunderstanding with Nilsson appeared to be an advantage. The hardest part of *Siegfried* for the tenor is Act One; by pushing it into the autumn we would be giving our Siegfried several months' grace and further time for study. We decided therefore to change the schedule in such a way as to make most of Act Three (including the final duet with Nilsson) in May, plus part of the second act; and to keep the remainder, including the whole of Act One, for the autumn. We told the news as quickly as possible to our Siegfried, who seemed greatly relieved.

Solti was conducting in Dallas in November 1961 and I wrote to him:

As you will know from my cable we have resolved the misunderstanding with Birgit, which was caused by a garbled cable and was certainly not her fault. The solution is simple: we shall put Act One into the autumn of next year and make Act Three in May. We can divide Act Two between the periods.

Our Siegfried seems aware of the responsibility we are imposing on him and swears he will be able to sing all the notes of Act Three perfectly accurately by the time you meet him again at the beginning of March. He nevertheless tells me that he reckons he can learn more from you in two hours at the piano than he can from anyone else in two weeks. What he really is saying is that he will guarantee proficiency so far as the notes are concerned before you arrive back in Europe, which will still give him two months to study the sort of expression you want. I only hope he means what he says.

In the meantime, our Gala *Fledermaus* had appeared, complete with comic turns by great operatic celebrities in the middle of the second act. I sent a copy to Flagstad, because I knew how much she liked the work. She replied:

> I received the really excellent records of *Die Fledermaus*. As I have sung Rosalinde about 98 times, last in 1926, I know the work very well and it is my favourite operetta. I am surely going to play it often. May I say that I do not find the celebrities adding to my liking, but otherwise I found everything wonderful.
>
> My health is slowly improving, but I get tired easily. As I can hardly play the piano with my left hand I am not eager to sing, either, so by now I am sure I will never sing any more.

However depressed she was, it seemed that the improvement in her health continued, and she managed another journey to visit her daughter in Phoenix. She returned to Kristiansand in the summer, where the Vienna crew had sent her postcards during the holidays. On August 7, 1961, she wrote:

> So nice to hear from you and to have greetings from the Vienna boys. I think of you all very often and with true affection.
>
> I am getting better every day and feel quite strong and well. I am singing every day, and improving. I am afraid I have lost the high tones above A, but my voice is getting stronger. I am practising the Brahms *Rhapsody*, the *Four Serious Songs*, Bliss's *Enchantress* and Elgar's *Sea Pictures*. Next week Ivor Newton visits me and I will ask his opinion and then ask him to tell you if I can still sing. I feel strong enough, anyway.
>
> I am longing for England and all my friends there, so I might make a trip in October or November or later. Have you recorded any Mahler Symphonies? I have No. 4 but would like some others.

I waited impatiently for Ivor Newton's return. His vast experience with singers and his immense knowledge of the capabilities of the voice, to say nothing of his long and close friendship with Flagstad would, I knew, lead him to give me a frank and honest opinion. He came back full of enthusiasm: the voice, he said, was still magnificent. His only reservation was about Flagstad's ability to cope with the strain of travel; but by some miracle, as with Kathleen Ferrier, the voice was remaining to the end.

On August 11 I wrote:

> I was so delighted to have your last letter and such a marvellous report from Ivor. I had hesitated before to ask if you had resumed singing, because your news last year seemed to indicate that you had really given it up.
>
> There is so much wonderful music available to you which does not range above the high A. I would love to think that we could work together again on anything you feel like singing. Is it the right time for me to mention the Fricka scene again?

On September 25 she replied from Oslo:

> At long last I can reply to your letter. I am at the hospital for a check-up and have been here three weeks and will be coming out Thursday. I have talked to my doctor about possible recordings and this time he thinks it will be all right, I am glad to say. I must admit that I tire easily, but otherwise I feel fine.
>
> I have been singing quite a lot at home, but it is difficult to judge if the voice is good enough for recording. I therefore plan to come to London to have a talk with you, take some coaching and maybe test the voice. I plan to come in November, as I understand you will be there then. . . .

The visit never took place.

By December, I was beginning to worry about our Siegfried. From time to time one or another of us called him up or wrote him letters of encouragement. It was all going fine, we were told; but whenever we inquired how *far* he had got, an impenetrable mist descended. By means of some astute international operatic detective work we discovered his schedule of performances, and concluded that he must have been working on *Siegfried* at some very odd hours, if he was working on it at all.

Early in 1962, on the pretext of trying out a new sort of microphone especially designed for him, we summoned him to London. The result confirmed both our expectations and our fears: the voice was magnificent, but of *Siegfried* he knew about as much as the studio cat. Some emergency action was necessary. I notified Mr. Rosengarten of the situation and recommended we should send our Siegfried to a teacher for a course of intensive training. This extra expense was unwelcome, but it seemed the only solution. I undertook to find a good teacher as close as possible to our Siegfried's residence (if he could be said to have such, for most of the time he was rushing about Europe performing everything and everywhere—except *Siegfried*, of course). Mr. Rosengarten agreed to the unprecedented step of paying for a tutor, on the grounds that the voice as such, on my recommendation, was such good material.

We found a tutor within a day, and arranged for our Siegfried to come back to London in a month's time for further tests. We also told the tutor that we wanted a progress report in three weeks, and when it came in it was good. True, our Siegfried had skipped a number of his lessons, but the tutor was as keen on the voice as we were. He thought the third act would be ready in time, and when the tenor returned in early March there was a big improvement. We seemed to be on course again.

In the "Siegfried" recording,
contralto Marga Höffgen sings Erda,
a role she has also sung on the stage
in both London and Vienna.

The rest of the cast was nicely in position. I was looking forward greatly to the chance of working with Hans Hotter, whom I had admired since the first time I heard him at Covent Garden after the war. His dignity, stature, and understanding of the Wagner idiom remained unchallenged in his particular field, and I was proud to think that he would at last appear on our label. Neidlinger was again our Alberich, though this time with a much smaller part than in *Rheingold;* and we had, sadly, made up our collective minds to change the casting of his brother, Mime, from Paul Kuen to Gerhard Stolze. I say sadly because everyone liked and admired Kuen; but the *Siegfried* Mime is a different pot of gruel from the *Rheingold* Mime, and Stolze's performances on the stage had been astonishing. On the rational grounds that pure judgment, not sentiment, should reign, we engaged Stolze. (He had, the year before, sung and acted magnificently as Herod in our recording of *Salome.*) Kurt Böhme was to appear again as Fafner, Marga Höffgen was taking over Erda, and we had the impudence to ask Joan Sutherland to sing the Woodbird. With an engagement book full of appearances all over the world as Lucia and Violetta and all her other star parts, and with all the major opera houses queueing for her services at any time or fee she cared to name, she agreed to come to Vienna and sing a part at which she had not looked since she was an unknown, undiscovered underling at Covent Garden. We were very moved by her acceptance. The prospect for *Siegfried* looked bright.

Then we received a message from the tutor. Our Siegfried had been skipping his lessons again; in fact, he had hardly been available at all since his last visit to London. What was worrying the tutor was not only that he would fail to learn what remained to be learned, but that he would forget what he had already learned. There was nothing to do, we felt, but to summon the wretched man back to London again, especially as by this time Solti had returned from the United States.

Our Siegfried was rather cross when we finally tracked him down, somewhere in the depths of Europe, where he was making another guest appearance. Didn't we trust him? If he had told us he would be ready, then he would be ready. We said that Solti would be in London for the last two weeks of April (the recording of *Siegfried* was scheduled to start in Vienna on May 6) and could be at our Siegfried's disposal for some final coaching. It then turned out that the tenor was so busy up to and including May 5 that the only time he could possibly come to London was during the Easter weekend (April 20). Reluctantly, Solti agreed to stay in London to hear the worst.

My major blunder was in not accepting the inevitable, there and then. Like Solti, like Gordon Parry, and like everyone else who had heard our Siegfried, I was haunted (and my judgment thrown) by the desire to hear this *kind* of voice in the part. To admit defeat at this stage, after an eight-month struggle and barely two weeks before the recording was scheduled to start, seemed cowardly. At its worst, it seemed a risk worth taking; but at that late hour, Solti was already inclined to think we should abandon him, and by the time he had had two rehearsals he was *convinced* we should abandon him. We agreed at any rate that any part of the second act involving our Siegfried was out of the question in May; our only hope would be to concentrate entirely on the third act, for it was imperative to complete the long final duet between Siegfried and Brünnhilde, since we would not have Nilsson in the autumn period. With a cloud of black depression over our heads, we decided we had better stick to our commitments and rely on even more piano rehearsal than usual to knock our Siegfried into shape. The oddest thing of all was that he was not at all worried, and could not think what was the matter with us.

In a major record company it is never possible to concentrate solely on one project at a time. The problems with *Siegfried* were only a minor part of Decca's vast international program, and in the tremendously busy months at the opening of the year I had been concerned about the total silence from Kristiansand, although I had sent one or two letters to Flagstad and several batches of records. I had heard nothing from Bernard Miles or Ivor Newton, though I was sure they would call me in the event of serious news. Then, on March 4, 1962, I had a letter. In all the years, we had addressed each other formally, but this one began:

Hans Hotter had been singing leading Wagnerian bass-baritone parts for over 20 years when he was engaged to sing the Wanderer in the Decca recording of "Siegfried."

Dear John (may I?):

Thank you for your letters. I am really ashamed that I have not written you before, but if it can be a consolation I have written very few letters lately.

I was in hospital over Christmas, and had a lovely and peaceful holiday, nobody knowing my whereabouts. Since then I have been in pain more or less but the doctors assure me I shall get better from the medicines I take, even if the medicines have some bad side-effects as well. I move with difficulty and therefore am afraid of travelling just now. I am trying to decide whether to go or not to Phoenix.

I sit in a good chair most of the time and read and embroider and, most of all, listen to records. I have stereo now and ask you to order for me all the records I have made with stereo. Furthermore, I would love to have any more Gilbert and Sullivan records Decca has made.

With kindest regards to all the others,

Love,
KIRSTEN

In the three and a half years that had elapsed since the completion of *Rheingold*, one major domestic change had taken place in our lives in Vienna. The storerooms in the Sofiensaal in which we had taken refuge for the editing of *Rheingold* revealed on closer examination to have been at one time an apartment, dating from the period when there had been a resident director of the hall. Most of us had grown tired of living in hotels for such long periods, and Gordon had the idea that the three of us—he, Erik Smith, and myself—should form a partnership and try to restore the Sofiensaal rooms to their original purpose. We approached Richard Postl, who, in addition to being the general director of the Sofiensaal, is a figure of major importance in Viennese business life, and obtained his permission to begin the conversion; without his approval, the idea would have come to nothing. We then obtained generous help from Decca; and within a week or two the business of removing the barber's chair, the bicycle, the sacks of corn, and the bundles of old paper began. The idea was that the three of us would live there whenever we were in Vienna separately or together; but there was plenty of room for itinerant Decca staff passing through Vienna and wishing to spend a night or two in something less formal than a hotel.

When we were first allowed to use the flat it consisted of large empty rooms; and on the Viennese principle of putting first things last, we installed a beautiful Schönbrünner chandelier in the lounge, even before we had chairs, tables, or beds. That was in 1960; and long before we arrived for the start of *Siegfried* in May 1962 the flat was comfortably habitable. Apart from giving some of us somewhere pleasant to stay, it served a useful musical purpose in that the large room we used as a lounge provided a perfect environment for piano rehearsals. Tucked away in a remote corner of the building, it was free from any sort of disturbance or interruption, and the artists felt able to come and go as they wished. There can be few other sitting rooms in the world that can claim to have been graced by as many distinguished figures from the world of opera; and in deliberately seeking to create an informal atmosphere we also gave ourselves a problem: the place was in danger of becoming a sort of musical community center—a rehearsal room, a social club, and a Decca office all at the same time. (In all the years, it has only been physically broken into once, and that was at two o'clock in the morning, when we were all in bed, by the late Jussi Björling. He was looking for a drink.)

Our point of departure in May 1962 was the third act of *Siegfried*. The intention was to begin with the opening of the act and proceed in sequence right up to the moment when Siegfried finds the sleeping Brünnhilde on the top of the mountain. As Birgit Nilsson would not be with us until May 14, we were then going to make certain episodes from Act Two involving Wotan, Mime, and Alberich, and then resume Act Three after Nilsson's arrival. Our Siegfried was still the big worry, and as soon as Solti arrived I suggested that we should change round the first two sessions: instead of recording the opening of Act Three with Wotan and Erda, we would start at the point of Siegfried's entrance, thus giving ourselves an immediate indication of the tenor's capabilities. Solti thought this was a good idea.

We made our usual orchestral tests, and by selecting certain passages where the scoring is similar, made comparisons between *Rheingold* and the sound we were now getting. They matched splendidly. (We had to remember that if we ever finished the *Ring*, and the Company decided to issue it as what the Americans call a "complete package," it was essential that the sound should be as consistent as possible throughout, no matter how many years separated the various recordings.) After the tests, our Siegfried went on stage with Hans Hotter, and we started.

Almost immediately, we knew the worst. The voice of our Siegfried was as splendid as ever, but up against the huge experience and artistry of Hotter he sounded grotesque. He knew the part, after a fashion, but the words were pouring out with no conception of meaning. This encounter between Wotan and Siegfried is one of the pivotal points of the *Ring*. It is a supreme dramatic encounter, and if it fails in expression, it fails altogether. It was failing very badly, but it was a first session and one learns not to panic on a first session. We did the best we could (at least a great deal of the material recorded by Hotter was first-class and could be used), and hastily scheduled a string of further piano rehearsals for our Siegfried; for as we had changed round the first two sessions, he had a day off from recording, and we had visions of chaining him to a piano.

As usual, when the chips are down, Solti was marvelous. He had to prepare for the next session (which was the Wotan/Erda encounter at the opening of Act Three) and rehearse the material with Hotter and Höffgen, but he found time to listen to every note our Siegfried had made on the first session, and set aside as many hours as he could to work with him at the piano. In our hearts we all knew it was a hopeless case—except that one kept going back to the tapes and acknowledging the sheer magnificence and power of the voice. If only . . .

The opening of Act Three went excellently the next day, and morale improved. Solti spent the evening rehearsing with our Siegfried, and told me afterwards that there had been a big improvement. He had not only taken him through the remainder of the scene with Wotan, which was scheduled for the next day, but had retraced his steps over the material we had covered on the first session. In view of the evident improvement, Solti suggested, and I agreed at once, that we should try the next day to record the entire scene, re-recording the material from the first session and going on without a break into its continuation. (It was a bit tough on Hotter, but I was able to assure him that in the event of vocal trouble we could always use what *he* had recorded on the first session.)

This meant that on May 9 we had to pack something like twenty-five minutes of material into a session, though half of it had been thoroughly rehearsed with the orchestra two days earlier. Our Siegfried arrived, apparently full of confidence, and the first take, though very erratic, showed promise. We seemed to be getting somewhere, slowly. Then he went to pieces altogether. The next take was, if anything, even more expressionless than his efforts on the first day. Gloom descended. There is a limit to the number of times you can ask artists to remake a passage lasting for twenty-five minutes; but Hotter, who was getting seriously tired by then, agreed to have one more attempt (the third) in the hope that our Siegfried would suddenly come to life. Hotter talked to him, Solti talked to him, and I talked to him. We did everything humanly possible to give him encouragement and to show him what was missing. But in the third take of the day it was not really possible to tell whether we had got through to him or not, for he simply ran out of voice, and that was the end of that.

We were now faced with two days without sessions before resuming *Siegfried*. In the whole of my career I have never been so worried, for

Scores open on their laps, Solti and
Culshaw discuss troublesome
passages that will need a brushup
rehearsal before the next take.

we had reached what seemed to be the point of no return. We had had three expensive sessions, and two of them could be virtually written off. Gordon Parry and I took Hans Hotter and his wife out to dinner that night and asked him, as an artist of such vast experience, what he thought. We had two free days on which to work on our Siegfried, after which he would face not only another remake of the scene we had tried to record, but also the difficult and tiring final duet with Birgit Nilsson, who could be with us for a maximum of three days. If we ran into trouble with that duet the whole of *Siegfried* would be held up for at least a year because of Nilsson's absence in Buenos Aires in the autumn. What was frightening me even more was the prospect of the first act in October; for if our Siegfried had prepared so inadequately, despite so much help, for the third act, what hope was there that he would do any hard work during the summer on the infinitely more difficult first act?

Hotter was extremely pessimistic, and equally frustrated. To have such vocal equipment as our Siegfried, to have a potential for which the operatic world had been waiting for twenty years—and to be able to do so little with it! We had come to the end of the line. It was my duty to call Mr. Rosengarten and tell him the alternatives: either we should cut

Solti warmly greets tenor Wolfgang Windgassen backstage at the Sofiensaal during the recording sessions for "Siegfried." Windgassen saved the day when he agreed to take over the title part at the last moment from an ill-prepared predecessor.

our losses and abandon the recording of *Siegfried*, or we should engage Wolfgang Windgassen to take over the part.

It is not so easy to abandon a major recording. The artists are under contract and the Company has obligations to fulfill. The idea of approaching Windgassen at this late hour was embarrassing in the extreme, for he was in Vienna at the time, singing at the State Opera, and must surely have heard rumors of what was going on at the Sofiensaal; and quite apart from embarrassment, there was the sheer practical difficulty that Windgassen was one of the busiest singers in Europe, and I doubted whether he had any free days at all for the next twelve months. The only thing to do was to face the situation and go and talk to him.

He was staying at the Hotel Europa, and with my colleague Christopher Raeburn I went to see him the next day. We had not met since Bayreuth in 1951. He is an intelligent man, and there was no point in telling him anything less than the truth, including the reasons why he had not been given the part in the first place. If he had wanted, he could have made us look extremely small, and he certainly had reason to be offended. Instead, because he is a professional and a very nice man, he just wagged his head and took out his diary. When I saw it, my heart sank: it was bursting with engagements, and not only in Vienna. Before we went any further, he said he would have to get on the telephone and talk to Stuttgart and Munich to see if they could possibly rearrange his appearances; but, as he wanted to record *Siegfried* more than anything else in his life, he would make it possible somehow.

We had another meeting later in the day. He had at least managed to solve the major problem, which was to make himself free for the three days when we had Birgit Nilsson. As for the rest, it would mean some radical rescheduling on our part to fit the sessions into his free time. He could not possibly have been more cooperative, and in not taking advantage of us he won our unstinted admiration. He saved the show.

But the show was not over yet, for I had to face our Siegfried, and quickly, before the news reached him via the Viennese grapevine. As luck would have it, it was one of those days when I could not get in touch with Mr. Rosengarten to tell him what was happening in Vienna and get his advice. I was very unsure of our legal position with our banished Siegfried, for he had a contract. On the other hand, we had more than enough evidence on tape to convince anyone of his inadequacy, and of the fact that he had not honored his part of the contract by learning his part properly. In London, one could have used the Company's legal machinery in such a situation; but in our Viennese outpost we had had no cause to summon local legal aid before, and in any case I did not want to give our Siegfried ideas. I simply wanted an impartial witness to sit in on the final encounter in the event that our Siegfried got heated and tried to pull any threats. I spoke to the British Embassy and explained the situation to a very bewildered official, and within an hour, at the time of the meeting, a witness appeared to take notes of our last encounter. Solti was also present.

I began by telling our Siegfried what I presumed he had already guessed: that his work so far had led us to the conclusion that to finish *Siegfried* with him in the title part would take many, many more sessions than the maximum of twenty which the Company had approved in its budget for the recording. This was out of the question. The choice therefore lay between replacing him in the title part, or continuing with greatly lowered standards and almost inevitably a bad press for the result, which would certainly do more damage to him, professionally, than to Decca. I proposed that we should agree amicably there and then to abandon his participation in *Siegfried*.

He took it very well. I am sure he knew just how ill-prepared he was, and just how appallingly this showed up against the experience of Hotter. I think he was relieved not to have to face the hurdle of the forthcoming duet with Nilsson, to say nothing of the prospect of spending the summer in preparation for the first act. All of us shook hands a little sadly with the owner of the best potential as a *Heldentenor* since the end of the war, and he walked out of *Siegfried* and out of our lives.

We spent the next day rescheduling *Siegfried* around the dates Windgassen had given us. By this time his agent had got in on the act and was much less inclined than Windgassen to make life easy for us. We were still in a corner because financial terms had not been agreed on, and Windgassen's first session was scheduled for the following afternoon. On the morning of that day—the session was at three—I managed to contact Mr. Rosengarten at last, who was understandably furious. Not only had we lost two sessions on account of a tenor I had recommended long ago, but we had paid quite a lot of money for the man's tuition; and Windgassen's agent was now making excessive demands if his artist was to take over the part in an emergency. This really did look like the end of the *Ring*. I think our conversation went on for about ninety exceedingly uncomfortable minutes. No sooner had we finished than Windgassen rang to ask whether he should come to the session or not. Solti and Hotter were on the other lines saying they could not record in three hours from now unless they knew *what* they were recording, and that depended on whether or not we, or Zurich, reached agreement with Windgassen's agent. It was too late to cancel the orchestra, anyway. Then Mr. Rosengarten came back on the phone and we went

Hans Hotter as the Wanderer is seen seated beside Mime's hearth in Wieland Wagner's 1955 Bayreuth Festival production of "Siegfried."

through our nightmare again. I think it was the worst morning of my professional life, and it did not make things any better to know that, basically, the whole affair was my fault for having had faith in the tenor, and for having maintained it against the odds.

It is a strange quirk of life that when things are going as badly as they were on that particular morning, nature sometimes steps in with an unpredictable bit of comedy which somehow helps to get events into perspective. When I finally came off the telephone at one o'clock, having been on it almost continuously since half past eight, and with the prospect of a session at three for which I had still to make a great deal of preparation, I remembered that when Gordon Parry had been ill some months earlier a Viennese doctor had prescribed some pep pills to keep him going through sessions for which he had no deputy. I suddenly thought that one of those pills might be my salvation on that particular afternoon, so I asked him where they were. They were in the drawer of his bedside table, he said, and as they were rather mild he advised me to take two. I went into his bedroom, opened the drawer, saw some pills, and took two, as he had suggested. Unfortunately, they were sleeping pills. Five minutes later, I was out cold.

Wisely, the others let me sleep until two-thirty and then, feeling like a zombie, I put my head under the cold tap and went down into the studio where the orchestra was already assembling. (It is remarkable how early the Vienna Philharmonic will turn up for sessions. Despite the huge amount of work undertaken by the musicians, it is quite common to find a number of them walking around the hall and practicing, anything up to an hour before the start of a session.) Solti and Hotter had arrived, and poor Windgassen was on the telephone outside the control room speaking to his agent, who in turn was speaking to Zurich on another line. Solti agreed that we should do everything possible to make up for lost time, and the obvious step was to make, once again, the scene from Siegfried's entrance in the third act through to the moment when he breaks the Wanderer's spear and begins to ascend the mountain. This would be the third time that Hotter had had to record this scene, but at least the whole thing was thoroughly rehearsed with the orchestra, and although it ran for about twenty-five minutes, we reckoned, with luck, to get another section of the third act recorded, if only as a test. (This would be for Windgassen—the opening of the scene on the mountain top, before he discovers and awakens the sleeping Brünnhilde. The long interlude between these scenes we would leave until one of the days when Windgassen was not available.)

Wolfgang Windgassen as Siegfried listens to the song of the Woodbird as he rests in front of the abstract construction representing Fafner's cave in Wieland Wagner's production for the 1965 Bayreuth Festival.

Windgassen was still on the telephone at three, when the session began, and was getting very red about the gills. Some sort of huge last-minute financial discussion was going on when suddenly he heard the orchestra strike up in the hall. He slammed the telephone down and said in German: "The hell with it! I'm going out there to sing!"

In the control room the effect was uncanny. We were hearing the same music we had heard so often in the past few days, under the same conductor and with the same Wanderer; but with the new Siegfried, it suddenly came to life. Certainly Windgassen's voice, as such, was neither as striking nor as powerful as that of our departed friend, and it was much harder to record and keep in balance. But behind every word lay experience and knowledge, and the conflict between Siegfried and the Wanderer became a dramatic entity for the first time since we had started. It was clear that for this recording Windgassen was going to make the effort of his life.

He continued to do so in the following days; steady, good-humored, and hard-working, he was a joy to work with. He told me on the day of the second session that he had resolved whatever differences there had been over the contract, but that he had one request to make of me, which he wished to broach man-to-man rather than as a contract point on which he could have insisted (and won). It was to the effect that if we ever got around to recording *Götterdämmerung*, we would invite him to sing the part of Siegfried in that work also. In front of the others, and with pleasure, I gave him my word—with the proviso that Decca had not yet decided to make *Götterdämmerung* (and I feared, after the troubles with *Siegfried*, that it never would!). Windgassen also said that if we completed the *Ring* with *Walküre* he would be happy if we chose someone else for Siegmund, as it was not one of his favorite parts. Nobody could have been more reasonable.

The troubles that Windgassen often experienced in the theater with Siegfried were not evident on the record. Although he was recording sections of difficult music anything between fifteen and twenty minutes in length, and repeating them two or three times on each session, he was not under the theatrical conditions which obliged him to conserve his voice. One of the reasons why there have always been so few tenors capable of sustaining the part of Siegfried in the theater is that the demands of the role are excessive. In his absorption with the character of Siegfried, Wagner seemed to have forgotten that although the *character* was supposed to be a sort of super-youth, the tenors who would be required to interpret the part would be ordinary human beings. In the first act of *Siegfried*, the principal character is on stage and singing all

the time except for the first few minutes and during the episode between Mime and the Wanderer. What is more, most of what he has to
do is heavy, declamatory singing, culminating in the exhausting forging
scene which ends the act. In Act Two he is on the stage for more than
two-thirds of the time, and much of what he has to do, after all the
shouting in Act One, is quiet and lyrical—which is already asking a lot
of the human voice. In Act Three he is on stage throughout, except
during the opening scene between the Wanderer and Erda. First he has
the long dramatic scene with the Wanderer at the foot of the mountain;
then comes his long solo scene when he discovers Brünnhilde asleep; and
finally, when he has awakened her, he faces one of the most exhausting
duets in operatic music, lasting for more than thirty-five minutes, opposite a dramatic soprano who is completely fresh because until that
moment she has not been required to sing a note! No wonder that, in
the theater, Windgassen and just about every other tenor who has tackled the part of Siegfried has taken trouble to find passages, especially in
the first act, where the voice may be conserved without unduly distress-
ing the audience. Under recording conditions, Windgassen did not need
or try to conserve his voice; and had I realized the year before how
fresh he would sound, and how hard he was prepared to work, I would
have saved myself and Decca a lot of trouble. When it comes to choosing a singer for a really difficult part, there is no substitute at all for
stage experience; and stage experience is what Windgassen, like his father before him, had.

I believe that Wieland Wagner has advanced the interesting theory
that towards the end of his life his grandfather realized that in the *Ring*,
at least so far as Siegfried and Brünnhilde are concerned, and in *Tristan
und Isolde*, so far as Tristan is concerned, he had asked too much of his
singers. Consequently, when he came to write his last work, *Parsifal*, he
took care to reduce the demands to more practical bounds. Parsifal is on
stage a very long time—but it is not a very long part; Kundry is on stage
quite a long time also—but the timing of her part in proportion to the
length of the work is small. The only long part is that of Gurnemanz—and it is written with extraordinary skill and awareness of the
limits to which that kind of voice may be taken. Certainly Wagner himself had terrible troubles in casting the *Ring* and *Tristan;* and it is possible, as his grandson has implied, that towards the end of his life he may
have realized that at least some of the troubles were of his own making.

Windgassen completed his big scene with Hotter on the first day, and
that evening our old friend Gustav Neidlinger appeared for his single
Siegfried session, which was scheduled for the next day. It is a short

part, for he has only two appearances, first with the Wanderer at the beginning of Act Two, and later in the same act with Mime. He also has a frenzied offstage laugh which is heard when Siegfried eventually kills Mime, but as that scene was scheduled for the autumn and as it seemed scarcely worth bringing Neidlinger all the way from Stuttgart for one maniacal laugh, we had decided to record his laugh in May and superimpose in the right place during the autumn sessions. As the laugh is offstage, where Alberich is supposed to be watching from the foot of a cliff, we rigged up another special acoustic device to add to the sinister quality of his laugh. This was the sort of thing Gustav adored, and once we were set up he would have gladly gone on for hours giving us his venomous laughs, each one more demoniacal than its predecessor.

This was not the only bit of superimposition in *Siegfried*, for Kurt Böhme, our Fafner, was not available at all for the spring period. He, too, needed a special acoustic, for in *Siegfried* he has turned himself into a dragon, and is only heard from the depths of his cave when he is aroused from sleep by one or another of the various intruders. It did not therefore worry us at all that he could not be with us for the opening scene of Act Two in May: we recorded the encounter between Wotan, Alberich, and the dragon without a single note of Fafner's vocal music going on the tape. In the autumn, when Böhme joined us, we planned to add his voice to the tape when we had discovered how to make it suitably hollow and cavernous.

What did worry us greatly on that day was the appearance of Gerhard Stolze, who came to make his very short Act Two sequence with Neidlinger. (All the rest of Mime's part was to be recorded in the autumn.) As I have mentioned, Stolze had sung Herod the year before in our recording of Strauss's *Salome*, and he had proved a "natural" so far as acting for the microphone was concerned. He had grasped in a few minutes what it takes many other artists a lifetime to learn—which is how to "work" a microphone intelligently, and that includes a knowledge of when to keep a good distance *away* from the thing. He had followed our stereo production of *Salome* to the letter, although it involved a great deal of physical movement for him, especially in the later scenes when Herod begins to have hallucinations. He had dashed about the stage and sung with great abandon and force; and the scope offered to him by the part of Mime in *Siegfried* was even greater.

Earlier in the year we had heard that Stolze had been ill, though there had been some mystery about it. We learned he had canceled some performances and that nobody had seen him for a while; and when these messages started reaching London we telephoned his wife, who reas-

Gerhard Stolze makes a fierce-looking Mime in the costume and makeup he wore for his appearances in the role at Bayreuth in 1968.

sured us, without saying anything further, that he would be available for the single *Siegfried* session in May and for the long series of sessions in the autumn. On that day in May he arrived at the Sofiensaal, and could hardly get up the stairs. He had had a polio attack. He seemed to have withered to half the size he had been the year before (and he was never very large), and one of his arms was all but useless. We wondered, when he arrived that day, how he would ever get through the taxing part of Mime.

Neidlinger was marvelous with him. We had wanted a great deal of movement from the two of them in this short scene, for on the stage these unholy brothers usually rush about all over the place. This was out of the question for Stolze in his condition, though his voice was as pungent and full of character as ever. There was only one solution (unless we were prepared to let the scene remain completely static), which was to get Neidlinger to make all his own moves while we "panned" Stolze—which means that although Stolze remained in one position throughout, we would move his voice over the stereo arc according to the production I had originally planned. It worked, for this short scene; and at the end Stolze came up to us and asked us to have confidence—he would be ready for the autumn, not only with his voice, but with his ability to move as well. We thought he was optimistic, but we were completely on his side.

By the end of that session we had done everything possible in the spring period until Nilsson arrived, and she was expected on the evening of May 14 for her first session on the 15th. In the meantime, we decided to make the long horn solo from Act Two with which Siegfried awakens the sleeping Fafner once again. Roland Berger, the first horn of the Vienna Philharmonic, with whom we have had a close friendship over the years, was scheduled to come and play, but he did not know that a few months before, when we were recording in Israel, we had met a young horn player of French origin who specialized in playing a ghastly parody of the sort of watery, wobbly horn sound which the French seem to adore and which is anathema to the Austrians. We persuaded our friend in Israel to give the weakest and most toneless performance of Siegfried's horn call imaginable, which we carefully preserved on tape and brought to Vienna.

Most horn players try to act the prima donna, and Roland Berger is no exception. He arrived at the Sofiensaal complaining that he was tired and needed beer before he could play a note. This being provided, he finally consented to play the long horn call as a test. When he came back to hear it, we played him the version we had made in Israel. His

Roland Berger, the Vienna Philharmonic's first horn, practices Siegfried's horn calls on the noble-toned but somewhat treacherous F horn still favored by Viennese players.

face was a picture. It was, he said, our lousy machinery. He became apoplectic. For any witness who did not know that we were good friends, it must have been an alarming scene. Finally, we told him the truth: and at that very moment the machinery *did* blow up, and quite seriously. Roland, mumbling about our utter incompetency, took himself off to the flat, drank several more beers and was found fast asleep in bed two hours later, after we had made the repairs. Then he gave the magnificent performance of the horn call which appears on the records.

The Viennese F horn has the advantage of unrivaled nobility of tone, and the disadvantage of being somewhat treacherous. (The Vienna Philharmonic is the only orchestra in Europe to retain the instrument.) Roland Berger's playing of the Siegfried horn call is a perfect example of why the Vienna Philharmonic is such a great operatic orchestra. The tone of the instrument itself certainly conveys Siegfried's heroism, but the approach to each phrase reveals Berger's instinct for drama—the ability to show Siegfried's changing moods of arrogance, tenderness, and resolution. This instinct is shared to some degree by every member of the orchestra, and has been acquired over the generations. It cannot be taught.

The next morning I had a cable from Birgit Nilsson to say that her husband had been taken ill and that she could not leave Stockholm as planned. Could we postpone the recording of the final duet until the end of the month? This was a bad blow, because the other forces involved were unchangeable. Neither Windgassen nor the orchestra could be free at the end of May, and Nilsson herself, as we already knew, was not available in the autumn. Once again, *Siegfried* was in serious trouble. I cabled back to Nilsson expressing sympathy but pointing out that my hands were completely tied: the utmost I could do was to stretch the existing period by one day, to include May 18, but beyond that there was no chance whatsoever in the immediate future.

The closing duet in *Siegfried* runs for about thirty-five minutes and we had scheduled it over three sessions. It is, as I have said, exhausting for both of the singers and for the conductor. The orchestra agreed to replace the session on May 15 with one on the 18th, and we waited helplessly for further news from Nilsson. A cable eventually arrived to say she would come to Vienna on the evening of the 15th. We were in business again, but not for long. Whether because of worry about her husband's illness or because she was just feeling out of sorts I do not know, but Nilsson was not herself when she arrived. She may not be the easiest person in the world to deal with on business matters, but her approach to singing is highly professional, and she is not the kind of artist who likes to indulge in imaginary ailments. In all the years, she has never of her own volition wasted as much as a second of our time or money. She said on her arrival on the evening of the 15th that she was not feeling well, and she did not look well. She looked even less well when she appeared for the afternoon session on the 16th, which was to begin with "*Heil dir, Sonne*," or Brünnhilde's awakening, which is a notoriously difficult passage.

She sang well enough, but not by her own standards. The vocal sheen and brilliance which is needed at this point in *Siegfried* every bit as much as in the Immolation scene from *Götterdämmerung* was missing; and she became quickly tired, which is unusual for Birgit Nilsson. All of us felt sorry for her and did what we could to help; but foremost in my mind was the knowledge that we had only two sessions to go, and that what we had done that day was not up to standard. She went back to her hotel to rest, and Solti canceled the piano rehearsal arranged for the next morning so that she would be completely fresh for the session. We also decided not to go back over "*Heil dir, Sonne*" for the time being, but to continue from the point where we had left off. The central part of the duet, though still arduous, is not as tiring as the beginning or the end, and we felt it would discourage Nilsson if we proposed that she should start all over again.

The next day the voice was showing signs of coming back, but was still not on form. Certainly some of the material was usable, and Windgassen was in excellent voice; but what was emerging was not the final duet with which we had hoped to end our *Siegfried*. There was just one session left.

I went to see Nilsson on the morning of the last session, but it was not necessary to explain anything to her. She is a very self-critical artist (which is why I think she considers it her right to be critical of other people, whatever field they work in), and she was clearly aware of the situation we were all facing. I said I was prepared to go over to the offices of the Vienna Philharmonic and see if I could get one extra hour added to the session that afternoon so that, if her voice came back on form, we might risk recording the *entire* duet during the session. (I had proposed the extra hour because I thought it would give her more time to rest between takes.) She said she was confident that she would be in better voice that afternoon, but did not think the extra hour would help, because nobody could possibly do the complete final duet more than twice in any circumstances. I knew when I left her that she was going to do her best.

Wolfgang Windgassen and Birgit Nilsson are shown singing the exultant final duet from "Siegfried" in this 1968 Bayreuth Festival performance.

It was a tense session. If you are forced to try and record thirty-five minutes of master material in three hours (less at least twenty minutes for the interval), you have to be doubly sure that *everything* that might go wrong has been eliminated. Gordon and the other engineers spent the whole morning and the lunch period checking and double-checking every piece of equipment and every microphone. Alberich's curse certainly seemed to be hanging over this first group of *Siegfried* sessions, and if anything went wrong that afternoon I was not looking forward to telling Zurich about it the next morning. Even the engineers had become demoralized, and on the face of it what we had set ourselves to do was impossible, at least if we were to maintain the musical standard of the rest of the recording. I told them we would know the answer by the interval, which I proposed to call later than usual.

The tension was terrific, but seemed to generate its own sort of white heat in the performance. By the time we came to the late interval I knew we were out of trouble. We had already made one glorious take of the duet, and the minor flaws that had occurred were easily correctable from the material we had made on the preceding days. I knew we were going to finish *Siegfried* (the troubles that would doubtless come in the autumn could not possibly be worse than those we had had in the spring), and so did the artists. After the interval they bounded back into the studio for what Solti always calls the "last chance"—the moment when you throw the vocal score aside and just sing with abandon. That is exactly what Nilsson and Windgassen did, and most of what is on the published record comes from that final performance. It has the right emotional quality—the sheer passion which envelops Siegfried and Brünnhilde as they look out towards their future. Hearing it back after that session, Solti came out with one of his classic bits of garbled English. "*It's animalig!*" he said. "*It's a perfect screaming!*" He meant that it had the right earthy, animal quality, and the screams are the musical sounds of love and joy which bring down the curtain on *Siegfried*.

Much later that evening, relaxing with Solti and Nilsson over drinks in the flat, we sent the following cable to Gustav Neidlinger in Stuttgart: RETURN TO VIENNA IMMEDIATELY TO REMAKE YOUR PART SIEGFRIED STOP STUDIO CAT ATE THE TAPE. After all that he had been through in the Sofiensaal, Neidlinger evidently did not think this was unlikely at all, and rang up at seven o'clock the next morning to say he would catch the earliest possible plane. When we told him it was a joke he roared with laughter and swore revenge. And he wanted to know how the Act Two sequence with Stolze sounded. If, he said, we had any reservations at all about it, he would willingly return in the autumn at his own expense. He was not thinking of himself, I am sure, but of Stolze. This sort of decency, this sort of consideration for a colleague in trouble, is rare in the world of opera, but Neidlinger is that kind of man.

During my absence in Vienna, my secretary had been sending regular batches of records to Flagstad but had received no letters from her. Shortly after my return to London, I spoke to Bernard Miles who told me that the news was bad. She had been in hospital for many weeks and he feared that she was unable to write, but he hoped that the doctors would let her return home before very long.

The Vienna trip that autumn was going to be long and tough. Before resuming work on *Siegfried* we had to make *Tosca* with Leontyne Price, Giuseppe di Stefano, and Herbert von Karajan conducting. Van Karajan also made a record of Christmas songs with Leontyne Price, which turned out to be one of those enchanting occasions when everyone can afford to relax and wallow in *kitsch*. Just before leaving London for a period that was going to keep me in Vienna almost continuously from early September to mid-December, I wrote what was to be my last letter to Flagstad:

Dear Kirsten:

  We have all been very upset to hear of your continued illness. This Friday we are all rushing off to Vienna to handle a very busy programme which includes the completion of *Siegfried*. We often think of you and the wonderful times we had together, and all of us are looking forward to a reunion. Meanwhile, I do hope you are making a steady recovery, and I know that all the others want to join me in sending love. . . .

The last letter I received from her was dated September 1, 1962. Her beautifully clear, flowing writing had badly deteriorated, but at least she was back home.

Dear John:

  It is difficult for me to write. I am still in bed and cannot move easily. I have been in bed four months now. I have been at home for three weeks and played records most of the time. I was delighted with the various "strange" ones, thank you. Güden was glorious.*

  I think of you often and of the boys and our nice times together. Please, send them all my greetings.

Love,
KIRSTEN

---

* We had sent Flagstad a recent recording of Hilde Güden, *Operetta Evergreens*.

Kirsten Flagstad with her "boys":
(left to right) Karl Brugger, Gordon
Parry, James Brown, Flagstad,
John Culshaw, Erik Smith
and Christopher Raeburn.

We were to begin the remainder of *Siegfried* on October 21. About two-thirds of the second act and the whole of the first had to be recorded and as, in a technical sense, both of these are far more difficult to record than the third act, we were praying we would be spared the sort of problems which had bedeviled us in the spring. I had spent a lot of time in the summer looking for traps: looking for anything which might unnecessarily eat up valuable session time, for in the back of my mind was the aim of finishing *Siegfried* in eighteen sessions instead of the scheduled twenty. By doing so we would still end with twenty because of the two wasted sessions at the beginning of May, but at least the budget would not have been exceeded.

Letters went off to every artist involved, detailing exactly what was planned for each of the autumn sessions. Where there was any ambiguity or doubt, the matter was raised now rather than later. I wrote to Joan Sutherland:

Running over the *Siegfried* schedule last night with Georg Solti, we discovered a most odd discrepancy concerning the Woodbird in two different editions of the score.

In all editions, quite correctly, the very first entry carries a footnote by Wagner which means that the phrase should be sung quite freely, i.e. not in strict tempo. This is perfectly in order.

However, in some editions of the score the next two entries of the Bird are also given the same marking, i.e. more or less *ad lib*—and this is certainly incorrect. What it all comes to is that your first phrases on the first entry can be as free as you like to make them, whereas the later entries are in a straightforward 9/8. I thought I would drop you a note about this because it is the sort of thing that can cause confusion and loss of time at sessions.

We were to begin with the scene where Siegfried encounters Fafner in the forest cave, and kills him, and we had to include all the passages for the Woodbird, as this was the only day that Joan Sutherland could be with us. To get an effectively frightening sound for Fafner, Gordon had rigged up a huge bank of about twenty fifteen-inch speakers, each with its own power amplifier, and installed the lot in the Blauersaal, which is a very resonant hall attached to the Sofiensaal. The effect we wanted was to be created through this resonance, for you cannot just amplify a small sound in the hope of making it seem huge (it will go on sounding like a small sound amplified). We also had to remember that Fafner's roars needed to be superimposed on an enormous orchestral climax.

Star soprano Joan Sutherland, seen here recording one of her major roles, sings the short but vital passages allotted to the Woodbird in the Decca "Siegfried."

Kurt Böhme, as Fafner, was to be enclosed in a small dead room with his own microphone and headphones which enabled him to hear what was being played in the main hall. He would also have a television set so that he could take his musical cues from Solti. In order not to tire Böhme's voice, I asked Erik Smith to go into the small room and roar like Fafner when he is attacked by Siegfried. When the roars began we would be able to make adjustments on the control desk and also to the microphones and speakers deployed in the Blauersaal. Getting the right sound on this sort of thing—to prevent it from sounding phony—can be a long and tricky business, but this time, and allowing for the fact that Böhme's voice would have a considerably greater output than Erik Smith's, the effect worked almost immediately. We were so delighted to have achieved it so quickly that we proceeded at once to deal with the Woodbird, and the sort of perspective we wanted to get on Joan Sutherland's voice. Joan was standing by to try it out for us with a piano in the main hall, and it was not until we were well on the way to getting what we wanted that someone remembered Erik Smith, still shut up in the small room and roaring away as the substitute Fafner.

The session went well. The contrast between Siegfried in the forest and Fafner in the cave and the Woodbird in the tree seemed to be in line with Wagner's wishes. At the playback, Böhme's dark voice boomed out with great menace and his roars during the fight sounded right. (If there is a single passage in the *Ring* that can be called manufactured, I think it is the short orchestral sequence covering the fight. Wagner wanted to get it over quickly; and he did.) Böhme did not greatly like the result. "I sound awful," he said.

"You're meant to," I told him. "You're a dragon."

He thought about that for a moment. "Yes," he said, "I know. But I'd like to be a *beautiful* dragon."

When we were recording this passage, or rather the passage which immediately follows the death of Fafner, I thought I spotted something which I had never noticed before in the *Ring:* the fact that it is precisely there that one hears the Siegfried motive for the first time with a drop of a seventh, instead of a sixth, in the middle of the phrase. From this point onwards it frequently appears in the version with the seventh, and most memorably so in the funeral march after Siegfried's death in *Götterdämmerung*. As far as I knew, this initial appearance after Fafner's slaughter had not been commented on before, and I went out of my way, in the essay I wrote to accompany the *Siegfried* recording, to draw attention to it. By killing Fafner and acquiring the ring, Siegfried had set the seal on his own fate, and it seemed typical of Wagner's subtlety to change Siegfried's motive slightly at that moment by substituting the ominous drop of a seventh for the normally bright and assertive sixth. As it is a horn phrase, I spoke about it to Roland Berger, who agreed it was an interesting point. Months later, long after *Siegfried* had been on the market, Roland told me he was convinced that the version containing the seventh had an earlier appearance in the *Ring*, but that for the life of him he could not remember where. He was going to play the *Ring* several times in the opera house during the season and he promised to look out for it: but it was not to be found. It was not until we were recording *Walküre*, three years later, that Roland came in one day brandishing a score. He had found the reference. The Siegfried motive, complete with a drop of a seventh, occurs in *Walküre*, Act Three, a moment or two before Brünnhilde hands the splinters of the sword to Sieglinde. Admittedly, it is not so clear as in *Siegfried*, and it is gone in a flash; but it is certainly there.

We spent the evening of that first day adding Böhme's voice to the opening scene of Act Two, which we had recorded in May with Hotter and Neidlinger. Böhme had to remain in his little room, while hearing over his headphones the edited version of the scene we had previously recorded. It, plus his own voice now sounding as if it came from the depths of the cavern, went onto a new tape which would in time become the master. (We had enhanced the impression of depth by getting

Bass Kurt Böhme, who recorded Fafner, also supplied the roars for Bayreuth's awesome monster in 1952.

Hotter and Neidlinger to sing away from the microphones and towards the back of the stage when they are calling to Fafner.) We also resisted any pressure to turn Fafner into a *beautiful* dragon, because whichever way you look at him Fafner is pretty disagreeable.

What remained to be done in Act Two covered three sessions, and compared with the first they were straightforward. From the recording point of view it is a pleasure to reach those parts of the *Ring* where nothing but musical concentration is required, and you are able to stop worrying about whether this or that device to produce this or that perspective is going to work or not. In those three sessions we completed all the Act Two scenes between Siegfried and Mime, and what is known as the Forest Murmurs. Stolze's promise had been accurate: he was well back on form and could move without difficulty, except for one arm which was still slightly paralyzed.

In the respite provided by those sessions, we were getting ready for the acute problems of Act One. Fortunately, it has only three characters—Siegfried, Mime, and the Wanderer—and all were at our disposal in Vienna for the days that were left. The technical requirements for Act One may be gauged by the fact that on the schedule I had quoted five special effects for Act Three, thirteen for Act Two, and twenty-eight for Act One, although it happens to be the shortest of the three.

We had given some thought, not entirely frivolous, to the question of the bear with which Siegfried makes his entrance in Act One. These days the bear is usually omitted from stage performances, despite the resulting absurdity when Siegfried speaks to, and drives off, a totally invisible animal. Our only hope of conveying the presence of the bear to a record audience (by any means other than that of the text itself) was to incorporate a sound—but nobody knew what sort of sound a bear makes. Some time before, we had enlisted the cooperation of London Zoo when we needed all sorts of animal noises for Beatrice Lillie's version of *Carnival of the Animals*, and before leaving for Vienna, Gordon Parry and some of his colleagues went down to the Zoo again and recorded a bear. (It seems that the only sure way to get a bear to make noises is to put a male and female in adjoining cages and then feed the female with honey. The protests of the male are then loud and unmistakable.)

We abandoned this effect as soon as we tried it over the music. It was unnecessary, and interrupted the music; and Wagner, though he wanted his bear to be visible on the stage, had not asked that it should bark. On the records, you can assume that the bear is present because it is talked about, but it still seems nonsense to omit it during a stage production without altering the text accordingly.

The noises which Wagner so carefully annotated in Act One of *Siegfried* should contribute, if effectively presented, to the dramatic tension. Mime's pathetic, futile attempts to forge the sword should sound in contrast to the certainty and vigor which Siegfried eventually brings to the task. Mime can only really express his anger by throwing things about (he is afraid of Siegfried, and of the Wanderer), and these actions, translated into sound, had to be part of the record. Even more important, we felt that they needed to be part of the *interpretation*, for if they could be done correctly they would contribute to the tension of the drama. It was necessary, however, to distinguish between those which could be done live (simultaneously with the music) and those which would have to be superimposed afterwards. In the former category came all the filing and beating of the sword, except that which is actually noted. My colleague Erik Smith, with Horst Berger (brother of Roland, the first horn of the Vienna Philharmonic) and two assistant percussionists, provided all the "on session" noises, including the moment when the white-hot sword is plunged into cold water. We had to experiment a great deal with the filing of the sword, mainly to decide when it should be rhythmical—i.e., going with the pulse of the music—and when it should not.

The big problem comes with the *notated* beating of the sword—from the point where Siegfried's forging song begins to the end of Act One.

At this point, Gordon's experience in Bayreuth in 1955 proved invaluable, for on that occasion the live-performance recording of Act One had been ruined by the hammering, which had been so loud and unrhythmical on the stage as to obliterate the voice of Siegfried. In the forlorn hope that the recording would be issued, the Bayreuth forces had reassembled at midnight specifically to record this particular scene under controlled conditions, with the hammering entrusted to a percussion player standing at Siegfried's side. It worked, and it was a variant of that technique which we adopted in Vienna.

This time, we recorded the sequence from the opening of the forging song to the end of the act without the notated beating. We then edited the sequence until it was musically in shape to everyone's satisfaction; and only then did we get Horst Berger to superimpose the sound of the beating of the sword on the large and small anvils. I find the result convincing, and so did the majority of critics, although a basic problem still remained unsolved. In the theater, no Siegfried that I have ever heard has been able to sing this very difficult passage and yet retain enough energy to give the mighty blows demanded by Wagner; still less has any Siegfried been capable of rhythmic precision in the rapid,

During a break in the "Siegfried" sessions, tenor Windgassen and percussionist Horst Berger clown around with some of the equipment that was used to provide the sounds for the notated beating of the sword in the forging scene.

lighter beating which follows. If the beating is imprecise, something—however small—is lost in the buildup towards the great climax at the end of Act One. This problem can be solved in recording by using an able percussionist, as we did; but, since Siegfried is not actually dealing the blows himself, the inevitable exhaustion, the sheer strain, is missing. Windgassen did his best to compensate (and we even gave him a sound-less rubber hammer to beat with!), but in the last resort an embarrassing choice remains. In this vital, long passage, does one want, in a recorded performance, a Siegfried whose vocal abilities are compromised because he has to beat out his own sword, almost inevitably with rhythmic inaccuracy? Or does one want a Siegfried who is vocally fresh through being unencumbered with the need to do two things at once? We chose the latter course, and I believe it was right.

The problem of keeping Siegfried in fresh voice throughout the opera is much less of a difficulty in the studio than in the theater, but it is still present. We arranged the Act One sessions in such a way that Windgassen was able to rest on alternate days, during which we concentrated on Hotter's long central scene with Stolze. It was all as smooth and steady as the sessions in May had been turbulent. There was a mildly anxious moment when Hotter, who had been working too much at the opera and giving several Lieder concerts as well, seemed to be running short of voice. Apart from that, and the protests of the percussion players who were exhausted after hours and hours of beating, banging, and filing, the first act of *Siegfried* went like clockwork. The final session was on November 5, and the second installment of the Decca *Ring* was safely on tape.

There were many miscellaneous sessions in Vienna during November of that year, and the editing of *Siegfried* was consequently delayed. Information from London and the United States indicated that a release date not later than April 1963 was envisaged, so we managed to have our first playback of the entire work in Vienna on December 3. The third act had been completely edited during the summer and did not need to be touched; but adjustments were still required in the first and second.

Our final playback in Vienna was on December 7, and the room was packed with friends from the Philharmonic. (In the case of a long work like *Siegfried* we arrange the playback rather on the lines of a Bayreuth performance. We start in mid-afternoon with the first act, and have a sixty-minute break for drinks; then comes the second, followed by a break for dinner, and finally the third.) We did not finish that evening until well after midnight, but everyone was very impressed. I wanted to ring Solti in London to tell him how well *Siegfried* had turned out, but knowing the vagaries of the Viennese international exchange, and fearing that it might take another hour for the call to go through, I postponed it until the morning.

When I finally reached Solti and told him how excited we were with the result, he sounded oddly subdued. Instead of his usual bounce, and a deluge of questions about whether this, that, or the other had come out as we hoped, he said almost nothing except: "I'm very pleased." In the end I asked him if anything was the matter. "I suppose you haven't seen the papers," he said. "Kirsten died last night."

The final playback of *Siegfried* also marked the end of a different aspect of our lives in Vienna. The control room in which we had worked almost since we first arrived in the hall, and in which we had recorded not only *Rheingold* and *Siegfried*, but *Aïda*, *Otello*, *Tristan*, *Fledermaus*, and *Salome*, among others, was due to be partly demolished and shortened by the management of the hall, who were interested in acquiring better backstage facilities for their dances, political meetings, and conventions. They offered, and we accepted, some adjoining rooms which were slightly larger, though it is always disturbing to have to change anything in a room, let alone change the room itself, when you have grown accustomed to the sound it produces and become familiar with its virtues and vices. We watched the builders tearing out our cupboards and demolishing the walls of the room in which so many of our battles had been fought, and it was a bit like seeing one's own house pulled down brick by brick.

Back in London there was much expectancy for *Siegfried*. Unlike *Rheingold*, which, until Terry McEwen blazed the trail, rested quietly in the studio, *Siegfried* was a center of attention as soon as the tapes reached England. By 1962, McEwen had gone to take over classical management in our New York office, and had been succeeded in London by Jack Boyce. Even before the tapes came back, Boyce had fixed a full playback for December 29 at five-thirty in the evening, and invited just about everyone who was likely to have a hand in selling, publicizing, or promoting *Siegfried*.

This was fine and welcome enthusiasm; but I was a bit apprehensive. *Siegfried* is very different from *Rheingold*, not only in content but in duration—it is almost twice as long. For those who are not accustomed to Wagner and who do not know the *Ring*, the absence of female voices for so much of *Siegfried* can lead to boredom. It moves much more slowly than *Rheingold*, and does not have so many obviously spectacular passages to display the technique of sound recording. In a sentence, I was afraid that many of those who had found, to their surprise, that

they could become caught up with *Rheingold* would find four and a
half hours of *Siegfried* simply too much. I feared that the people whose
influence we most needed to sell *Siegfried* would go away saying that
Rheingold had been a flash in the pan, and that the new piece was boring except for the converted.

I went to Jack Boyce and proposed that we should announce and
hold *two* playbacks at the studio, one consisting of the entire work, for
which we would announce the running time of each act, and the other
of excerpts lasting about an hour and a half. We would leave it to the
individuals concerned to decide which playback they attended. As it
happened, both were full, and some people came twice.

The release date was to be April 1963, and up came the Wagner Society again to ask for a pre-release playback. After the *Rheingold* experience I was not too keen, but the sales and promotion people felt
strongly that it should be done. This time it was in a long narrow hall in
the Charing Cross Hotel, and I did my question-and-answer bit in the
second intermission in order to escape quickly at the end. There was
one other playback before the public release, and that was at the Nor-
breck Hydro in Blackpool, where that great enthusiast Ivan March was
running his (now defunct) annual weekend conference. I think "convention" would be a better word for these remarkable gatherings,
which drew people from all over the country to listen to demonstra-
tions and lectures given by all the major record companies. I had introduced *Rheingold* before its public release during the 1959 conference;
and now in 1963 I was to talk about *Siegfried* and play excerpts for an
hour.

I had been given the period from 1130 to 1230, and had been asked to
finish promptly in order to let the audience have a drink before lunch,
which was at one. I asked if the people from other companies who were
preceding me had also been told to finish promptly, and was assured
that was so. The first speaker, at 0930, overran by ten minutes, and by
the time the next man from another distinguished competitor had got on
the stage and decided what he wanted to say, it was 1050. At 1200, half
an hour after I was supposed to have started, he was still dribbling on,
and people were leaving the hall in droves. I could see myself getting up
there at about 1220 and talking to an audience of six. But short of physically dragging the man off the platform there was nothing anyone
could do. (If I had thought he was doing it out of a rather nasty competitive spirit, to keep Decca off the platform until people were likely
to leave for drinks and lunch, I would not have minded so much; but he
was so overcome by his own eloquence, or lack of it, that I don't think
he gave the clock a thought.)

He finally wound up at 1215. I went round the back with my colleague who was to work the tape machine, and Philip Hope-Wallace who was to be in the chair. When we walked through the hall there cannot have been more than twelve people there; yet when we went on the stage five minutes later, having got the tape in order, the hall was full enough to burst. (I hoped that the competition was watching!) Hope-Wallace cut his introduction to the minimum, and I said that as we had barely forty-five minutes before lunch I was not going to talk at all: I would merely announce where each *Siegfried* excerpt came from, and let the recording speak for itself. At one o'clock, when the last notes of the duet from Act Three had sounded, there was applause for about two minutes. I reckoned we had sold a few sets that morning; and the only really angry person was the barman, because he did no business at all.

Siegfried is a six-record set, which makes it much harder to sell than *Rheingold*, which is only three. On the other hand, you do not have to sell as many *sets* to reach a total of as many records. People who are trying to make up their minds about whether or not to buy a large multi-record set are undoubtedly influenced by the critics, and we were wondering whether the notices would be anything like as good as they had been for *Rheingold*. We need not have worried. Alec Robertson led off in *The Gramophone* with the following sentence:

> This first complete recording of *Siegfried* is, I feel confident, the finest recording, as such, of opera that we have had so far, and one that embodies a magnificent performance of the great work. . . .

In the course of a review that covered several thousand words, Roberston had almost nothing adverse to say. Like many other critics, he picked out Fafner:

> Böhme's already large voice is powerfully magnified and emerges with a cavernous sound, with a result as legitimate as the powerful speaking trumpet prescribed by Wagner, who also cued in the dragon's roars and dying groans. These roars become quite frightening in the combat scene, for the great beast seems to be in the room with one, and coming towards one. . . .

After praising Solti and the Vienna Philharmonic for their achievement, Robertson singled out Roland Berger for his playing of the horn call in Act Two. So did Burnett James in *Audio Record Review*, adding: "The fire and lyricism of Solti's conducting, and the brilliantly accomplished playing of the Vienna Philharmonic constantly brings the

Roland Berger, James Brown, his wife Elizabeth, John Culshaw and Horst Berger (partially visible at lower right) play a game of roulette in the Sofiensaal apartment during off-hours.

work vividly to life. Here is the true Wagnerian sound, the splendour and the passion. . . ." *Consensus* gave its highest rating and said: "Yes, it is terrific; terrific without gimmick or vulgarity, a great artistic achievement as well as a great dramatic thrill . . . the effects are not overdone and it must be a poor soul who cannot thrill to Fafner's appalling roars. This staggering technical achievement is worthy of the high artistic endeavour of this triumphant performance. . . ."

Back in *The Gramophone*, in a later, retrospective review, Desmond Shawe-Taylor was the first to have any major reservations. After writing: ". . . it justifies in most respects the immense enthusiasm with which it has been received. Not even in the theatre have I been so conscious of the extraordinary variety and beauty of Wagner's orchestration which Solti, the Vienna Philharmonic and the Decca engineers have between them realized with amazing fidelity . . ." he went on to find a number of faults in the vocal performances. Hotter came in for criticism, and so did Stolze. The rest he liked, more or less, and he concluded: "Joan Sutherland's Woodbird, a piece of ritzy casting, has come in for criticism on the ground that her travelling instructions to Siegfried are far from clear. Well, I admit that she is no station announcer; but in point of fact the part is curiously difficult to articulate, and others don't do it much better."

Reactions from abroad were almost universally ecstatic, and we got another *Grand Prix Mondiale* from the French. (That made five to date, for we had also received them for *Aïda*, *Tristan*, *Salome*, and *Rheingold*.) In the course of a long review in *High Fidelity* (New York), Conrad L. Osborne wrote: "*Siegfried* is, to my mind, Solti's finest recorded accomplishment to date. All told, a solid production, and a welcome plug in one of the more deplorable gaps in the catalogue. On to *Götterdämmerung*, please."

On to *Götterdämmerung*.

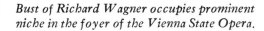

Wagner and the Vienna Opera

Although the Viennese have the reputation of being musical conservatives, they took Wagner to their hearts at an early date. Johann Strauss Jr. played the *Tannhäuser* Overture at his outdoor concerts in the early 1850s, and Johann Herbeck, later to be director of the Vienna Opera, led his own arrangements of choruses from *Tannhäuser*, *The Flying Dutchman* and *Rienzi* long before the local premières of these operas. In 1857 *Tannhäuser* had its stage première at the suburban Thalia Theater and proved so popular that the playwright Nestroy wrote a parody of it. Soon after, *Dutchman* and *Lohengrin* followed at the Kärntnertor Theater, then the city's main opera house. It was in Vienna in 1861 that Wagner heard *Lohengrin* for the first time. *Tristan* almost had its première in Vienna, but trouble with singers ended the project. By this time Wagner was such a hero with the Viennese (despite the opposition of their major critic, Eduard Hanslick) that *Meistersinger* was slated to open the grand new opera house on the Ringstrasse. Difficulties in producing the huge work forced a delay, and the house was inaugurated on May 25, 1869, with *Don Giovanni;* but *Meistersinger* was mounted not long after. It was the first of a procession of works that established the Vienna Opera as one of the leading exponents of Wagner's music, a position it holds to the present day.

A standing ovation followed the gala performance of Beethoven's "Fidelio" that opened the rebuilt Vienna State Opera on Nov. 5, 1955. The auditorium resembles the bombed-out one but is airier and less ornate.

The foyers and grand staircase escaped damage in 1945 air raid. The chandeliers and vaultings, gilt ornamentation and coffered ceiling are those Wagner knew when he supervised productions at theater in 1875.

Two hundred debutantes and their escorts perform a polonaise at the opening ceremonies of the 1969 Opera Ball. Staged in the Opera House itself (whose auditorium and stage are joined to form a huge dance floor some 170 feet long), the ball is the culmination of Vienna's annual carnival season. The president of Austria and members of the government preside from what used to be the royal box. The 6,000 revellers dance to Strauss waltzes played by five orchestras.

CHAPTER FOUR

1964 Götterdämmerung

ON THE LAST DAY of June 1944 there took place the last performance in the old Vienna State Opera. It was *Götterdämmerung*. Professor Otto Strasser, who until his retirement at the end of 1966 had been president of the Vienna Philharmonic for many years, recalled that performance for me.

"The bombardment of Vienna was beginning. Already in June shells were falling on the outskirts of the city, and every member of the orchestra knew that *Götterdämmerung* was going to be our final performance in the old house. It was *Götterdämmerung* in more senses than one: it was the end of an era. I know, I was there; and everyone had this same feeling. Knappertsbusch conducted,* and I think it was one of the greatest performances of his life....

"The bombing of the center of Vienna began on September 10, 1944, and the State Opera was destroyed—all but the shell of the building—on March 12, 1945. We saved all our instruments by storing them in the Musikvereinssaal and in the cellars of the Burg Theater."

Professor Helmut Wobisch, the vice-president, took up the story:

"We had a great Wagner tradition in Vienna, the legacy of Richard Strauss, Wilhelm Furtwängler, and Hans Knappertsbusch. But after the war, with the exception of a *Walküre* production at the Theater an der Wien, we did not play the *Ring* at all until Decca began the *Rheingold* recording in 1958. Von Karajan began his first cycle in the theater *after* the recording, so the younger generation in the orchestra had never played *Rheingold* until they came to the Sofiensaal.

---

* Not Karl Böhm, as stated in the *Concise Oxford Dictionary of Opera*.

STAATSOPER WIEN

Freitag, den 30. Juni 1944

Preise II

DER RING DES NIBELUNGEN

Ein Bühnenfestspiel für drei Tage und einen Vorabend
von Richard Wagner

Dritter Tag:

Götterdämmerung

In drei Aufzügen und einem Vorspiel

Musikalische Leitung: Hans Knappertsbusch

Spielleitung: Erich v. Wymetal

Personen der Handlung

Siegfried	Dr. Julius Pölzer *Staatsoper München*
Brünnhilde	Helena Braun *Staatsoper München*
Gutrune	Daga Söderqvist
Hagen	Herbert Alsen
Gunther	Carl Kronenberg *Staatsoper München*
Alberich	Adolf Vogel
Waltraute	Elisabeth Höngen
Die drei Nornen	Else Schürhoff / Elena Nikolaidi / Daniza Jlitsch
Die drei Rheintöchter	Esther Réthy / Aenne Michalsky / Elena Nikolaidi
Die drei Mannen	Egyd Toriff / Karl Ettl / Roland Neumann

Bühnenbilder und Kostüme nach Entwürfen von Alfred Roller

Nach jedem Aufzug eine größere Pause

Anfang 16 Uhr   Ende 21 Uhr

Das Publikum wird gebeten, sich vor Beginn der Vorstellung beim
Erscheinen unserer verwundeten Frontsoldaten in der Mittelloge von
den Plätzen zu erheben.

The performance of "Götterdämmerung" (above) that ended the Vienna State Opera's 1944 season proved to be the last ever in the old opera house. With his Thousand Year Reich collapsing, Hitler ordered all theaters closed a few days later; and on March 12, 1945, an Allied air raid left the building the tangled wreck seen at right.

"There is a very big difference between the sound and style of the Vienna Philharmonic playing Wagner, and that of any other major orchestra. The difference is in the tradition taught in our schools, especially for the brass players. We have the big, broad German style which is handed from generation to generation by our teachers in the Academy, so in that sense the young players who had never played *Rheingold* knew what to do because it was in their blood. What we like so much about Solti is that he understands and agrees with this tradition, and allows us to play in the way we have studied, and not in some other way which, forced upon us, would be foreign to our style, to our tone—to everything. I just want to add this: the brass players have by now played the *Ring* under many conductors, but they tell me that the only conductor who really knows how *they* have to play a *motiv* from

Wagner correctly is Georg Solti. The Hungarian is the only one who really has the right rhythm. . . ."

Almost exactly twenty years after that final wartime performance of *Götterdämmerung* in the old Vienna State Opera, we were to embark, in Vienna, on the same work; for even before the success of *Siegfried* was established I had been given approval to try to set up *Götterdämmerung* for 1964. This, all of us knew, was to be the big challenge, for no other part of the *Ring* posed so many artistic and technical problems. Even before we started, it looked like it would be the most expensive recording ever made, partly because of the length of the work, but also because it is the only *Ring* opera to require a huge chorus (in Act Two), and because we wanted to assemble the sort of dream cast that is unlikely to be encountered in the theater.

While I was trying, with my colleagues in Zurich, to coordinate the cast we wanted for two periods in 1964, another major development was being put forward for consideration by Gordon Parry and Jimmy Brown. They were very conscious of the risks involved in moving to the new control room in the Sofiensaal, but they knew that they would have at least a year to get used to it before *Götterdämmerung* started. What they had in mind, and what they had been working on in their spare time, was the idea that the new room should contain a permanent installation of brand-new equipment which they would design specifically to meet the sort of requirements we had imposed on ourselves in Vienna.

The old equipment had done us proud, and indeed was to continue to do so for at least another year. There was nothing wrong with it, except that it had not been built to accommodate many of the techniques we were using. It could be adapted for such techniques, but only at the cost of time and nerves. Some of the fantastic hookups we imposed on the equipment had to be seen to be believed, but if anything went wrong the problem of fault-tracing became acute. The machine was being used for something for which it had never been designed.

There are two ways of making records: the lazy way, and the other way. I have attended opera sessions run by other companies, and at some of them neither the producer nor the engineer has left his seat from first until last. After one such occasion I went out for a drink with my opposite number, and when he asked me for my impression, I could not resist saying that everyone seemed to be taking life very easy. He shrugged. "Why should we bother?" he said. "Once the tapes are back at headquarters they are out of our hands and the selection committee does what it likes. Whatever *we* do that is not strictly conventional—as the critics want—will be wrong. So we just give them the music plain and let them get on with it."

What had clearly emerged from the success of *Rheingold* and *Siegfried* was the fact that if one could create a "sound picture," to use a clumsy term, it was possible to bring the listener closer to the music and the drama. It is not easy to define just how this can be done, but it is not only by technique. No amount of juggling with microphones, no amount of technical trickery will make a "sound picture" unless the artists themselves are willing to enter the scheme of things and rethink their performances *within the new medium.* I would not deny Gordon and Jimmy an ounce of the credit they richly deserved for what we had already done together; but without the cooperation of the artists, and without a conductor who was wholly in sympathy with what we were trying to achieve, their efforts would have been wasted. We knew that the cast we had in mind for *Götterdämmerung* would be just as cooperative as that of *Rheingold* and *Siegfried;* but the technical problems from our end were far greater, and any loss of session time on a project as expensive as *Götterdämmerung* was unthinkable. This is why Gordon and Jimmy had drawn up a design for a highly advanced control desk, or "mixer," which would enable them not only to produce all the effects and perspectives required, but produce them in a tenth of the time imposed by the old machine.

It was not directly my affair, but I did not think their chances were high. The new mixer and its ancillaries were going to cost as much as the opera itself, and the old machine had proved its capabilities time and time again—why take the risk of a change, especially in the middle of the *Ring?* There was also the tricky question that Gordon wanted the machine to be built in Vienna, so that he and Jimmy, as co-designers, could keep an eye on every stage of its construction and make sure that it incorporated everything we might need for the future. At a time when every Decca team was crying out for new and different equipment of one sort or another according to the needs of the location—and it should be remembered that Vienna is only one location among many—it did not seem very likely that the plan would be approved.

The chief of the Decca studios is a very remarkable man, who has not so far entered this story as much as he deserves. Arthur Haddy possesses vast experience, knowledge, and judgment, and he is a great believer in the delegation of authority. He also has an extraordinary eye for talented staff, and retains their loyalty by delegating responsibility wherever it is deserved. In 1956 he had all but dumped Gordon and Jimmy in

Vienna, and told them to get on with the job. He did not breathe down their necks: in fact, in the ten years that I have been working in Vienna, I doubt if he has visited us more than three or four times. He was satisfied with the work; he had a good team; so he left it alone. He came into the picture only when a major technical decision had to be made, or when we returned with something substandard, which, mercifully, was not very often.

Gordon, who has considerable powers of persuasion, so convinced him about the need for the new mixer that Arthur Haddy put it up at once to the chairman, Sir Edward Lewis, who gave immediate approval not only for the machine as such, but for its construction in Vienna. It was an exciting prospect: suddenly, we would have at our fingertips what was likely to be the most advanced and unorthodox piece of recording equipment in the world, and it would be installed in time for *Götterdämmerung.* The design was strictly Decca's, but the assembly and construction of the machine were to be done by Wiener Schwachstromwerke. The contract was signed, and work began in 1963.

Apart from its versatility, the new mixer incorporated a new seating deployment for those who had to use it. One of the problems with the old machine was that its design, in common with the majority of its type, left practicable room for only one engineer. We had found, over the years, that in dealing with a complicated operatic score, one pair of hands was insufficient, so the engineers had adapted the old machine to enable Gordon to work the orchestral controls while Jimmy handled the voices. (The idea, still prevalent in Germany, that the musical man, or producer, should himself handle the controls is, in my opinion, absurd. It is impossible to read a score and several meters at the same time: it is impossible to exercise musical and technical judgment at one and the same instant. The concept of the *Tonmeister,* as he is called, is a typically German invention, and more often than not the occupant of that exalted position turns out to be a frustrated conductor who has been shrewd enough to pick up a smattering of technical knowledge and so find a way to earn a living.) One of the troubles with the setup on our old machine was that Gordon, on the orchestral department, was in the middle, with Jimmy, handling the voices, on his left; which left me on the right. The structure of the machine would admit no variation, and to give Jimmy a vocal cue I had either to lean right across Gordon, possibly obstructing his view of the meters, or yell like mad when the music was loud. And because the machine was not designed with a view to all the complicated effects we required, it was sometimes necessary for me to operate an effects control myself. (The organ pedal during the first eight minutes of *Otello,* with von Karajan, which we

Arthur Haddy, chief of the Decca studios, helped clear the way for construction of a new, more versatile control desk, or "mixer," for the Sofiensaal studio.

had pre-recorded in Liverpool Cathedral, is another case in point, for Gordon and Jimmy simply ran out of fingers capable of reaching accessible knobs to control—in addition to the organ—an orchestra, solo voices, onstage chorus, offstage chorus, wind, cannon, and offstage trumpet.)

The design of the new mixer put the producer in the middle, with one engineer on each side of him. Gordon was now on the left, still controlling the orchestra, and Jimmy on the right, with the voices and effects channels under his fingers. Furthermore, the tape machines were to be in a separate room, though visible through a large glass panel. They could be worked by the third engineer or, if necessary, by remote control from the mixer itself. After years of frantic improvisation, it seemed at last that we would have an instrument more than capable of fulfilling whatever requirement we desired. It was typical of Decca that the decision was made so quickly, and without qualification.

In Zurich, Leon Felder was as usual responsible for booking most of the artists involved in *Götterdämmerung*, and he realized from the start what a vast operation it was going to be. In April of 1963, I had sent him a full cast list with suggested alternatives. Certain castings were, of

The Sofiensaal's new mixer, with its formidable array of buttons, switches and slide controls (above), enabled John Culshaw and Gordon Parry (right) to produce all of the special sonic effects required for "Götterdämmerung" more efficiently than with the old console.

course, indisputable: Nilsson, Windgassen, and Gottlob Frick (as Hagen) had to be in the cast or there was no point in starting. We built the plan around their availability, and Solti's. Gustav Neidlinger was no worry, because his part in *Götterdämmerung* is so small that we would need him only for one day. And now that our dream of Flagstad as Waltraute would never be fulfilled, I wanted at all costs to have Christa Ludwig, who sang the part occasionally, but incomparably, on the stage.

The biggest headache was the casting of Gunther. The trouble with Gunther is that he is an important, but weak, character. He is on the stage quite a lot, but he does not have a great deal of rewarding music to sing. Because of this, the part is often given to whatever second-class baritone happens to be around, and so an already weak character becomes weaker than Wagner intended. And just *how* weak should Gunther be? I began to wonder if the weakness, which is so often commented upon by critics, might not be more attributable to the sort of performance the part usually receives than to the part as written. But Gunther's weak reputation was established, and no first-class baritone I could think of was likely to touch the role.

In the recording of Benjamin Britten's *War Requiem*, I had worked for the first time with Dietrich Fischer-Dieskau, and had marveled at his seriousness, modesty, and sheer technique. The huge reputation he enjoyed was not to be smirched by those critics who, having "discovered" him, were currently in the process of trying to knock him down. ("This month's Lieder record by Fischer-Dieskau," one of them had recently sneered, "is not among his hundred best.") You do not get on close terms with an artist new to the Company in the course of one series of sessions, and I feared that the mere mention of Gunther to Fischer-Dieskau might cause him to lose faith in Decca's judgment forever. But I had to take that risk, for I could already imagine what he might make of the part, although he had never sung it on the stage. His reply was an immediate and definite yes. He knew and loved *Götterdämmerung*, and I think he saw what might be made of Gunther. The character may be weak, but he is still a king and he plays a vital part in the action. He is also a tragic character, though the tragedy of Gunther is usually swamped by the more dramatic events involving Brünnhilde, Siegfried, and Hagen. This, we hoped, would not happen with Fischer-Dieskau in the part.

As dates and contracts began to clarify, the division of *Götterdämmerung* over three periods emerged. The first period, scheduled for late May and early June 1964, would be devoted to the whole of the long first act, except for the Gibichung scene (Fischer-Dieskau was not available in the spring). This was fine, because the Gibichung scene is an entity in itself and could easily be left until the autumn. Also in the first period we planned to record the opening scene of Act Two, between Hagen and Alberich. The second period, between October 26 and November 5, would see the completion of Act One with the Gibichung scene, and the recording of all those parts of Acts Two and Three *not* involving Brünnhilde (for Nilsson was not available until later). The final period, from November 15 to 26, would therefore concentrate on Act Two, from Brünnhilde's entrance to the end of the Act; and on whatever was left from Act Three, including the Immolation scene. It was not a bad schedule, for although we had to jump about a bit from act to act, the scenes within the acts were not in themselves broken up. And at least we were starting at the beginning and ending at the end, which is a rare thing in opera recordings.

Throughout 1963, work progressed on the new control desk, and before the end of that year I was taken to have my first glimpse of it. Delivery and installation had been arranged for the middle of April 1964, exactly one month before we were to begin *Götterdämmerung*. As it was too much to hope that there would be a respite during that month in order to allow the engineers to get completely familiar with the workings of the new mixer, it was arranged to move the old gear out of the new control room and install it in another room, where it would be operated by another crew from London. As insurance, the Company decided to keep the second crew in Vienna for the whole of the first part of *Götterdämmerung*, which would therefore be recorded in duplicate: there would be a version from the old equipment on which *Rheingold* and *Siegfried* had been recorded, and a version from the new equipment which was about to be installed.

Six months before we were to start on *Götterdämmerung*, I circulated to all concerned a detailed list of the requirements for the first period. We had learned a lot of lessons from our experiences with *Rheingold* and *Siegfried*, but the demands of *Götterdämmerung*, and the challenge it presented for an imaginative use of sound, remained enormous. The following points were among the notes:

> Act One. The Norn scene.
> I would like us to think about a special sound for this whole scene, at least on the voices: something a bit coloured, empty or doom-laden to fit the opening mood and key of the piece (E flat minor/C flat minor as opposed to the E minor/C major for the same music in *Siegfried*). This would make

Dietrich Fischer-Dieskau smiles at a comment made by Georg Solti during a "Götterdämmerung" playback. For the recording, the busy German baritone agreed to sing the small but significant part of Gunther, a role he had never sung on the stage.

a big contrast with what is to follow in the next scene—the Brünnhilde/Siegfried duet, which we must make as radiant and focussed as possible. The question is: dare we sustain *any* sort of coloured sound on voices for about twenty minutes?

The First Norn will be on the extreme right, the Second Norn extreme left and the Third dead centre. There will be no movement, except at the end when the rope breaks, when the ladies must come together in the *centre* and disappear downwards. (The coming-together, and the fact that they are supposed to bind themselves together with the rope, is usually omitted on the stage today, presumably because Wagner allowed only three bars for the whole business.) Shall we cut and move them to the middle? I'd rather not if you can do it without interruption. The descent effect will have to be same one we used for Erda in *Rheingold*. (By the way, all full scores known to me, and most miniatures, wrongly indicate the entire first narrative as the province of the Third Norn, whereas it obviously belongs to the First. It's a misprint that has never been corrected, and a bad one.)

Brünnhilde/Waltraute scene. We must get some really beautiful *distant* thunder (bars 12, 13 of third scene). It needs to be beautiful because the scoring is very light and any defects like rain or birds or traffic will show up hopelessly. As Waltraute approaches, we can consider replacing Wagner's cues for lightning with the thunder brought a little closer. Waltraute's offstage call is a Blauersaal job, so we shall need to be set up in there. But I've worked out that she has time to get from the Blauersaal over to the main stage in time for her cue with Brünnhilde, so we shall not need to interrupt the take.

There is supposed to be a sort of thunderbolt crash just before Brünnhilde leads Waltraute on. It comes over very heavy orchestration. We must discuss what noise, if any, to put in here. And in general, I think we can do some very imaginative sound treatments to reflect the changing emotions of this magnificent scene, especially at the end.

End of Act One. The stage horn at the end (before Siegfried comes on) will need no strengthening with trumpets or anything else if Roland Berger has an early night and if we put him in a separate hall where we can control the sound. But—and this is important—the passage is terribly tiring for Birgit, even with her stamina. Should we therefore consider putting the horn on afterwards?

Now comes the most difficult of all the effects, which never comes off in the theatre because in his time Wagner was asking the impossible, and since it became possible people have stopped trying. We should be able to bring it off. All we have to do is to make Windgassen sound like Fischer-Dieskau gone wrong. The sound of the disguised Siegfried needs a dark colouration, imparting a baritone timbre to the tenor, and has *nothing* to do with echo. At the very end the voice has to revert to normal when he takes off the Tarnhelm, but I suppose we could cut at that point and disconnect whatever sort of magic box you have been using.

Act Two. Hagen/Alberich scene. At the end of this scene the voice of Alberich has to fade into the distance and yet retain clarity. (It should be as if he has been speaking of Hagen in a dream, and the dream is dispersing with the coming of daylight.) What about getting Neidlinger into a vocal box, like *Rheingold*, for his last lines, so that we can control both the quality and the direction of the voice? I don't think this should be a conventional exit at all: the voice should dissolve slowly, and if we can get the right sort of sound I'd be glad to do without any special directional effect. He's got to vanish aurally, but it must not sound like a fade.

These were only some of the points in the first sequence of sessions, and in early January we began a series of production meetings to try and sort them out. What was very much in our minds was the feeling that we had to do *better* than we had done in *Rheingold* and *Siegfried*, partly because Decca had so unhesitatingly supplied the new technical installation, and partly because it is never any good just to repeat yourself. There would inevitably be some people ready to object strenuously about our efforts to change a tenor into a baritone by electronic means at the end of Act One. *It does not happen in the theater* would doubtless be the phrase thrown at us from certain quarters. There is an answer, however. It does not happen in the theater because nobody has tried to make it happen; but *the idea is in the score*. When the drugged and deceived Siegfried goes back up the mountain wearing the Tarnhelm, he is required by Wagner to adopt the guise, stance, and *voice* of Gunther. (He must sing, according to Wagner's directions, in a rougher, deeper voice.) Wagner helped his tenor as much as possible by writing the part as low as he dared, and by avoiding any lyricism in the vocal line; but I would hazard a guess, based on a knowledge of Wagner's enthusiasm for any new and effective way of bringing about the ends he desired, that he would have jumped at the possibility of using a throat microphone if such a thing had existed in his lifetime. The essence of the scene is that the disguised Siegfried must sound frightening to Brünnhilde, and anything which darkens or coarsens or, in an ideal world, *lowers* the tenor's voice is a step in the right direction. We knew that on a record we could do it: we could, in effect, alter the actual structure of Windgassen's voice by rearranging the overtones in such a way as to impart a baritone timbre. No transposition of key would be evident on the record. Whatever the purists might say, we were convinced that Wagner, had he lived to know the possibilities of sound recording, would have demanded the use of every obtainable modern technique when it came to the object of conveying his works in a dramatically effective way on records. (Since the record appeared I have read a number of explanations claiming to show how we did this effect, and not one of them has been right.)

The new equipment was installed in April 1964 and between then and the start of *Götterdämmerung* a series of tests and parallel recordings took place. By the time the artists assembled we knew that the sound coming from the new gear matched what we had produced in the past, while giving us a flexibility and versatility which would have been impossible on the old equipment. But, though none of the artists knew it, our younger colleagues James Lock and John Mordler came over from their usual location in Geneva and recorded the whole of the first part of *Götterdämmerung* on the old equipment just in case an undetected bug got into the new gear.

The trio of Norns: Grace Hoffman, Anita Välkki and Helen Watts.

We had an excellent trio of Norns to begin the work. It is beyond my comprehension how some people who otherwise claim to like the *Ring* still manage to find this scene boring. It can be boring if it is badly conducted or badly sung, and one should really hear it with the last triumphant notes of *Siegfried* clearly in mind: for it is their antithesis. When Helen Watts began to sing the first line, we knew we had got the sound we wanted; and so great an impression did she make that within a day she was summoned by von Karajan to the Vienna State Opera and engaged on the spot for the Salzburg festival. (News spreads quickly in Vienna, via the orchestra of course.) Grace Hoffman was our Second Norn, and the Finnish soprano Anita Välkki, who normally sings Brünnhilde, appeared as the Third. Nilsson and Windgassen arrived that day, for on the next session they were to start the dawn duet which, with the orchestral interlude known as Siegfried's Journey to the Rhine, concludes the prologue to Act One.

The sessions rolled along on schedule. We were anticipating every possible trouble and complication, but nothing happened. It was slightly unbelievable. Nilsson and Windgassen were both in fabulous voice, and our use of the new equipment for an offstage effect worked perfectly the first time we tried. This was Roland Berger again, playing Siegfried's distant call after he has left Brünnhilde on the mountaintop. The

Roland Berger gets his cue for Siegfried's offstage horn call in the Rhine Journey by following conductor Solti's beat over closed-circuit television.

whole thing—the atmosphere, the working conditions, the morale—was a far cry from what had been going on in the same place exactly two years earlier, when we were struggling against the odds with *Siegfried*, Act Three. The scene between Brünnhilde and Waltraute, with Christa Ludwig at the top of her form, went without incident, and so did the end of Act One, which at this stage was recorded with Nilsson only, in order to allow us to add Windgassen's transformed voice later on. The gods, it seemed, were with us; and they stayed with us through the final session of the first period, when Frick and Neidlinger evoked the proper sense of evil for the opening scene of Act Two.

As soon as the sessions were over we set to work at once on the editing and effects, especially the thunder required for the beginning and end of the Waltraute scene. Of all effects, thunder is the least predictable. Manufactured thunder—i.e., thunder produced by recording a different sound, like wooden planks being dropped or broken, and then playing it back at a much slower speed—tends to sound artificial. On the other hand, real thunder is often accompanied by heavy rain and other incidental noises which would have no place in *Götterdämmerung*: one of our very best bits has the unmistakable sound of a London fire engine in the middle! Out of an accumulation of recorded thunder amounting to over one hour, we were only just able to find the few seconds or so we required, including the very distant thunder which Wagner demands in the interlude between the second and third scenes of Act One. On the stage, Brünnhilde is alone on the top of the mountain where Siegfried had left her. She is radiantly happy, waiting his return; and she is looking at the ring he gave her. The orchestra softly plays motives from the third act of *Siegfried*, and from them it is almost possible to read her thoughts and memories of the awakening, and her love for Siegfried. Suddenly, and quite softly, the Valkyrie motive is heard, together with the sound of distant thunder; she looks up, but returns at once to the contemplation of the ring. The motive and the thunder herald the coming of Waltraute, who will implore Brünnhilde to give up the ring.

The music makes perfectly good sense without the thunder, but it adds to the dramatic tension to have the right kind of thunder in place, which is why Wagner wrote it in the score. We had to search for hours to find a roll which was distant and ominous enough, and we knew it had worked like a charm when, much later, we played the whole scene to Solti. He was following the score, but when the distant thunder sounded he looked up—and out of the window! He was convinced it had come from outside.

Then we did our transformation of Windgassen, who was baffled but intrigued. When it was finished, and without saying what we had done, we played the result to Frick and Neidlinger and asked them to say who they thought was singing opposite Nilsson. (We admitted that we had done something strange to the male voice.) Frick thought it might be Hotter, and Neidlinger guessed it was Fischer-Dieskau. When we told them it was a transformed Windgassen, they were aghast, and demanded to hear the scene again. They then wanted to know how it was done, but that was a secret we were keeping to ourselves.

The knowledge that the first *Götterdämmerung* period had gone so calmly and successfully made us doubly determined to be ready for the much more complicated sessions in the autumn. And one particular problem had not been tackled at all.

In the second act of *Götterdämmerung*, at the point where Hagen summons the Vassals, he blows a call on an instrument which Wagner describes as a steerhorn. His calls are answered by two other steerhorns deployed offstage right and left, which sound just before the full chorus of Vassals bursts on the stage. A month or two earlier, I had written to Wieland Wagner in Bayreuth to ask him what type of instruments he used in his current production and, if they were not the original instruments as used by Wagner, did he know what had become of those instruments and what they were like? I received no reply, doubtless because Wieland Wagner had enough problems of his own in getting ready for the 1964 festival. I therefore asked our Munich office to get in touch with him personally and see if an answer could be obtained. The reply came quickly by cable: WAGNER SAYS STEERHORNS ARE THREE TROMBONES PLAYED ON THE STAGE NOT IN THE ORCHESTRA.

This was the easy way out, but the more we looked at the score the more it became clear that if Richard Wagner had wanted trombones, he would have written for trombones. What he wanted was something to symbolize the primitive power of Hagen: he wanted a coarse, even unmusical, sound (shades of the *Rheingold* anvils again!). A steerhorn, which I took to mean a sort of cow-horn, would make that sort of sound; but the problem was not just to find three instruments, but to find ones capable of playing the three notes written by Wagner—C, D flat, and D. I wrote to just about every opera house I could think of where *Götterdämmerung* had been produced in the past few years, and from those that replied the answer was always the same: we use trombones. Gordon Parry also was convinced that trombones would make the wrong sound: they would be too smooth, too civilized, too *musical* for what Wagner had in mind.

In the summer I went to Bayreuth, and one night I told Wilhelm Pitz, our chorus master, about the steerhorn problem. He said he would speak to Wolfgang Wagner, who might have the time to look up the files in Wahnfried and find out what his grandfather had used. Instead, Wolfgang Wagner was able to help us in a much more practical manner. He made an appointment for us with an elderly gentleman called Otto Mahler, who turned out to be a professional instrument maker who had a small workshop near Bayreuth. Mahler remembered the original instruments well—both the sound they made and what they had looked like. I asked him where they were, and he said he had seen them carried off by American soldiers after the war, at the time when the occupying troops turned the Festspielhaus into a vaudeville theater. It would have made a nice adventure, but I could not see Decca allowing me to comb the length and breadth of the United States looking for three purloined steerhorns, so I asked Otto Mahler if he could help us.

He was obviously a dedicated man, and a real craftsman. He had brought along a strange, fat trumpet the likes of which I had never seen before. He demonstrated it to me and to Pitz, playing long blasts on the note C like the Hagen call from Act Two. I thought it was just what we wanted: it was coarse and harsh and dark in timbre. But it was not right, Otto Mahler said. He had brought it along merely to give an idea of what the real steerhorns from the days of Richard Wagner had sounded like. I then asked him outright if he could make a set of steerhorns for us, and have them ready by October. He looked a bit shocked, but said he would try. As soon as I got back to London, I sent him a confirmation that we wanted the instruments, and asked him to start work on them as soon as he could.

A number of outstanding details had to be cleared up during the summer. One of them I raised in a letter to Leon Felder in Zurich:

> Birds. I expect you will be as surprised to receive a letter on this subject as I am to find myself writing it. We have had terrible trouble during the first part of *Götterdämmerung* with a colony of birds nesting in the roof of the Sofiensaal. The creatures begin to sing every time the orchestra starts, and if the music happens to be quiet you can hear them clearly on the tape. I don't know whether it's the Sofiensaal's responsibility to get rid of them, or ours, but something will have to be done before we start again. I'd better tell you that we have tried all the obvious things like firing rifles and putting up scarecrows, but they are Austrian birds and they like the music. The Sofiensaal cat is a lazy brute, too. . . .

The chirpings had been particularly grotesque in the very quiet music at the beginning of Act Two, and as we had never had trouble like this before it was clear that the birds had somehow found a way to get inside the rafters, between the ceiling of the hall and the roof. During the summer they were somehow driven out and all the holes plugged. We had no more birds in the autumn.

Meanwhile, an important development was taking place on the periphery of the *Götterdämmerung* recording. Much earlier in the year, Gordon Parry had come up with the idea that this recording, because it was the largest and longest ever undertaken by the industry, would make a good subject for a television film. This seemed a fine idea in every respect but one—which was that we were all too busy to cope with something which would obviously need a great deal of negotiation and administration. Mr. Rosengarten thought it was worth investigation, and Jack Boyce, of our classical promotion department, put out feelers in various directions. One of the commercial networks showed mild interest at first, but it was eventually the BBC, and specifically Humphrey Burton, from whom we got the sort of enthusiastic response we thought the idea deserved. The whole thing was to be a co-production between the BBC and Radio Austria, and it was conceived as a sixty-minute documentary to be called *The Golden Ring*. From the start, the idea was that Radio Austria would provide a unit of technicians and OB (outside broadcast) cameras, using video tape, while the BBC would provide a 16-mm. sound-on-film camera unit, a separate sound unit, and the film's producer, who was to be Humphrey Burton. It was envisaged that the finished film would be dubbed into various languages in addition to the basic versions in English and German.

The negotiations proved a nightmare. They started in the early spring, and by the end of the summer were no nearer an acceptable solution. It had at least been agreed that, if the thing happened at all, the best period would be the last, for it contained the more spectacular parts of Act Two and the final scene of *Götterdämmerung*. The Austrians had therefore reserved a unit to cover the period from November 15 onwards, but in the late summer they wrote to Burton to say that unless all outstanding matters could be immediately resolved they would have to withdraw the facilities, which were in demand for another project. The curse seemed to be working again, and when we set out for Vienna to record the last three sections of *Götterdämmerung*, nobody knew whether there would be a television film or not.

Wilhelm Pitz, who was to prepare the *Götterdämmerung* chorus for us, is a charming man and to my mind the greatest chorus master in the world. To watch him at work is not only a lesson in choral training, but a study in psychology. An uninformed observer might be excused for thinking that Pitz was not earning his money, for he infrequently raises his voice and his manner is always subdued. But by the time he has finished with a chorus, one need have no doubt about the result. He knows how to reveal whatever good qualities any particular chorus has; and he knows how to minimize its weaknesses. He is a very great choral trainer.

We had had many discussions about the size of the chorus for Act Two, and Gordon was pressing for a decision in order to arrange the microphone setup. I wrote to him in Vienna on September 25:

> I have been looking up the long and rather involved correspondence between Pitz, Felder and myself on the *Götterdämmerung* chorus, and the final conclusion was that at its maximum strength for Act Two it would consist of 90 people, comprising seventy male and twenty female voices. I know this is a lot smaller than the figure we orginally discussed, but Pitz has pretty well convinced me that he can do a better job with 90 picked voices than with a mass of 200 nondescript voices. He obviously knows what he is doing, and he has ample rehearsal time at the beginning of October to select the voices he wants. So allow room for 90 on the stage unless you hear otherwise.

This time, however, Pitz did change his mind, and after one or two rehearsals he rang me to request permission to increase the size of the chorus to one hundred men and thirty women. I did some cunning rescheduling, and figured that with any luck we might be able to eliminate one chorus session altogether, thus avoiding any extra expense for the larger chorus. Zurich had no objection, so we went ahead.

About that time I received a letter from Otto Mahler enclosing a photograph of the steerhorns he had made. He had played them to Wieland Wagner, who wrote him a charming note on September 1 to say that he was very pleased with the result. Wagner said he found the sound interesting, original, and even rather frightening. In his letter to me, Mahler added that it had been a nerve-racking and time-consuming task, ". . . but now I am pleased to have been able to simulate completely the sound of a roaring bull on these horns. I have spared no effort to produce something completely unique for your Vienna recordings. . . ." The instruments were already on their way to Vienna; but in the meantime our old friend Morris Smith, the orchestral manager at Covent Garden, revealed that he too could put his hand on a set of instruments which had been used at one time or another in *Götterdämmerung* productions at the Royal Opera House. I asked permission to borrow these as well, for although they were not true steerhorns, I felt they might come in handy in bolstering and assisting the tone of the new Bayreuth instruments. Morris Smith was coming to Vienna anyway to see some of the *Götterdämmerung* sessions, and willingly gave us permission to borrow the horns.

The period immediately before the second sequence was frantic. When I arrived in Vienna the choral rehearsals were in full swing, and Otto Mahler's instruments had arrived. They were being tried by various players using all sorts of mouthpieces, and the sound they made was just what we wanted. Never again would any of us be able to hear that passage from Act Two played in the theater by trombones without fuming at such careless disregard of Wagner's intentions. (And in case anyone imagines that record companies have more money to spend than opera houses, it is worth mentioning that the cost of the instruments was modest, and would be a pittance for any opera house with a large enough budget to stage *Götterdämmerung* at all.) We sent a congratulatory telegram to Otto Mahler.

Benjamin Britten was in Vienna, rehearsing with Istvan Kertesz and the Philharmonic for a performance of the *War Requiem* which was to take place two days before *Götterdämmerung* resumed. We had promised to install our closed-circuit television equipment in the Musikvereinssaal so that the distant boys' chorus would make its proper effect, which it did; though any such extramural activity adds a great deal to the strain of preparation. Leontyne Price was passing through Vienna, full of her forthcoming engagement at Covent Garden for the Visconti production of *Trovatore*. Little did we think, in wishing her good luck, that within a month she, who had nothing whatsoever to do with *Götterdämmerung*, would unwittingly almost bring us to a halt.

The list of special requirements for the autumn sessions ran to six closely typed foolscap pages, and every point referred to a specific demand by Wagner. The more one studies his scores, the more one realizes what a master of stagecraft he was, and it mattered very much to

*Chorus master Wilhelm Pitz (above)
urges on his male choir (left) during a
rehearsal of Act II of "Götterdämmerung."
Pitz, founder of London's Philharmonia
Chorus, has also directed the Bayreuth
chorus since the festival resumed in 1951.*

him that his ideas should be followed. We ran a series of tests to get effective positions for the various offstage horn calls, for they are not meant to sound all the same. (The steerhorn near the opening of Act Three is not the same sound as the steerhorns in Act Two.) Admittedly, these are minor points, but they are cumulative in their effect on the whole design. It is precisely because the work is so huge and demanding that one should not pass lightly over any detail.

While work progressed smoothly on the Gibichung scene which would complete Act One, and on the relatively easy scene from Act Three in which Siegfried narrates the events of his life to Hagen, we were planning for the big choral episodes to come, and for the extraordinary, brief solo scene for Gutrune which follows the funeral march. That scene is a minor masterpiece in itself. Although it runs for only two minutes and thirty-three seconds, it is not only a point of balance and repose within the structure of the act, but also the source of some potent images for the audience. We have heard nothing of Brünnhilde since the vengeance trio at the end of Act Two. Siegfried, after his encounter with the Rhinemaidens, has been slain by Hagen on the banks of the Rhine, and his body is being borne back to the Gibichung Hall to the thunderous accompaniment of the funeral music. Then follows the short Gutrune scene. She is alone in the vast hall, and she is frightened. Wagner's scoring, after the richness of the funeral march, drops to the minimum, pointing the atmosphere in the dark and empty hall where Gutrune wanders. Was it Siegfried's horn she heard in the night? She thought she heard Siegfried's horse neighing, and a bitter laugh from Brünnhilde's room awakened her. Was it a nightmare, or did it happen? She had seen a figure wandering down to the shore of the river, and it must have been Brünnhilde, for her room is empty.

Then, into this desolate scene breaks the triumphant Hagen, calling for lights and flaming torches to reveal the body of the dead hero to his betrothed. It is a brief, masterly, indispensable scene, and we sought to convey the loneliness and helplessness of Gutrune by placing her in an acoustic indicative of the emptiness around her. We rehearsed Claire Watson for hours in this scene, until she knew her movements by heart. She is a fine actress, and the note of fear she was able to induce in her voice was caught and heightened by the open acoustic we had decided to use. It was an exceedingly tricky scene to bring off successfully, but in the end we were pleased with it. (It is worth mentioning that in the 1965 production of *Götterdämmerung* at Bayreuth, Wieland Wagner cut the scene altogether, presumably with the agreement of the conductor, Karl Böhm, and proceeded directly from the end of the funeral

Hagen (Gottlob Frick, center) and Siegfried (Wolfgang Windgassen, right) huddle with a colleague during a break.

march to the entry of Hagen in the final scene, thus saving two minutes and thirty-three seconds in a work that runs for two hundred and sixty-five minutes. It is staggering enough that Wieland Wagner could not see the point of the scene within the structure of *Götterdämmerung;* it is even more staggering that his conductor agreed to such a cut. I can imagine what Knappertsbusch would have said.)

For the opening scene of Act Three we had acquired a splendid trio of Rhinemaidens: Lucia Popp, Gwyneth Jones, and Maureen Guy. The latter pair came from Covent Garden, and were to arrive in Vienna on November 3 for sessions on November 4 and 5. On the evening of November 2, when we had just finished the scene where Siegfried is killed, Solti received an urgent telephone call from Sir David Webster, the general administrator of the Royal Opera House, Covent Garden, to say that Leontyne Price had just canceled her engagement for the new *Trovatore*. Giulini and Visconti were already in London and expecting to start rehearsals for the production immediately, and both had decreed that Gwyneth Jones was the only acceptable replacement for the indisposed Price. It was therefore imperative for us to release Jones from her *Götterdämmerung* contract and try to find a replacement Rhinemaiden in Vienna.

It was a tricky position for Solti. He wanted Gwyneth Jones in *Götterdämmerung* as badly as I did, but he was musical director of Covent Garden and owed an allegiance to his own house in a time of crisis. I went over to the State Opera in Vienna to find out who might be available to take over the part of Wellgunde at short notice, but there was no one of any consequence available, and it was far too late to start digging around Europe. I also knew that alternative dates were not acceptable to the other two singers, for they both had immediate engagements outside Vienna. I told Solti we could not release Gwyneth Jones. We would guarantee her return by some means or other on the evening of November 5, which would mean that for two days Giulini and Visconti would have to manage without her. I also rang Gwyneth herself in London and said that while we all appreciated what a break the *Trovatore* was going to be for her, she would bring *Götterdämmerung* to a grinding halt if she did not come to Vienna. She said she would come—after all, there was plenty of *Trovatore* to keep the others busy for two days without her.

John Culshaw (right foreground) fondles the Sofiensaal cat at a cocktail party in the recording team's flat during the "Götterdämmerung" sessions. Others include (left to right) Gordon Parry, Roland Berger, Birgit Nilsson, Gottlob Frick, Dietrich Fischer-Dieskau, Claire Watson, Dieter Warneck (Fischer-Dieskau's secretary), Humphrey Burton (BBC-TV producer).

They turned out to be a splendidly matched trio, and by the middle of the session on November 5, I knew that the scene would be finished in time. We had a car waiting to take our London-bound Rhinemaidens to the airport as soon as they had finished, though the girls could get back that evening only by flying on three different airlines and changing planes twice. Just as the last notes were ringing out we received a cable from Sir David Webster: WE WOULD APPRECIATE THE RETURN OF GWYNETH JONES AND MAUREEN GUY AS SPEEDILY AS POSSIBLE. The following reply went back to him by return: WEIALALA STOP TWO RHEINMAIDENS LAST SEEN SWIMMING YOUR DIRECTION WITH FAVOURABLE CURRENT GREETINGS HAGEN CULSHAW AND ALBERICH SOLTI.

Suddenly, all the obstacles that had been in the way of the television program seemed to vanish overnight. A series of summit meetings in London, Zurich, and, so far as the BBC and Radio Austria were concerned, Vienna, resolved all the problems but one, which was planted neatly in my lap. The artists had not yet been approached, so would I please get their agreement?

In the event, it was not at all difficult, for no money was involved. Any of the principals could have sabotaged the whole idea by insisting on payment, but as I was in the pleasant position of being able to say that nobody in the cast was going to be paid, and that by refusing to appear an artist would be denying himself or herself the most valuable sort of publicity, there was very little argument. It was also made clear to everyone that absolutely nothing would be specially "staged" for television, and they were requested to try to ignore the cameras as much as possible.

This was the essence of Humphrey Burton's idea for *The Golden Ring*, and it was a good one. When the idea was first discussed in the spring I had been nervous of the amount of time we might lose through having camera units all over the place; and the engineers had been worried lest the noise of the cameras and the sound of their movements might interfere with the recording. At that stage, Burton was thinking of having three special TV sessions after we had finished *Götterdämmerung*, and on those three sessions all of us—artists, orchestra, and staff—would *pretend* to be making the recording we had in fact already made. This scheme was quickly dropped. It might have been possible for the artists, but our side of it would have looked hopelessly unreal. What Burton really wanted to get into his film was the urgency and tension of a big session, and that is something which you cannot possibly contrive at will. It became clear to all of us that his film would have to be made on the spot during actual sessions; and if there was technical interference, we would have to find a way around it.

Filming was to begin on November 15, at the start of our final, and heaviest, *Götterdämmerung* period. Burton arrived from London with his camera crew and a sound unit; the Austrians, with their big cameras, had already started their installation in the Sofiensaal. (The Austrian cameras were recording their material on video-tape machines located in a control van outside the hall. You can play back the video tape in a similar way to audio tape, so that from time to time, when there was a moment to spare, we were able to see what material the Austrians had got. The BBC unit was using 16-mm. film, and was therefore much more mobile: it concentrated on the scenes at the airport, in the flat, in Solti's hotel, and in the city of Vienna itself.)

We had occasion to call for help from Adolf Krypl as soon as the BBC unit arrived, for someone at the London end had forgotten to obtain any import permits for the equipment, and the entire crew became stuck in the airport. Krypl went off in his car and worked another miracle on behalf of the BBC, while the Austrians, back in the hall, were rigging up the powerful lights which would be required for the cameras they were using. As soon as I saw them I thought we were in for trouble, for I remembered the time when some comparatively innocuous lights were fitted up for some still photography we required, and the orchestra had protested vehemently: the lights were too dazzling, and it was impossible to read the music. I had warned the TV people about this problem, and had been told it would be possible to "bounce" the light off the ceiling, in which case nobody could complain about dazzle; but for some reason which I did not clearly understand it now seemed that "bouncing" would not work. It would have to be direct light, shining almost straight down towards the musicians.

I felt sure I knew what was going to happen. At the very beginning of our next and most complicated session, involving orchestra, full chorus, soloists, and offstage steerhorns, there would be a riot in the orchestra because of the lights and we would lose anything up to half an hour before settling the matter one way or the other. We simply could not afford that risk, and so I got on the telephone and asked the Philharmonic to send down some members of its governing committee to decide there and then whether the lights were acceptable or not. If they were, well and good—and the committee would have decided in lieu of the orchestra; if they were not, the TV people still had the next morning to think up another method of lighting the hall.

In the end, we developed a very amicable relationship with the TV crews, both Austrian and British; but at the beginning it was very hard to make them understand that they were, so to speak, guests at a party, and that the recording had to take precedence over everything else. We told them we would give them every possible cooperation, but they must understand that nothing could ever *stop* for the sake of TV, whereas TV would have to stop instantly if it ever interfered with our work. They were not used to such conditions and for the first day or two the atmosphere was a bit frigid. But as they began to understand the pressure under which we were working, and as the results of the video-tape playbacks showed that the tension of the occasion was being captured visually, they quickly settled down to the conditions.

A Radio Austria crewman focuses his camera on the orchestra from a Sofiensaal box during the filming of "The Golden Ring," the TV documentary about the making of the "Götterdämmerung" recording.

We had made one ruling from the start, and that was that the re-corded music should be taken from our "lines"—i.e., that it would be our sound, not theirs. We were all aware that the sound reproduction on the average home TV set is appalling, but we still wanted our *balance* to be established on the program. Even so, the whole Sofiensaal was grotesquely wired for sound. One of the BBC units was concerned solely with random sounds and conversations, and we had agreed to wire up all microphones and telephones in the control room so that they were permanently live, and the BBC sound unit was able to pick up everything we said, whether or not an on-off button had been pressed. This was alarming, but they promised to use discretion in the selection of material, and I am relieved to say that they did. Things often get said in the control room which are not for public ears.

In the ten days between the second and the last sequences of *Götterdämmerung* we edited the Gibichung scene and so completed the long first act which had mostly been recorded in the spring. The result was more than encouraging. Windgassen was, if anything, in better voice than he had been during *Siegfried*, Claire Watson was a charm-ingly pure and feminine Gutrune, Frick as Hagen was the embodiment of evil, and Fischer-Dieskau as Gunther surpassed even our expectations. Indeed, if there was any doubt at all at this stage, it concerned the ques-tion of dramatic balance. Was the performance of Gunther too strong, too powerful? None of us really thought so, but we made a mental note to watch this point in the big scenes from the second and third acts which lay ahead. In any case, it would only involve a frank discussion

*Recording the scene
where Hagen summons
his vassals in the second act
of "Götterdämmerung."
Two players in the Blauersaal (left)
provide the offstage effects
sounding their steerhorns on cues
relayed via closed-circuit television.
Another steerhorn player (right)
stands next to Gottlob Frick
on the main stage
and supplies those notes
supposedly blown by Hagen.*

with Fischer-Dieskau, whose intelligence and instinct for what is dramatically right would lead him to adjust any such emphasis at once. As it turned out, his performance was a masterpiece of dramatic gradation. Gunther's nobility, his standing as a king, is maintained right up to the moment in the second act when, with a fearful conscience, he recalls that he swore blood brotherhood with Siegfried. His moral breakdown from that moment until he is killed by Hagen is all the more terrible because his weakness has not been evident from the start. It is a performance that still grows in stature and tragedy every time I hear it.

The first day of the final group of sessions was pandemonium. It was the big choral session from Act Two, the scene where Hagen summons his private army, and we were taking it up to the moment when Gunther arrives with Brünnhilde on his arm. It is a marvelous scene, but full of traps. It needs a huge choral sound and an orchestral sound to match: big, loud, rich, and clear. Hagen's voice has to come through this texture, and it is the scene where the steerhorns are involved.

We placed the two offstage steerhorns in the Blauersaal with closed-circuit television. Another player, with the C steerhorn, was to stand on the main stage next to Hagen and blow the note whenever indicated in the score. We called the players down for a morning rehearsal, to find the hall crawling with television people. There were cameras and cables everywhere. To make the recording, *we* had a staff of five; but at one point the combined forces of the BBC and Austrian TV amounted to more than forty. It was all very disturbing, and more than once that morning I cursed the day that the television idea was born.

As television cameras record the scene, Solti conducts his combined forces in one of the climactic moments of "Götterdämmerung": the oath on the spear from Act II.

The session was to begin at three. Although I had had clearance from the Philharmonic's governing committee, I was still apprehensive about the orchestra and the lights—after all, a dispute between the orchestra and its own committee could still waste valuable time. But Professors Wobisch, Strasser, and Barylli had done their work well, and there was not so much as a murmur; on the contrary, several musicians commented on how much easier it was to read the music. With the Vienna Philharmonic, it is never safe to predict anything; and surrounded by a battery of cameras, the players were on their best behavior.

We started on time. This was the most anxious moment for Humphrey Burton, for I had told him not to let the Austrians switch on their cameras until we gave a signal. We wanted to have normal conditions until we were sure that our own equipment was working properly, after which we would let the TV people start their machines; and if the cameras made a noise, that would be the end of TV filming, for that session, anyway.

The cameras were switched on, and everyone listened intently. There was not a sound. They could make their film "live," and we could get on with finishing *Götterdämmerung*. It was a great session.

By this time Birgit Nilsson was back with us again, and in splendid voice. We had been thrilled with her work in the first act during the spring and, as usual, what impressed us so much was that she had again rethought and reworked the *Götterdämmerung* Brünnhilde, changing an inflection here or a piece of phrasing there, so that what she was recording was not just a carbon copy of every other performance she had ever given. This has been true of everything Nilsson has done for Decca, and it is an admirable trait. After all, as the world's leading Brünnhilde and Isolde, she has no need to change and rethink anything at all; but she does so, constantly, because she is a very intelligent artist.

It is not easy to get close to her. Professionally, she is very easy to work with and will consider any suggestion you care to put up. Socially, she is great fun and loves a party. But the personal warmth one felt with Flagstad is somehow missing, and it is hard to gain her trust. I have the deepest admiration for her voice, her artistry, her intelligence, her sense of humor, and her incredible stamina, but I still don't know, after all the success she has had in our *Ring*, whether she thinks the records are any good or not.

Because of her broad sense of humor, and because of the intensity she puts into her work, it had become a tradition to play a joke on her during any opera we recorded. She looked forward to this, and tried to anticipate what we were up to. As soon as she arrived in Vienna for the last part of *Götterdämmerung* she began to try to find out what we had planned; for she remembered that nothing had happened in the spring.

There is a moment towards the end of the Immolation scene when Brünnhilde calls for her horse Grane, on which she will shortly ride into Siegfried's funeral pyre, and we decided to produce a live Grane at that moment. (Adolf Krypl knew a man who had a horse, etc.) I was worried in case the sound of the orchestra, which is extremely loud, might cause the horse to panic, so we arranged a couple of rehearsals during which the music of the Immolation scene was played at deafening strength over loudspeakers in the hall, while the horse, which had had to climb a lot of stairs to get into the hall at all, was led backwards and forwards across the stage by its owner. On the first occasion it seemed nervous and disturbed, and kept pawing the ground with one of its front legs; I began to think we had better drop the idea. On the second occasion it remembered that we had all got pockets full of sugar, and took no notice at all of the music. When it came to the day, we had arranged an elaborate system of signals to the street below, so that the horse need only enter the hall at the last moment, and so might be spared any last-minute attack of stage fright.

We need not have worried. None of us knew very much about horses, but we had reckoned without our horse. It knew exactly what to do, and that it was the center of attention. As Nilsson sang the cue "*Grane, mein Ross!*" the wing doors of the stage opened and our Grane trotted out, tail up, in complete command of the situation. Nilsson almost fell over with surprise, and the orchestra cheered. By the time we had got the horse off the stage and restarted the take, we had lost exactly fifty seconds on this whole incident, but we had gained enormously in a different sense: for there are times when it is necessary to lower the temperature in order to make it rise even higher. You cannot sustain the pitch of intensity required by *Götterdämmerung* without, once in a while, doing something preposterous and even childish. This is why, in the theater, artists involved in long rehearsals for productions of the *Ring* get up pranks which they would never need to think of if they were preparing, say, *Tosca*. It is a form of safety valve, though I do not expect anyone to understand this except those who have been exposed to such powerful music hour after hour, day after day, and night after night.

Everyone was afraid of the Immolation scene. It had to be the climax not only of *Götterdämmerung* but of the whole cycle. By some means

Birgit Nilsson, having just called for her horse Grane during a run-through of Brünnhilde's Immolation, is astonished to see a real live Grane trotted out onto the Sofiensaal stage. It has become a tradition to play a joke on Nilsson during opera recording sessions.

we had to make the sound richer and larger than anything in the rest of the work, and we seemed already to have reached the limit of what was possible with the end of the second act. The really big problems arise after Brünnhilde has sung her last lines, for it is a question of balancing the huge orchestra so that the last, miraculous intertwining of the motives can be heard clearly and with the utmost beauty of sound. This is no occasion for tricks. We took refuge in one of the basic principles of recording—the fact that if the sound in the hall is correct, and with the right positioning of microphones, the sound on the record will also be correct. Solti worked on every section of the orchestra in turn, building the layers of sound, explaining the need for clarity in the basses, and searching for the ideal balance in the brass department. (We experimented with various orchestral deployments between trumpets and trombones and Wagner tubas before finding one which enabled all sections to give the maximum sonority without forcing the tone.) In the end we recorded five different versions of the last five minutes of *Götterdämmerung*, and spent the evening analyzing the results with Solti. We were on the brink of what we wanted, but it had not yet been achieved. On the final session, we would get what we all hoped for.

I had not told Solti of my intention to superimpose the sound of the collapse of the Gibichung Hall, because only a short time before we had had one of our few professional disagreements over a rather similar matter. At the moment just before Brünnhilde's entrance in Act Three there is a stage direction by Wagner to cover the moment when Hagen, having slain Gunther, attempts to take the ring from Siegfried's finger. The dead arm rises, and Hagen falls back with a cry of horror; the women cry out with fear. Then Brünnhilde enters with the line *"Schweigt eures Jammers jauchzenden Schwall!"* ("Cease your cries of grief!"), and these words make nonsense unless someone has uttered a cry of some sort. For some reason Solti was against any sound at that point, possibly because he felt it might interfere with the hushed music that accompanies Brünnhilde's entrance. At the time we had more urgent things to worry about, so I determined to add the sound of the cries afterwards. (I felt sure that Solti would accept the point as dramatically valid once he had heard it done properly, and this turned out to be true, although he still does not let his singers do it in a stage production.)

With the idea of the collapse of the Gibichung Hall I was on somewhat less secure ground. First of all, none of us had the slightest idea how to do it convincingly; and second, it was not indicated *as a noise* in the score. There was equally no reason why Wagner should have thought of mentioning it as a noise, for in demanding what amounted to the collapse of a substantial stage set he was assured of any amount of noise by the nature of the requirement. (The Covent Garden production after the war used to be especially effective at this moment, for the great pillars of the ancestral home really did come toppling down in huge segments; and even in the 1951 Bayreuth production the noise on our unissued recording is quite spectacular.) We experimented for days to get a convincing sound, but nothing seemed to work. We tried thunder, forwards and backwards; we tried dropping heavy objects and then adjusting the playback speed to alter the sound. Each one of us could hear in his own mind the right sort of sound to go with the music, but nothing we tried was acceptable. We had reached the point of deciding to omit the noise altogether and admit defeat when Jimmy Brown, on his way home one night, heard on his car radio what he swore was the perfect sound for the collapse of the Gibichung Hall. He immediately got in touch with the German radio station responsible for the program and begged to borrow the tape. The rest of us remained doubtful, but several days later Jimmy arrived with a short piece of tape supplied by the station, and an hour or two later played us the result of his labor. It

Nilsson gives her all recording the last lines of Brünnhilde's Immolation, the culmination of Wagner's colossal four-opera cycle.

was perfect. I doubt if we would ever have succeeded in making up a sound which was so effective, dramatically speaking, yet which somehow did not disturb the flow and power of the music. Solti did not hear it until months later at a playback in London, and I was expecting an objection from him—for it is the only case in the entire *Ring* recording where we incorporated something that is merely *implied* by Wagner. To my great joy Solti liked it, and agreed that some nonmusical sound can be justified, dramatically, at that moment.

We were coming to the end of the schedule. The television people, whose existence we had virtually ceased to notice in the pressure of work, were excited by the material they were getting. Burton was already talking about a ninety-minute film in place of his original conception of sixty minutes. The artists had cooperated splendidly by giving interviews about Wagner in general and *Götterdämmerung* in particular. Only Fischer-Dieskau, it seemed, was unwilling to be interviewed, and one day Burton came to see me to ask if I would intercede to persuade him. I said I knew that he loathed interviews, but that I would try. He was reluctant, but finally agreed on condition that it would take place privately in our apartment; and it was during that interview, when he was asked how he saw *Götterdämmerung*, that he described it remarkably as "a family tragedy." His portrayal of Gunther certainly fits that conception.

We said our farewells to Fischer-Dieskau and to Windgassen, and came to the last session. At this point every note of *Götterdämmerung* had been recorded, but there were six unsatisfactory sections which constituted essential remakes. As there was no possibility of overtime on that session, and no hope of continuing the next day, I prepared a schedule for Solti which would show him exactly what had to be done, in what order, and within what time. It is the only way, for otherwise too much time is unwittingly spent on the *first* pieces on the list, while the last pieces never get made at all. The list went as follows:

TIME	MUSIC	NOTES
1500	Third Act. Section "A"	Rehearse/Record.
1510	Second Act. Section "A"	" "
1525	Third Act. Section "B"	" "
1610	First Act. Section "A"	" "
1635	*Interval*	
1700	Third Act. Section "C"	Rehearse: 20 mins.
		Record : 10 mins.
1745	Third Act. Section "D"	Rehearse/Record.
	End of Session	

The end of the Immolation scene was ringing out for the last time. The television cameras zoomed in toward Birgit Nilsson on the stage as she sang the final lines, and when, later, we saw that part of the film we were all greatly moved. Out there, in the cold lights of the studio, without stage costume and with only the proscenium curtains as a background, she seemed to become Brünnhilde, so caught up was she in the emotion and the music. Somehow that moment seemed to justify the methods we had slowly evolved during all the sightless hours in the control room, and we loved her for it.

It was over, and we could not quite believe it. We had some champagne with Nilsson and Solti, and we drank to *Walküre* and the eventual completion of the *Ring*. Then we did something utterly idiotic.

We had been working on *Götterdämmerung*, on and off, since May. We had just completed the most strenuous part of the recording. Instead of taking a break from it, even if only for a day or two, we plunged at once into the rest of the editing, working like people possessed, to get the opera strung together, however roughly, and hear how it came over in a complete performance. Also, we were working to a deadline, as I had to leave to meet Mr. Rosengarten in Geneva in early December. Although we had not really recovered from the sessions, we worked from early morning until late into the night, day after day, assembling the second and third acts; and the day before I was to leave for Switzerland, we had our first playback to ourselves. It was the most foolish thing we ever did, for we had had too much of *Götterdämmerung*. Our ears were tired, and we had all spent far too long in a small and smoky room. At the end of the first act, Gordon said: "It's no damn good. It doesn't work. We've messed it up." At the end of the second act, we were all in the deepest gloom and almost inclined not to play the third. But we did, on the pretext of getting a timing, and at the end we were convinced it was a disaster. Each one of us, in his different way, felt he had failed in the challenge of his life, and I went off to Switzerland the next morning in the blackest mood of my career. At that stage, nothing would have convinced any of us that we might be wrong.

To make things worse, we had gone badly over the budget, which was why I had been summoned to Geneva. I don't think that Mr. Rosengarten, who knows me very well, had the least idea how I felt that day; for although I dislike exceeding a budget in any circumstance, it is doubly appalling to have done so and yet be convinced that the result is poor. I did not tell him that; I could not. Decca had equipped us with everything we asked for from the very inception of *Götterdämmerung*. We had a brand-new technical installation, and a flawless cast; we had worked without intrusion or obstruction and had been helped by the administration all along the line; and yet it seemed certain that we had let Decca down, and were about to deliver something that was not only vastly more expensive than *Rheingold* or *Siegfried*, but vastly inferior to them as well. I could not think how it had happened, except that somehow we must have become complacent and oblivious to the standards we had set ourselves in the past.

And yet . . . on the way back to London, I wondered if it could possibly be as bad as we thought. If one man has absolute authority on a session, to the extent that anything or everything he wants must be produced, it can be very serious indeed if his ears or his judgment go wrong. But that was not the way we worked, and it simply did not seem likely to me that five of us could simultaneously take leave of our senses and produce a thoroughly bad record of *Götterdämmerung*.

Someone on the crew would surely have rebelled; for although the producer is responsible for what money is spent and how the time is allocated, we have always worked in a very democratic way and encour-
aged any sort of constructive criticism from any quarter, no matter how
humble.

When I got back to London, I rang Gordon in Vienna at once, with
the single request that neither he nor anyone else on the crew should say
a word about our misgivings until *after* the final editing had been done.
I felt we all needed time and a change of atmosphere before coming
back to *Götterdämmerung*, and there was Christmas ahead. So we made
a plan to return to Vienna on Boxing Day, absolutely incognito, in
order to finish the rest of the editing—and there was much to do—in
peace and quiet. Had the orchestra known of my return, there would
have been dozens of telephone calls and interruptions by visitors, so we
vowed to make it a secret, and to put *Götterdämmerung* out of our
minds until then.

When we got back to Vienna after Christmas we knew as soon as we
played the first tape that we had been utterly wrong. The thing
sounded fabulous. Now, refreshed by the break and with no interruptions, we worked long and pleasurable hours re-editing and correcting
and putting in the effects which we had omitted on the sessions to save

*Nilsson reacts physically to something
she has just heard during a
"Götterdämmerung" playback.
Windgassen and Frick look on at right,
while Culshaw and Solti stay buried
in their scores at left.*

time. Each day brought a new revelation of superb conducting, or playing, or singing, and this time we knew we were not fooling ourselves.

The New Year is a great period for celebration in Vienna, for there is the famous Vienna Philharmonic New Year Concert, conducted by Willi Boskovsky, and there is always a ball in the Sofiensaal. We kept away from both; indeed, we hardly left the control room except to go up to the apartment to eat and sleep. Day by day, the master tape was growing, and we fixed on January 8 as the day for the final playback, when we would reveal ourselves and invite our friends from the Philharmonic. Work was progressing so well and with such a result that one evening early in January we decided to go out for dinner for the first time since our arrival. We went to a modest restaurant where we were unlikely to meet anyone we knew, and indeed we did not meet anyone at all; but the next morning the telephone rang early, and it was Professor Wobisch. "You think you can keep a secret from me?" he said. "Not in Vienna," I told him, "but how did you know we were here?" "Oh," he said, "it's in the paper this morning that you were all seen at a restaurant last night." It could not happen in any other big city in the world, but it happens all the time in Vienna.

For the playback on January 8 we invited as many of our Philharmonic friends as we could accommodate. I have never looked forward as much to any playback, for by now the depression of a month ago had completely gone. We had spent the last few days adding a few remaining effects: Hagen smashing the drinking horn from which Siegfried and Gunther have drunk blood brotherhood in Act One; Siegfried's gasp when Hagen strikes him dead in Act Three; and the noise of the collapse of the Gibichung Hall as Brünnhilde rides into the funeral pyre.

I did not follow the score during the playback. I knew that the tapes contained all the best material we had made, and now it was time just to listen, and get involved again in the drama of *Götterdämmerung* in the way that we intended the listener at home to get involved. The first act, although it runs for over two hours, seemed to go in a flash; and, as Andrew Porter had once said about *Rheingold*, one seemed to be among the actual characters, rather than listening to a group of brilliant performers. Towards the end, our trick of turning Siegfried into the false Gunther worked out in its context just as I had hoped: the shock came not so much with the first line as with the last, when Siegfried, having removed the Tarnhelm, reverts to his normal tenor voice.

The great span of Act Two seemed perfectly proportioned: the dark beginning, the excitement of the big choral scene, the tension of the passage when Brünnhilde sees the ring on Siegfried's finger and knows she has been betrayed, and, above all, the final vengeance trio. In all the years, it seemed that we had never had such conducting, and such superb orchestral playing. And it was not just good professional playing of the kind which one has a right to expect from any major orchestra. Much more than that, it was infused with that special intuitive, indefinable quality which is the hallmark of the Vienna Philharmonic, and the Vienna Philharmonic alone. There is a moment in Act Two, shortly after Gunther appears with Brünnhilde, when the violins quietly enter with Gutrune's theme; and the *way* they enter, the way the bows are placed on the strings, the sweetness of tone, the phrasing with its slight but unanimous rubato and portamento—all this adds up to something which can neither be calculated nor taught. It is the result of tradition in the very best sense of that word: it is instinctive musicianship, and it gets to the heart of the music. Time and time again this sort of detail added its magical touch to the performance. I do not think there is a sound in the world so magisterial, and yet so tragic in character, as that of the Vienna Philharmonic horns as they remind Gunther of the oath he once took with Siegfried. The tone speaks so directly and with such emotional power that it almost becomes articulate and makes the words redundant.

Later when the last chord of the third act had finally died away, we sat in silence that was not contrived. The impact of the great work, and the sense of involvement in it which each of us in that small audience had felt, was too intense to lead anyone to speak for a while. Finally, Roland Berger got up. He said, "There's nothing to say, is there? It's unbelievable. I think we all need a drink. . . ."

The playback in the London studio a month later was no less remarkable in its effect, this time on people who had not heard a note of the recording before. I had explained to the sales and promotion people that before deciding to place *Götterdämmerung* on twelve sides we had given serious thought to the possibility of ten. It *is* divisible, just, over ten sides, but several of the "breaks" in that deployment are poor and some of the timings, bearing in mind the sheer volume of much of the music, undesirably long. We had therefore settled for twelve sides, whose average playing time was about twenty-three minutes, and everyone agreed that this was acceptable.

About this time we had a call from Humphrey Burton at the BBC to say that the video tapes from Austria had arrived and work was in progress on the editing of *The Golden Ring*. Adding the video-tape material and the 16-mm. film gave a total of something like twenty hours of film and tape, which had to be edited down to make a program lasting either sixty, seventy-five, or possibly ninety minutes. A week or two later a party of us went over to the TV Centre and watched the film in its current state: it was running for rather more than four hours! I could see that Humphrey Burton had a problem on his hands, for so much of the material was so good that he was understandably reluctant to cut. Most of the difficulty derived from our technique of recording in long takes of up to fifteen minutes, during which one expects some dramatic tension to be generated—and dramatic tension is the very stuff of television. But you cannot just have *moments* of such tension: you have to let the scene play, and allow the music, and the metamorphosis of the artist into the character he or she is portraying, emerge gradually for it to make its effect. It was obvious to Burton that the only way to get the film into any sort of manageable proportions would be to cut whole, long sections and dispense with them entirely. He found this heartbreaking, for he loved the music. But somehow it had to be reduced to ninety minutes or less, and ruthless scissors were required.

Meanwhile, the test pressings of *Götterdämmerung* were coming through from the factory, and so excellent was the result that I thought I would send a test copy of the Immolation scene to Birgit Nilsson, who was then in New York. It was a stunning performance, and the recording played perfectly. Nilsson's great voice rang out over even the heaviest orchestral passages, and I thought it was probably the best thing she had ever done on records. Certainly she had never *sounded* better, and I thought it would please her to hear the disk and realize in advance what acclaim she would receive when *Götterdämmerung* reached the market in May.

The next thing I knew was a telephone call from my colleague Terry McEwen in New York, to say that he had spoken to Nilsson—who was furious. The record was terrible, she said, and her voice was inaudible. She would be writing to me directly about it, but she wished to register an immediate protest. I was stunned, and asked McEwen what he thought, although he had already sent me a cable on behalf of his colleagues in London Records, Inc., to say that *Götterdämmerung* was the greatest operatic recording in history. He was utterly confused by Nilsson's reaction. I asked him to go and see her, and find out on what sort of machine she had played the disk.

That evening, after having played an identical copy of the record at home and found it as good as ever, I got into the car and visited friends in various parts of London, all of whom had vastly different kinds of equipment, ranging from an extensive and virtually professional setup to

John Culshaw plants a big kiss on Birgit Nilsson's cheek as he congratulates her for a job well done.

a modest portable stereo player. I did not tell any of them what the trouble was, but invited their comments, especially on the balance between voice and orchestra. No fault was apparent when the record was played on any of the machines that evening—though one person said that, if anything, Nilsson's voice was slightly too *loud* to be realistic. I could not imagine what had happened in New York, but when I tried to call Nilsson she was not prepared to speak.

Her letter came in a day or two, more or less implying that the balance she had heard in Vienna was false, and that on the finished record she could hardly be heard. She sounded, she said, like a weak Pamina. It was a very angry letter indeed. I knew that I would be seeing her in Vienna shortly, and sent her a cable imploring her to reserve judgment until then, when I knew we could convince her that the record, far from being a mess, did full justice to her voice. Terry McEwen called again and said that she had been playing the record in her hotel bedroom on equipment which, in his opinion, was highly suspect; but she had refused to go with him to the office of London Records or to his home to hear it under normal conditions on a properly adjusted machine.

Solti was conducting in Israel at that time, and I wrote to him:

> The build-up for *Götterdämmerung* seems to be enormous. I have a cable from London Records saying that they find it the greatest operatic recording ever made, and here in London I have never known such a favourable response, nor so much enthusiasm from those who are going to sell the work. The TV programme is going out on May 16th on BBC 2, and Humphrey seems sure we shall get a repeat on BBC 1 later in the year. I am going to the U.S.A. at the end of April to try and help the promotion of the record there.
>
> There is only one bad piece of news. Birgit has heard the Immolation scene in New York and refuses to listen to any more of the set. She insists that the orchestra is too loud, and is hinting that she will not make *Walküre*

Fischer-Dieskau points out an interesting passage in the "Götterdämmerung" score to soprano Claire Watson, who sings the role of Gutrune in the recording.

next year. I cannot find anyone who agrees with her about *Götterdämmer-ung*, and I am not talking about people in Decca or other "interested" parties. I have even tried it out on one or two voice fanatics—the sort of person who never listens to the orchestra in opera anyway—and even they don't agree with her. I do not know whether you would think it worth-while to send her a cable yourself, expressing astonishment at this reaction. For myself, I am completely at a loss because I sent her the record just to please her and show her what a magnificent job she had done. But it has upset her terribly, which upsets me, and her arguments don't seem to make any sense at all. . . .

Humphrey Burton called me a day or two before I was hoping to leave London for the Easter weekend. Would I spend the weekend with him at the TV Centre and give him a hand in cutting scenes from the film? I told him I knew nothing about film editing—but that was not his problem. The film was now down to something just over two and a half hours in length, and he had settled for a running time of ninety minutes. The problem was that he still had several sustained musical sequences, and as they were all excellent, he needed help from someone outside to determine which ones were to be thrown out. I was glad to help, though I wished Gordon and some of the others had been in London.

We saw the film in its current state, and I did not envy Burton. Two and a half hours went by very quickly, and to have to get rid of sixty minutes seemed impossible. We could lose the big Act Two scene between Hagen and the chorus—but with it, inevitably, would go all the film covering the steerhorn story. We could get rid of the rehearsal and final take of the trio from Act Two—but the performance, and the film-ing of that sequence, was too good to throw away. Humphrey sug-gested we should start from the other direction, and decide what was really essential, and then cut out the rest. After a long day we settled for the Hagen scene; a short sequence between Claire Watson and Fischer-Dieskau which showed, since it was repeated several times, how a passage gets molded into shape; the whole of the trio from Act Two; the death of Siegfried and the funeral march; and finally, the latter part of the Immolation scene. These would constitute the musical content of the film, while the rest would be concerned with sequences in the re-cording room, interviews with artists and staff, and a brief look at the Viennese background to set the whole thing in its right context. It was a fine selection, but it was sad to see so much good material from the rest of the film being consigned to oblivion.

Birgit Nilsson was making a record of Scandinavian songs in Vienna that April with my colleague Christopher Raeburn, and I flew out to see her about the *Götterdämmerung* affair. In London, Arthur Haddy was convinced that she must have been playing the record on some wholly inadequate or badly adjusted equipment in New York, but I still feared that she would refuse to listen in Vienna, on the grounds that somehow, in the control room, we were faking the sound in order to impress her. Haddy then had a brilliant idea. There is a small battery-driven machine on the market which, though not by a long way capable of producing anything like the real sound of the record, nevertheless gave a tolerable indication of what was there and had the huge advantage of being easily portable. Haddy suggested I should take one of these to Vienna and give it to Nilsson to use where she liked. If, after that, she still maintained that her voice was inaudible, there was nothing further any of us could do.

I met her in the Sofiensaal at the end of her first session, but she said she did not wish to talk about *Götterdämmerung*. I replied that after seven years of work together she owed it to us to listen to what we had to say. She had made what amounted to a severe professional criticism, on which she was not prepared to go back; but at least she might give us a chance to put our case. With that, she agreed to come into the control room, and we showed her the record we were going to play, which was identical to the one I had sent her in New York. We then played parts of the Immolation scene as she requested, and she agreed it was fine—but it was the room and the equipment that made it so, she claimed, and it would not sound similar in another room, and on another machine.

I produced the little machine Haddy had given to me, took the record off our turntable, and played it on the portable. She look astonished. After a minute or two, Gordon suggested she should take the portable machine and the record back to her hotel and listen to the whole scene without anybody around to try and persuade her one way or the other. She agreed, and I said I would telephone her in one hour. And when I did call, she was a different person. It was fine—the voice was all there and the orchestra was not too loud. She could not think what had happened in New York. She was very nice about it, and we let her keep the gramophone because it seemed to please her.

I shall never know what was the matter with the machine in New York, but the moral of this tale is clear: if a major recording produced by one of the big companies sounds seriously deficient in one way or another, technically speaking, the chances are more than likely that the fault is with the playback equipment and not with the record. In one form or another this sort of problem is the daily bane of classical recording executives, and nobody knows how to solve it except by making the public more conscious of what constitutes good sound. And not only the public—for, only a few years ago, one of the major critics complained in print that our recording of *Tristan und Isolde* was feeble in the bass, and that as the bass line in *Tristan* is extremely important the recording failed in a major way to measure up to what Wagner had written. I could not let that pass, and invited him to bring his review records to a neutral meeting point, which in this case was the Rimington van Wyck shop in Cranbourne Street, where the late Fred Smith was in charge. I knew that Fred stocked first-class equipment: the sort of equipment on which a major critic *should* be reviewing a major recording. The critic was astonished by what he heard: for there was plenty of bass, and in the right proportion. We then sent an engineer to look at the critic's equipment, and found not only a serious deficiency on the bass side, but also that he was reviewing all his records with the bass control fully retarded, and the top control fully advanced. Yet he had blamed the record, and had never given a thought to his machine.

I went to America at the end of April, and the British reviews were sent over as soon as they appeared. They surpassed anything we might have expected, and most of them were long enough to go into the performance and the recording in great detail. A few sentences from the main reviews will give an idea of the tone:

The Gramophone (Alec Robertson): "The success of this performance and recording is total and triumphant: here is the greatest achievement in gramophone history yet."

Records and Recording (Thomas Heinitz): "I doubt whether any other conductor in the world today could have produced so brilliant and vital a performance from the orchestra or obtained results of such uniform excellence from even this great cast. Nothing like this *Götterdämmerung* has ever before come out of a recording studio."

The Observer: "Yes, I know it costs a fortune, but it's worth every penny. Simply getting this huge work on disc at all must have caused unprecedented administrative headaches; but to have it so beautifully prepared and homogeneously realised is nothing less than a triumph."

The Times: "Another major triumph for Decca's incomparable engineers. . . . this combination of superlative orchestral playing, splendid singing and brilliant recording has given rise to a set which does full justice to the most gigantic of all operatic conceptions."

The Gramophone (retrospective review by Desmond Shawe-Taylor): "All in all a glorious achievement, which it will be difficult to equal and almost impossible to surpass."

Financial Times (Andrew Porter): "Gush is unattractive and seldom convincing, but I must risk it here. Not since my student days have I felt so passionately about the *Ring* as after hearing this new *Götterdämmerung*. By the end one is overwhelmed—and questioning all the standards by which one thinks and works and lives.... It is another Decca landmark in gramophone history. The recording as a whole is magnificent: big, faithful, sensitive, rich and exactly balanced...."

This immensely gratifying reception by the British press was paralleled abroad. As each country in turn released *Götterdämmerung* the reviews flowed in with accolades that were almost embarrassing. There was hardly a dissenting voice anywhere.

In New York my colleagues at London Records had arranged a reception for the critics to be held on the afternoon of April 26, during which excerpts from *Götterdämmerung* would be played. That same day I had lunch with a senior executive from another American company, who went to some trouble to tell me that our Company had made a mistake in planning the reception. The critics, he said, would not come, because they did not like to be seen together at such affairs. The best we could hope for would be a few gossip columnists looking for bits of information about the artists. I was half inclined to think him right, until I actually reached the reception, which was packed—and packed with the big names. The New York *Times* and *Herald Tribune* had sent their critics; Roland Gelatt of *High Fidelity* was there, and David Hall of the rival *Hi-Fi Stereo;* and Irving Kolodin of the *Saturday Review*. It was a remarkable turnout in honor of the new recording; and the equipment (which had been set up with real professional skill by the president of London Records, Mr. Toller-Bond) did full justice to the records. I was very proud of our recorded offspring that day, and thrilled by the enthusiasm and emotion it seemed to generate wherever it was played.

On May 16 *The Golden Ring* was shown for the first time on BBC 2. I had seen it a day or two before at a press showing, and thought that Humphrey Burton had done a fine job of enclosing the musical scenes in a narrative of the recording which seemed far shorter than its ninety minutes. It was uncanny, too, for in the intervening months I had as usual forgotten how things had actually looked in the studio, and hearing the records no longer reminded me of the Sofiensaal. On the film, it all came back: the tension, the doubts, and the occasional flash of something extraordinary achieved.

The film was well received, and Humphrey rang me the next day to say that he expected to get a repeat on the much larger BBC 1 network before the end of the year. (Meanwhile, the German version was almost finished, and negotiations were in progress with a number of other countries interested in showing versions dubbed into the appropriate languages.) It caused a great deal of comment, including the following agonized protest in the *Songwriters' Guild News:*

> Believe it or not, the BBC is said to have made a film of this massive Wagnerian work (*Götterdämmerung*). The intention is that this should be shown on Eurovision and wherever else they can place it. Why pick on *Götterdämmerung?* Can the BBC find no British work of comparable stature to film? If not, surely they could have commissioned one. . . .

Our sales were going well at home and abroad. In June a cable came from America quoting the sales so far, and adding: THIS OUTDOES EVERY-THING IN RECENT YEARS STOP WE ARE DELIGHTED AND FULL OF FAITH. I was reminded of a comment I had read some years earlier, attributed to Walter Wanger, the film producer. Faced with some appalling financial crisis on whatever film he was making, and doubtless pushed to an extreme, he is said to have remarked, "Nothing is as cheap as a hit, no matter how much it costs."

It was too early yet to call *Götterdämmerung* a hit, but it was certainly off to a flying start, and we were already preparing for *Walküre,* and the completion of the Decca *Ring.*

Sir Georg Solti: Master

"Is there a greater conductor alive today?" The question, asked by a critic for *The Gramophone,* was purely rhetorical for many thousands of music lovers. To these people, Georg Solti is, quite simply, the greatest living conductor. It is a role for which he has been preparing since childhood. Born in Budapest in 1912, he studied piano, composition and conducting under four Hungarians of worldwide stature: Dohnányi, Bartók, Kodály and Leo Weiner. He made his first concert appearance as a pianist and could have had a brilliant career as a virtuoso. But Solti had already zeroed in on his true metier: he wanted to be a conductor. His first opportunity came when he received an appointment with the Budapest Opera.

In 1936 and 1937 the young maestro realized one of his fondest dreams when he was invited to assist Arturo Toscanini at the Salzburg Festival. Toscanini was Solti's idol and to work with him on *The Magic Flute* and *Falstaff* was to acquire his sense of mission, his constant search for musical perfection. Years later, when Solti heard a private recording of the 1936 *Magic Flute* (besides assisting in its preparation he also played the glockenspiel), he reaffirmed his admiration for Toscanini, even though his own ideas about the opera had diverged considerably from those of the great Italian.

Just before the outbreak of the war, Solti went to Switzerland to attend the Lucerne Festival, where Toscanini was conducting. He planned a two-week visit and ended by remaining there for six years. Unable to resume his career as a conductor, he again turned to the piano and won first prize in the Geneva International Piano Competition in 1942.

Nonetheless, after the war he lost no time in returning to the podium. In 1946 he was appointed Musical Director of the Bavarian State Opera in Munich. In 1952 he became Artistic and Musical Director of the Frankfurt Opera, which he led at home and on tours to Paris and the Florence May Festival. In 1959 he was invited to conduct *Der Rosenkavalier* at London's Covent Garden and created such a sensation that he was offered the musical directorship of the Royal Opera. His duties began in 1961.

Solti brought the company to a pinnacle of artistic achievement in a series of dazzling new productions that included Wagner's *Ring* cycle, *Tristan und Isolde* and *Die Meistersinger;* Mozart's *Don Giovanni, Marriage of Figaro, Magic Flute* and *Così fan tutte;* Richard Strauss's *Salome* and *Die Frau ohne Schatten;* and Arnold Schoenberg's *Moses and Aaron.* In 1970 he took the Royal Opera company on their first major European tour.

Solti had by then been directing opera companies for almost 25 years and, like Toscanini before him, wanted to move out of the opera house and into the concert hall. Not that his symphonic urges had been stifled: during this quarter-century he had made guest appearances with many of the world's

of the 'Ring'

greatest orchestras, including the Vienna Philharmonic, the London Symphony and London Philharmonic, and the New York Philharmonic. But with his appointment in 1969 to the musical directorship of the Chicago Symphony Orchestra, Solti inaugurated an important new phase of his career. Within a brief period he restored the Chicagoans to the splendor they had known under the late Fritz Reiner: their concert version of *Das Rheingold* was the sensation of the 1970-1971 concert season.

Chicago has had to share its superstar with other cities. In 1971 Solti was appointed principle guest conductor of the London Philharmonic, and in 1972 he took over as Musical Director of the Orchestre de Paris. This would be more than enough to keep most mortals fully occupied. But Solti the dynamo also intends to spend one month each year directing a new production at Covent Garden and has also taken on the post of Musical Advisor to the Paris Opera.

Solti's recordings are a testament to his wide knowledge and musicianship. In the symphonic category his Beethoven, Bruckner and Mahler recordings are outstanding. And his opera recordings tend to obliterate the competition. He is the only conductor to have been honored nine times with the French Academie du Disque Award of the Grand Prix du Disque Mondiale for his recordings of *Das Rheingold* (1959), *Tristan und Isolde* (1961), *Salome* (1963), *Siegfried* (1964), *Götterdämmerung* (1965), *Die Walküre* (1966), *Elektra* (1967), *Der Rosenkavalier* (1969) and *Tannhäuser* (1972). His last award was also given in recognition of his silver jubilee as a recording artist for Decca/London.

Although he is a thoroughly international figure, Solti holds British citizenship and lives (if the term can be applied to so peripatetic a person) in St. Johns Wood, London, with his attractive young wife and their daughter. Recently he became a Commander of the British Empire and in 1972 he was knighted.

Midway through his first Chicago season, Solti received a musical knighthood from critic Robert C. Marsh, who wrote that his "sense of drama and melodic line . . . recalls Toscanini more than any other conductor before the public today." And from New York *Times* critic Harold Schoenberg comes affirmation: "Certainly nobody today conducts Wagner with such strength and color, such a grand line and feeling for tradition."

Sweet strings and rich brass

"Recording the *Ring* with the Vienna Philharmonic had much to recommend it," says Maestro Solti, seen here making a new *Parsifal* with the orchestra in the Sofiensaal. "First of all, as an operatic orchestra, they have the music in their blood. Then there is the particular sweetness of tone cultivated by the string players—an almost Viennese sweetness passed down from generation to generation. And the brass sound is rich and mellow. These qualities make it an ideal orchestra for the *Ring* operas, which are not so much woodwind as string and brass operas."

The Vienna Philharmonic is a unique institution. Its members play regularly in the Vienna State Opera orchestra. In their spare time they emerge from the pit to play a series of subscription concerts. These, along with tours and recordings, place them on a par with the world's best symphony orchestras.

In addition to its regular Saturday and Sunday morning concerts, the Vienna Philharmonic celebrates each New Year with concerts devoted to the music of Vienna's beloved Strauss family, a tradition that dates back to 1928. The New Year's Day concert proved such a success that a New Year's Eve concert was added in 1952. Both are among the major musical and social events of the year. The concerts are held in the flower-bedecked Grosser Musikvereinsaal.

CHAPTER FIVE

1965 Die Walküre

"ALL GOOD SINGERS beasts and should be burnt; and all bad singers burnt anyway." This swift and effective solution to the problems of opera in the modern world was put forward by Solti one day in Vienna when I was having the familiar battle with a singer who did not want to turn up for a session. The rules and obligations by which mankind in general conducts itself do not apply to the world of singers and, I am told, racing drivers. There are characteristics which are shared by singers of every kind and every nationality, and which vary only in degree from voice to voice and nation to nation. Latin tenors carry the traits to an extreme: for most of them live in a sort of yellow-submarine world from which they emerge only occasionally to protest vehemently about the total lack of consideration bestowed on them by the rest of mankind. Basses run them pretty close in the selfishness stakes; and, contrary to popular beliefs, the ladies are far more reasonable than either category of men.

These reflections are prompted by the realization that throughout the *Ring* recording we had no troubles at all with what is commonly thought of as the operatic temperament. Birgit Nilsson's objections about the *Götterdämmerung* test pressing were not hysterical—she was convinced something had gone wrong, and was right in making her views known. We had occasional moments of irresponsibility, like the one which prompted Solti's remark: for the singer in question pleaded leave of absence from an important session because of a rehearsal at the State Opera at which her presence was mandatory. It then turned out that she was actually going to the hairdresser, and we were able to call her bluff. And there were others who, knowing they had heavy sessions on which their voices were to be recorded for posterity, would still accept every engagement it was physically possible to undertake and arrive at the sessions tired and in poor voice. All the same, this sort of trouble was minimal, and in all the sessions it took to make *Rheingold*, *Siegfried*, and *Götterdämmerung* we had had less trouble, and less loss of time, than one would accept as routine on any two sessions involving Italian singers.

Christa Ludwig, who sings Fricka in the "Walküre" recording, is seen here as she appeared in the part in the 1967 production by Herbert von Karajan at the Metropolitan Opera.

The problem of setting up *Walküre* for the late autumn of 1965 was that of avoiding an anticlimax. It was the work on which we had, so to speak, cut our teeth in 1957; it was the work which, in 1950, had first convinced me of Solti's outstanding ability as a Wagner conductor. It was the most popular part of the *Ring* cycle, and the only one which existed complete in competitive versions; but after the monumental *Götterdämmerung* we had to condition ourselves to the fact that *Walküre* was different in almost every respect—a gentler, more lyrical piece which must be approached on its own terms as part of the cycle. There was no point in trying to outdo *Götterdämmerung*. Our object was to make a *Walküre* which would take its place logically between *Rheingold* and *Siegfried* in the Decca *Ring*.

It seemed a long time since our "pilot" *Walküre*, Act Three, in 1957; and when it came to the casting of Fricka, I was reminded of all the correspondence with Flagstad, and of our scheme to record her *Walküre* Fricka as long ago as 1959 and put it in cold storage until such time as we had permission to record the whole work. Now that she was dead there was one name which came at once to mind—Astrid Varnay. The *Walküre* Fricka would lie in the very best part of her voice, and she had all the experience and the temperament to play the part superbly. We approached her very gently, not wishing to offend an artist who had been a great Brünnhilde and Isolde, and who was still an incomparable Ortrud in *Lohengrin* and Herodias in *Salome*. We reminded her that Flagstad had learned the *Rheingold* Fricka especially for the recording, and we would be proud to think that the mantle of the part could now pass to Astrid Varnay. In any case, we simply wanted her to be part of our *Ring*. To my extreme sorrow, she turned it down—or, rather, imposed conditions which, through our prior commitments to another artist, we could not possibly accept. I do not know who advised her, but I feel sure it was a mistake. She had no reason to grant any favors to Decca, and she may well have felt bitter that we had recorded her major roles with Flagstad and Nilsson. I had hoped she would see that for once it wasn't a question of business or bargaining, but of sentiment.

As soon as we knew there was no hope of convincing Varnay, we turned unhesitatingly to Christa Ludwig, who had sung so superbly as Waltraute in *Götterdämmerung.* I wanted at all costs to have Hans Hotter as Wotan, for although he was now approaching the end of his career he still had no serious rival as the *Walküre* Wotan or the *Siegfried* Wanderer. (I was not disturbed by the fact that George London had sung the *Rheingold* Wotan for us in 1958, because I have always felt that *Rheingold* required, dramatically and musically, a young-sounding Wotan, and the part had never really suited Hotter, at least during the years since the end of the war.) I knew that Hotter suffered from asthma, and that on a bad day he could develop a wobble in the voice that distressed some people much more than it distressed me; but it seemed essential to get his performance on record. To more than one generation, he *was* Wotan, in voice and looks and manner.

Our Sieglinde was not hard to find, for Régine Crespin had the voice, the sensitivity, and above all the femininity required by the part. One was tired of hearing matronly Sieglindes, who looked and sounded like Siegmund's mother; on the other hand, the part needs a real voice, and calls for considerable acting ability. Siegmund was more of a problem,

Continued on page 222

Régine Crespin has sung Sieglinde in leading opera houses throughout Europe and America. Here she is shown in the San Francisco production of "Walküre."

John Culshaw's producer's schedule for the recording of "Die Walküre," shown here, gives some idea of the complex nature of recording a complete opera. The chart shows, first, those singers who will be needed for each session (indicated with check marks); then any special requirements, such as the steerhorns on Nov. 9; and unusual orchestral requirements, such as the six harps that will be necessary on Nov. 3 and 4. The portion of the act to be recorded is then indicated by references (in boxes) to the rehearsal numbers in the full orchestral score as well as to the pages these cover in the full and vocal scores. Finally, the approximate timing of the ground to be covered is shown in minutes and seconds. The references to "Trov.," "Fig.," "Zaub.," etc., at the bottom of the chart for most sessions are abbreviations of the operas the orchestra must play on those evenings at the State Opera: "Trovatore" on Nov. 8, "Figaro" on the 9th, and so on. An extra evening session—such as the one on Nov. 17 written in at the top of the chart—can sometimes be scheduled simultaneously with an opera performance provided the work in the theater (Mozart's "Zauberflöte" in this case) employs a relatively small orchestra. The frequent crossings-out and reshuffling of sessions toward the end of the recording period give evidence of the last-minute planning that was necessary to make up for lost time and bring "Walküre" in on schedule.

	FRI	SUN	TUE	WED	THUR	FRI
SESSION NO.	1	2	3	4	5	6
DATE / TIME	OCT. 29th	OCT. 31st	NOV. 2nd	NOV. 3rd	NOV. 4th	NOV. 5th
BRÜNNHILDE						
WOTAN						
SIEGMUND	✓	✓	✓	✓	✓	✓
SIEGLINDE		✓	✓	✓	✓	✓
HUNDING	✓	✓				
FRICKA						
WALKÜREN						
SPECIAL REQUIREMENTS	1 TRUMPET No PERC.	No FLUTES No TRUMPETS No PERC No HARP				
ORCHESTRA SPECIAL REQUIREMENTS	ONE HARP	CELLO AND BASS SECTION !!		SIX HARPS	SIX HARPS	
	ACT ONE	ACT ONE	ACT ONE	ACT ONE	ACT ONE	ACT TWO
	29 4 – 47 6	9 13 – 29 8	START – 13	47 – 64 6	8 62 → END	49 – 62 ACT 2 167
	ACT I	ACT I	ACT I	ACT I	ACT I	
	K 38	H 10		55 F	U 70	167
	55 F	38	H 8	V 71	SCHLUSS ACT I.	190
FULL SCORE PAGES	32 – 51	15 – 32	1 – 16	51 – 82	80 – 112	201 – 221
VOCAL SCORE PAGES	32 – 47 (28) – (43)	15 – 32 (14) – (28)	1 – 16 (1 – 14)	47 – 68 (43) – (59)	65 – 85 (59) – (77)	149 – 164
APPROX. TIMINGS =	14' 00"	13' 00"	13' 00"	12' 00"	10' 00"	11' 00"

FIDELIO

WALKÜRE

XTRA
CT III
271 — 12 288
S (possibly —5)
+ REMAKES (LIST)

	W	Tu	F	Sat NO ORCHESTRA REQUIRED ↓	M M	M	T	W	Th	Fri F
	NOV. 10th	NOV. 11th	NOV. 12th	NOV. 13th	NOV. 15th	NOV. 16th	NOV. 17th	NOV. 18th	NOV. 19th	NOV. 20th 19th
	✓	✓	✓	●	✓	CUE	✓	✓	✓
	✓	✓	✓	✓	✓	✓	✓	✓	✓
	✓									
					✓					
	✓ (ON)	✓ ON AND OFF	✓ (ON)	OFF ONLY						

ACT ③
12 288
— 300
12·30

ACT II
START —
103
+
125 —
134
4·45 +
6·45
11·30

ACT III
300 —
END
13·00

ACT II
1 148
— 170
12·00

| | EDIT 4 TRACK AFTER SESSION !!!! | | TRACK | | | | | | |

TRACKING FOR WALKÜREN HELMWIGE, SIEGRUNE, ROSSWEISE, GRIMGERDE

	ACT THREE	ACT THREE	ACT THREE		ACT TWO	ACT TWO	ACT TWO	ACT TWO	ACT THREE	ACT THREE
	4 29	START	12 53		23 27	15 53	START	5 15	67	83
	— 53 1	— 29 3	— 67 4		— 33	— 50 10	— 15 6	— 15 27	— 33 8	END
	243 2	ST.	260		102 6	5 134	13 296	ST. — 103	1 148	7 283
	261 1	243	283		125 4	148	END	+ 125 — 134	170	296
	342— 375	273— 342	375— 398	AS FOR NOV. 11th	158—133 172 153	172— 204	143 END 146	145— 133 163 82—163	398 178 449 204	445 398 — 457 420
	241— 278	199— 241	276— 301		116— 129	128— 151	86— 104	104— 119	301— 319	318— 334
	15'00"	11'00"	13'00	—	10'30"	14'00"	12'00"	13'00	13'00	12'00"
	ZAUB.	BRASS REH. TOSCA AM (2) OK with Opera if O.K.	OTH.	TRAN.	ARIAD ORCH REH. AM.	BALLET ORCH A.M.	ZAUB MAG BUTT	ROCV ZAUB	JEN TROV	FORZA

for it is a curious and difficult role which lies for much of the time at the lower end of the tenor voice. It is not really suitable for a high baritone, and it is not really comfortable for most tenors. (As I have mentioned, Windgassen sings it occasionally on the stage, but he was not very keen on the idea of recording.) While we were making *Götterdämmerung*, Wilhelm Pitz suggested, half as a joke, that I should mention it to Fischer-Dieskau, for although he might never perform it on the stage he could certainly manage it under recording conditions. It turned out that the idea was not new, for Fischer-Dieskau had thought of it himself some years earlier and promised me that he would take another look at the part and let me know as quickly as possible.

Reluctantly, he turned it down, and I could see his reasons. Our choice then turned to James King, the young American tenor whose career was developing at a great pace. Although really a high tenor, King had in the lower notes of his voice that dark, baritonal quality essential for a good Siegmund, and he was a very sensitive musician. He came and sang for us in London in the early months of 1965, and we had no hesitation in engaging him. And for the eight Valkyrie maidens we cast a wide net all over Europe in order to catch a really outstanding ensemble for the opening of Act Three.

Because *Walküre* poses far fewer technical problems than any other part of the *Ring* we had decided, and Solti had agreed, that this time we would record the work in a single period, between October 29 and November 19, concentrating at first on the opening act which calls for only three characters. On the day we were scheduled to start, it would be eight and a half years since the same conductor and orchestra, in the same hall and with the same staff, had recorded Act Three of *Walküre* with Kirsten Flagstad, and so laid the foundation for the *Ring* cycle which was now nearing completion.

The success of *Götterdämmerung* continued during the quiet summer months when people usually spend less money on records. The French awarded another *Grand Prix Mondiale*, and the Dutch honored *Götterdämmerung* with their coveted Edison prize. The German critics awarded it their main prize. In Vienna, Karl Löbl wrote a review which showed how completely he had grasped our aim of producing a recording in a way that differed completely from efforts of other companies.

In June of that year, Tillett and Holt Records, Ltd., of Wigmore Street, which was a relatively new offspring of Ibbs and Tillett, Ltd., the concert agency, put up the idea that extracts from

*James King, who recorded the
part of Siegmund in "Walküre,"
also appeared in the role during
the 1968 Bayreuth Festival.*

Götterdämmerung should be played one evening in the Wigmore Hall,
and that Solti and I should be present with the engineers to answer questions from the audience. Such was the demand for tickets that Tillett
and Holt asked us if we would appear on two consecutive nights with
the same program. It was a slightly traumatic experience, as we were all
involved with the recording of Verdi's *Don Carlo* at the time, but the
sound installation which had been fixed up by the Vienna engineers was
as good as I have ever heard in that sort of hall, and when it came to
questions the audience was far from reticent. Somebody who had attended the *Ring* cycle at Covent Garden the year before got up to point
out how much better Windgassen sounded on the records than on the
stage, and then proceeded to question the morality of our methods. On
the stage, he said, the tenor gets tired, especially in *Siegfried*. Wagner,
being an intelligent man, must have known this and therefore must have
expected his tenor to sound wearier and wearier as the evening progressed. Was it not therefore contrary to Wagner's wishes to create
conditions in a recording by which the tenor was able to keep in fresh
voice throughout the work?

"No," Solti said. "It's very simple. I will explain it to you in three
words: *Wagner was mad!*" When the laughter had subsided, he explained that Wagner, in the heat of composition, had not considered the

question of a singer's stamina, though he had to face the problem, even to the point of unwillingly sanctioning cuts, when it came to staging his works. To be able to have a tenor in fresh voice throughout a performance was something that every tenor, every conductor, and every stage producer dreamed about; but it was unlikely to happen, even in a generation better endowed with *Heldentenoren* than the present. It was therefore only in a recording that one could hear a voice from first to last in the condition that the composer had imagined it while writing the work. And far from being morally questionable, it was a huge advantage for the recording over the stage.

Sitting there on the stage listening to the questions and helping to answer them on two successive nights, I was struck by the nature of these audiences. These were not the people who would have come to such an event even ten years earlier; these were people, many of them young, who were acutely aware of the changes that had come about in the world of recording and in the sort of experience a good record could impart. Their questions were serious, and they were not ready to

accept evasive answers. If such audiences could assemble in the middle of London on two warm July nights to hear and discuss a recording which had been on the market for over two months, I felt that the future for the serious classical record looked good. On every side there were indications that it was being taken more seriously than at any time in its history.

On October 26, when we were already in Vienna preparing for *Walküre*, Hans Knappertsbusch died. He had had a bad fall the year before, and had never really recovered. It is not often that there is a true bond of affection between an orchestra and a conductor, and especially so in the case of an orchestra with so long and proud a tradition of its own as the Vienna Philharmonic. The older members still talk with awe about Furtwängler and Richard Strauss. They speak with profound respect for the memories of Erich Kleiber and Clemens Krauss and Bruno Walter. For others, still living, they have mixed feelings ranging from loathing to admiration. But for Hans Knappertsbusch, they had love.

Georg Solti and John Culshaw answer questions about the recording of the "Ring" at a lecture-demonstration in London's Wigmore Hall shortly after the release of "Walküre" in 1966.

To make matters even more poignant, we were recording Bruckner's Seventh Symphony with Solti when the news came through, and the work had been among Knappertsbusch's favorites. At the start of the second session Professor Otto Strasser, the president of the Vienna Philharmonic, told the news to the orchestra and asked them to stand in silence for a while. Some of the players were in tears. Then Solti said to the orchestra:

"I can only add a personal note. Of all the people who might have had reason to resent my appointment in Munich after the war, there was one who had more reason than anyone else: that was Hans Knappertsbusch. There was in fact one man who really helped me, in my inexperience: that was Hans Knappertsbusch. He was a father to me. . . ."

Some days later, on November 11, Solti conducted a memorial concert in the Musikvereinssaal. It consisted simply of the funeral march from *Götterdämmerung*, and the slow movement of Bruckner's Seventh Symphony, separated by one of the most beautifully written and spoken tributes it has ever been my privilege to hear. The highest praise I can give to Professor Strasser's speech that morning is to say that it matched its context, and was worthy of its place between two musical masterpieces.

I had never heard the Philharmonic play with such heart-rending beauty as on that morning. Bruckner had completed the slow movement of his Seventh Symphony after the death of Richard Wagner, and now it was being played in memory of a great Wagnerian. Every man played as if making his own personal tribute in the only way possible: that of producing the most exquisite tone imaginable. And to us it seemed that the mantle of the great tradition of Richter, Muck, Richard Strauss, Furtwängler, and Knappertsbusch had now passed to Georg Solti.

We began *Walküre* with trouble, but it did not last long. Régine Crespin called from Paris to say she was not feeling well, and wondered what the chances were for a postponement for several days. I said that we could give her one day only, for although she was supposed to sing on the first session, I reckoned that by the time we had settled the orchestral sound and made sure that it matched the rest of our *Ring* cycle, we could easily use up the rest of the session with James King, who was already in Vienna and with whom we had never worked before. I told Crespin it was essential that she should join us not later than the evening of October 29, and she seemed grateful.

It did not take long to settle the orchestral balance and match it with the earlier recordings, and King found himself on the stage sooner than he expected. We concentrated on his big Act One monologue, with excellent result: his dramatic cries of "*Wälse! Wälse!*" were as thrilling as his expression in the tender moments was moving. Above all, it was a thoroughly masculine voice, and we knew it would be the perfect counterpart for Crespin's feminine Sieglinde.

The first act of *Walküre* is one great lyrical outpouring, as if Wagner, having rightly held back the flood of passion during *Rheingold*,

Solti leads the Vienna Philharmonic in the memorial concert for Hans Knappertsbusch at the Musikvereinssaal.

could not restrain it any longer. We had no effects to worry about, and were able to concentrate with Solti and the singers on producing what we hoped would be a ravishing sound. Crespin's command of German, and of German expression (which is the result of work with her husband, who is an authority on German literature) again astonished the orchestra. It may have been Crespin's complete confidence and command which suddenly caused James King to have inhibitions and doubts, though she was an excellent colleague and never tried to score points off him. (And Frick, who had never heard King before, was wildly enthusiastic. "*This* is the tenor we've been waiting for!" he announced to all and sundry.)

There was nothing seriously wrong with King, but by the fourth session he had become noticeably less expressive than at the start, and was willing to admit the fault. It is a very curious thing that although America has produced a large number of distinguished singers whose presence has enriched the European operatic scene since the end of the war, they all seem to share a particular trait. It is a strange sort of inhibition concerning details of breathing and the correct "placement" of the voice which can become an obsession in some cases, and which at an extreme divests the performance of dramatic intensity. It may be something to do with having to work in a foreign language, and therefore not "feeling" the language as one would a native tongue. Something of this had got into James King, but fortunately we were not dealing with someone like our late-lamented Siegfried, for King is an intelligent and balanced human being; and we knew what to do. I arranged with Solti to finish the first act a bit ahead of schedule, in order to give ourselves forty-five minutes of free time. After the interval on that session we had seemingly finished the first act, and King and Crespin were expecting to rehearse and perhaps record the Act Two scene scheduled for the next day. Instead, we pulled the old trick: we told them we were going to remake the latter half of Act One in a continuous take, and asked them to throw their scores away. They had both done their parts on the stage many times, so they could sing from memory; and if anything went wrong, we had plenty of cover in the material already made.

I think they were a bit shocked, but out they went. Just before we started, with only just enough time left on the session to record such a long stretch of music, I went out on the stage to encourage King to sing his head off and stop worrying about niggling details. He knew what we wanted, and I knew he was going to do it. He had only one request—he wanted to leave out a short passage ("*Dich selige Frau...*") because we already had a superlative performance on an earlier take and by omitting it he would be fresher for the rest of the act. I told him that was fine, and warned Solti not to stop at that particular passage just because King did not sing. In the rush, I forgot to tell Crespin.

From the first bars, the performance came to life. Without scores, and with the comforting feeling that whatever happened we could put together a fine performance from what we had already made, the two artists sang like the lovers they were meant to be. They handed their phrases one to the other with tenderness and passion, and you could feel Solti and the orchestra entering the mood of the scene in a way that had not happened earlier. It was going to be a great take. When King came to "*Dich selige Frau*" and, as we had arranged, did not pick up his cue, it even gave me a bit of a shock, so caught up was I in the performance; but whatever shock I had was nothing to Crespin's. She too was completely immersed in the abandon of the performance, and when her partner failed to come in she looked at him with horror (I could see the stage on the closed-circuit television), stamped her foot, marched across the stage, and kicked her innocent Siegmund on the shin before getting back to her own position in time for the next cue.

"I was *furious* with him!" she said at the end, when I went out to explain what had happened. She then gave him a kiss, and they laughed about it; but the take itself was no laughing matter. It had everything

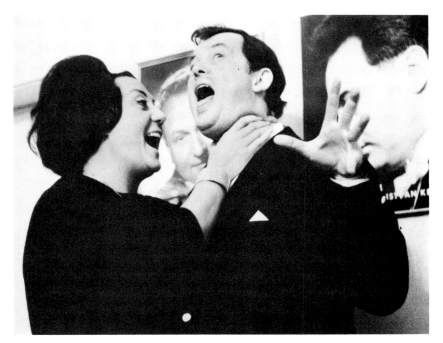

Cutting up behind the scenes: Soprano Régine Crespin's attempt to strangle her tenor, James King, seems to win the smiling approval of another tenor, Wolfgang Windgassen, whose picture hangs on the wall at the back.

we wanted—the beauty of two great voices, the sound of the orchestra at its best, and all the passion and abandon that Wagner had wanted for that enchanted spring night.

Nilsson was to arrive on November 8 and Crespin had to leave on the 10th, so in the days of the overlap it was essential to make the only two scenes they had together: the end of the second act, and the ten-minute sequence in Act Three when Brünnhilde, while handing the shattered remains of the sword to Sieglinde, tells her that she will bear Siegfried, the hero. (We had a telephone call from Ljuba Welitsch to ask if she might come and hear the session, and as always she was a very welcome guest. One of our regular duties is to bring kippers to Vienna for Welitsch.) James King was also leaving on the 9th, and so it was a congested period. We had followed the first act with the scene between Siegmund and Sieglinde in Act Two, though it is really her scene rather than his.

This portion of John Culshaw's full score for "Götterdämmerung" shows how the producer's copy gets heavily marked with cues and editing directions during the planning and making of a recording. The marginal notes serve to remind the producer about various offstage cues and indicate that the voices of the Rhinemaidens should gradually be panned sonically from center to the right and then to left to suggest their swimming about in the river.

Prompted perhaps by what had happened with the end of Act One the day before, Crespin surpassed herself in the remarkable episode of Sieglinde's hallucinations where she imagines she can see Siegmund torn to pieces by Hunding's dogs. This scene leads to the meeting between Brünnhilde and Siegmund known as the *Todesverkündigung*, which we had recorded years ago with Flagstad and Svanholm as a fill-up for the *Walküre*, Act Three, album, and it was now scheduled for Nilsson's first session on November 8.

In studying this scene before the recording started, I had noticed a curious discrepancy between editions of the score. It is necessary to explain that *full* scores of the *Ring* are extremely difficult to find and almost impossible to buy. They are in limited supply and have not been reprinted in Western Europe for very many years. It is always possible to hire a full score, but from the producer's point of view this is very unsatisfactory. In the course of making a major opera it is unavoidable that the control score gets heavily marked with cues and editing directions, and these must be preserved. In the months preceding each *Ring* recording I became involved in a frustrating and time-consuming search for a legible secondhand full score which, when run to earth, was always outrageously expensive. I had heard, however, that *Walküre* had been reprinted in a limited edition in Eastern Europe, and I managed to find one of these reprints in Vienna. On superficial examination it appeared identical to the standard Western edition and I assumed for a while that it had been made from copies of the original plates. The page numbers were the same in both editions, and each page contained the same number of bars and the same music.

Closer examination began to reveal startling differences. A notoriously bad misprint of the sword motive in Act One which appears in the Western edition (and which is often played as written there, despite its false rhythm) was correctly printed in my Eastern edition. Certain dynamic markings present in my score were missing from the other, as were several stage directions which might well be important for us, as in two cases they clearly involved offstage sounds. All the indications were that my Eastern score was a *later* edition than the other, as one would assume from the single example of the corrected sword motive.

The two directions which immediately concerned us appeared in the *Todesverkündigung* scene. Toward the end, Brünnhilde tells Siegmund that, contrary to Wotan's orders, he will live and that she will protect him. Hunding is approaching, intent on Siegmund's death. "*Hörst du den Ruf?*" Brünnhilde asks urgently ("Do you hear the horn call?"); and the stage direction in the libretto and in the Eastern score says *Horn calls are heard in the distance at the back.* A little later, when Siegmund is leaving the sleeping Sieglinde to go and face his pursuer, the stage direction immediately before *"So schlumm're nun fort"* asks for *Repeated horn calls from all sides.*

Despite these instructions for horn calls in the two places I have mentioned, no actual *music* for the passages appears in either the full score or the stage music parts. Across the bars in question, in both instances, there is a crescendo on C for the Wagner tubas in the orchestra, but it is not related, rhythmically speaking, to the steerhorn call which Wagner wrote out in full, several times, a little later in the act when Hunding approaches the place where Siegmund is waiting. And, when it appears, the Hunding call is a clear variant of his own motive from the first act.

At this stage I decided it was necessary to ask Bayreuth for help, and accordingly sent a long cable outlining the discrepancies and requesting information. The reply was interesting, but did not solve the problem. It was claimed that the two stage directions were not contained in the first published Schott score (1873–74) which was personally supervised by Wagner. (How then to account for the mistakes in that edition?) Bayreuth also said that the first *draft* of the score which is still in the archives does not contain the instructions; and it was confirmed that the final copy of the full score, which was presented to King Ludwig, had been missing since 1945. But the two stage instructions *are* in the private edition of the *Ring* text, pages 58 and 59 (Zurich, 1853), and appear again in Volume VI of the *Collected Poems and Writings*, pages 75 and 76 (Leipzig, 1872). It was therefore the conclusion of the Bayreuth archivist that the two directions had been transferred to the score from either the Zurich or the Leipzig publications. By whose hand, and with whose authority? Had Wagner written them in his libretto, the proofs of which in both cases of publication he doubtless corrected, and then forgotten to insert them in the score? For such a thorough composer, and bearing in mind the direct reference to the horn calls in the text at both moments, this seemed very unlikely.

It was a tricky problem. As we saw it, there were three possibilities. We could record the two short passages exactly as written and without any stage music; but in doing so, we would be ignoring two clear directions which appeared both in the Eastern edition of the score (which we had established as the more accurate of the two, musically speaking) *and* in the published libretto. Or we could insert across the bars in question a brief, offstage reference, very distant in perspective, to the Hunding motive (it would, of course, have to be a C, which is also its pitch when, a little later, Wagner *does* write it in the score). Or we could intensify and alter the perspective of the *orchestral* Wagner tubas, by increasing the number of instruments, placing them very distantly offstage on either side, and making them repeat the C with a crescendo on the sustained note.

The first of these proposals struck us as too negative. Wagner did not write instructions in his libretti for nothing, and the directions appeared in what now seemed to be the more accurate edition of the full score, which he had presumably checked and approved. But the second proposal seemed too presumptuous. (I am fairly convinced myself that Hunding's actual call *is* required at these two points, and that stage music did exist and was subsequently lost. But it is one thing to feel fairly convinced, and another to start writing music into a masterpiece; and the evidence in favor, though reasonably strong, was not enough to justify such a course.) We therefore settled for the third choice, which did not involve altering a note of the music, but at least made the tuba music as written sound like the distant call to which Brünnhilde, and then Siegmund, refers.

Finally, I would hazard a guess about how this confusion arose. I do not think that, in writing the original score, Wagner inserted horn calls at all at these two points. He began to *write* Hunding's call where it now appears in the printed score, just after Siegmund has left the stage in quest of Hunding. Then he subsequently noticed the ambiguity of Brünnhilde's and Siegmund's references to a call which was not in the score, whereupon he added the brief stage directions to indicate that distant calls were required at those points. But as Hunding is still a long way off, and as the bars in which the two calls are to be heard are extremely brief, it is possible that the effect did not work in the theater. For the horns to be heard at all, at least when Brünnhilde refers to them, they would have to be closer than Wagner desired, for Hunding does not arrive in the ravine for another five minutes or so; and my guess is that either Wagner or another stage director struck out the reference from the original score and destroyed the stage music, in case what was printed there should cause a false entry by being mistaken for the later calls.

The mystery of the score remains, however. For if the Eastern edition is printed from the original plates, how is it that the Western edition, which on that assumption came later, has more actual mistakes in the music? And if the Western plates were the first, did Wagner himself, having corrected the musical errors, add the stage directions for the offstage calls which appear on the Eastern plates? The matter will probably never be cleared up until the manuscript is discovered. Meanwhile, the compromise we adopted for the recording seemed the only acceptable resolution, short of ignoring the issue altogether.

We were not yet finished with steerhorns, for we had to think of the notated calls which announce Hunding's arrival at the end of Act Two. The calls are offstage and approaching, but must be loud and full. The note is C, but our C steerhorn from *Götterdämmerung* was not in the right octave, and when we tried to get in touch with Otto Mahler in Bayreuth we discovered that he had closed his instrument factory and taken up viniculture instead. (When we had made the *Todesverkündigung* scene with Flagstad and Svanholm we had used bass tubas for the call. They were quite powerful and effective, but altogether too musical for what Wagner had in mind when he wrote "steerhorn".) Then Gordon had a brilliant idea. He suddenly remembered those huge elongated horns, about fifteen feet in length, which are still used in the Swiss Alps to summon the cattle over great distances. They are usually carved from wood, with most of the outer surface bound with a fine cord, and the bell is often decorated with

In a side corridor of the Sofiensaal, American trombonist Terry Cravens plays the alphorn for the offstage calls that announce the approach of the pursuing Hunding at the end of Act II of "Walküre." The earphones provide him with his cues.

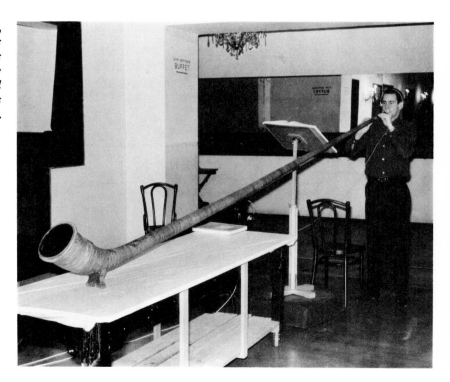

local shields or a simple painting. Because of the distance over which the sound has to carry they are capable of making a considerable noise, and we reckoned that we could mold the sound into something appropriate for Hunding.

I remembered that Decca had a recording crew in Geneva at that time, and called my colleague John Mordler with the request that he should find a Swiss peasant with the right sort of mountain horn capable of playing a low C. He should also find out what it would cost to persuade the peasant to bring his instrument to Vienna for a couple of days. In such a situation it is always advisable to have an alternative plan, so I called Leon Felder in the Zurich office and asked if he would be kind enough to make the same sort of investigation in his canton. The results were startlingly quick and unexpectedly comical.

In the control rooms in Vienna there are two telephones with outside lines. Within an hour Leon Felder called me back from the Zurich office to say he thought he had what we wanted. The man was a policeman, not a peasant, and had won several prizes for blowing the sort of horn we needed. He was at that moment in Felder's office assembling the monster, and would be ready to blow it down the telephone at any moment. At that instant, the other telephone rang—it was John Mordler from Geneva, complete with a Swiss peasant and an even longer horn which would shortly be blown into *that* telephone. To add to the confusion, there was in Vienna at that time a superb American bass trombone player called Terry Cravens, and he, armed with *his* instrument, was with us in the control room ready to play a C against which we could compare the pitch of the instruments in Zurich and Geneva.

In the race to assemble the instruments, the policeman in Zurich won by a short head, and so far as one could tell over the telephone he was making a splendid sound. Unfortunately, it was an F, and his attempts to sustain and blow a rhythm on C were perilous. We thanked him and got back to the Geneva telephone, over which the most startling noise was emerging. (It nearly deafened me, so I hate to imagine what it must have been like at the other end.) And it was a C, or at least within shooting distance of C, and we knew that the error in pitch could be overcome by adjusting the mouthpiece. I asked John Mordler to make whatever arrangements were necessary for the man to come to Vienna, and then to call Mr. Felder for financial approval. He did all that, but the comedy at the Geneva end was not quite over. When our peasant discovered that John was talking to a *director* in Zurich, it was almost too much for him. He explained that he was the village champion and must at all costs play his championship piece over the telephone to Mr. Felder. In vain did John try to explain that Mr. Felder was in charge of financial administration and was not concerned with musical abilities. Furthermore, Mr. Felder was an extremely busy man with a hundred problems much more pressing than the ambitions of an alpenhorn player who was going to Vienna to play a succession of identical repeated notes. But the man was adamant. The fee was not of major importance; neither was the question of travel and living expenses; what he wanted was to play his party piece to Mr. Felder over the telephone, and play it he did, twice. As I was to discover very soon afterwards in Vienna, and Mr. Felder doubtless discovered then, championship pieces especially written for the alpenhorn, which can best be described as a *reluctant* instrument, are not quite as extended as the average Bruckner symphony, but they seem to go on far longer.

The little man arrived in Vienna with his instrument the next day. He had never flown, nor had he been out of Switzerland before. We watched as he slowly assembled the horn on the stage of the Sofiensaal and blew a series of earsplitting notes which nearly dislodged the chandelier. They had an arbitrary sort of pitch, and one of them was definitely a C. The problem was to find it, for most attempts would produce something disagreeable in the vague region of C before settling down, somewhat unsteadily, on the note itself. We asked the man if our American trombone player could have a go, possibly with his own trombone mouthpiece; and as soon as he did, we knew we had got what we wanted. Out came a proper C, and with it the menacing Hunding rhythm in a tone which we believed would have sent Wagner into transports of delight. It was far from beautiful, but we were not seeking a beautiful sound; it had terrific penetration, so we knew we could afford to put it well offstage without any risk of its being drowned by the orchestra. The only problem was to coax our peasant into letting Terry Cravens play the thing.

It was then that he told us how he had played his championship piece to Director Felder over the telephone. As we were eager to do anything to please him, we sat around on the stage while he played it for us. It went on and on. Just as it appeared to be settling on what might be described as a very democratic tonic, it would veer off again in another direction. To grasp the form of the piece, or even of a phrase, was made difficult because, as certain notes had to be coaxed out of the instrument by trial and error, they were preceded by a long pause and much flexing of the lips and puffing of the cheeks. (While all this was going on, the piece stopped altogether and might, for all we knew, have finished.) When at last it was over our friend pointed out that this year's championship piece, which we had just heard, was possibly less good than last year's—which, without further ado, he proceeded to play. I am ashamed to report that it sounded exactly the same to me.

By this time we were resigned to a long recital, but someone eventually brought out the score of *Walküre* and pointed out the line where Hunding's horn is written. Then a terrible realization dawned on us—our man had not the slightest idea how to read music! We did not wish to offend him, so we made great play about how difficult *Walküre* is for *any* instrumentalist, but especially for the steerhorn with its row of repeated C's. He peered at the score and seemed to agree. We then suggested that as our American trombonist had undertaken the part hundreds of times before—which of course he hadn't—it might be safer and quicker to let him play the Swiss instrument. To my relief, our visitor agreed at once—to his relief, I imagine. He was a charming little man, and we bundled him and his instrument off to Switzerland the next day, where he could go back up his mountain and tell his neighbors how he had recorded Wagner in Vienna.

The end of the second act is a hard part to record, but we were pleased with the result. It required one of our very complicated hookups, in that all sorts of different acoustics and perspectives are required to cover the action. There is Hunding's horn, loud and growing closer; there is Siegmund first in one offstage position and then, by Wagner's decree, in another; there is Hunding, first heard offstage but not yet in contact with Siegmund; and on the stage itself is Sieglinde, awakening to find that her nightmare has become reality. There is a thunderclap, and then the sound of Brünnhilde's voice as she appears in the air above Siegmund, followed immediately by the sound of Wotan's voice as he stands above Hunding. All this takes place in an extremely fast tempo, and the cues follow one another at an alarming rate. (From the purely technical point of view, it is the hardest two minutes in *Walküre*.) We made a mess of the first take, largely because until you have had a chance to try a scene like this with the artists giving full voice rather than the half-voice which is used in rehearsal, it is almost impossible to gauge how the *relation* between the perspectives is going to work out.

At the very end of the act, Wotan has the famous passage beginning "*Geh' hin, Knecht!*" and ending with the words "*Geh'! Geh'!*"—at which command Hunding sinks dead to the ground. Ever since I first saw Hotter on the stage, I had known this was one of his greatest moments: the immense dignity and power of the angry god whose favorite daughter had disobeyed him came across the footlights with that sort of magnetism, or hypnotism, which only the greatest artists can command.

Hotter's performance conveyed still more than that—the unspeakable grief of a father who has been forced not only to ordain the death of his son but also to witness the fatal fight and to intercede in order that Siegmund shall die. His final words to Hunding—his "*Geh'! Geh!*"—become neither a shout nor an order, but the words of a man driven to the limits of experience. There is nothing left for him except to vent his fury on Brünnhilde.

It was moving to find that on the session, after a lifetime's experience as Wotan, Hotter was still trying to rethink the phrase. Did Wagner

Recording the third act of "Walküre": the disobedient Brünnhilde (Nilsson, center foreground) asks Wotan (Hotter, right above) what her punishment is to be as her sister Valkyries listen. Man following score in foreground is assistant producer Christopher Raeburn.

want the first emphasis on "*Knecht!*", or would it sound more contemptuous, or even ironical, to put the emphasis slightly on "*kniee*"? He tried "*Geh'!*" half a dozen different ways to see which might be the most effective. Even from an artist as charming and sympathetic as Hotter, it is a little unnerving to be asked advice about something which had been second nature to him for so long; but it is something you cannot forget quickly. Throughout *Walküre* his concern from first until last was with Wagner's Wotan, and not with Hotter the personality. It was an honor to have him in the studio.

The second hardest passage to record in *Walküre* is the opening of the third act—the so-called Ride of the Valkyries. We had found out long ago, in 1957, that the opening always *sounds* wrong when you first record it, and when you look at the score the answer is plain to see: there is no bass until shortly before the voices enter. Wagner visualized his maidens flying through the air on horseback, and therefore wrote a loud but *light* sound. I am sure Solti was right in feeling that it should not be too fast: a magisterial sort of pace is surely appropriate for the maidens who are bearing the bodies of dead heroes to Valhalla. And there are plenty of records in existence to prove how few conductors can get the rhythm right, for if one accent is misplaced at the start the whole piece will remain unrhythmic throughout.* Though perhaps the best-known popular excerpt from the *Ring*, it is not considered by many critics to be one of Wagner's better inventions; but I recall discussing it once with Benjamin Britten, who is by no means an ardent Wagnerian, and agreeing with him that *in its context* it is an excellent and effective piece, for it builds up the necessary tension for the arrival of Brünnhilde and Sieglinde.

As in all such scenes in the *Ring*, Wagner gives exact details of what he wants in the way of staging. At the opening, four of the maidens are on stage, and four more will be heard approaching from offstage as the scene progresses. The elaborate scenic requirements did not of course concern us; but it was obviously important to make the offstage voices convey, as far as possible, the picture of the Valkyrie maidens flying through the air on horseback as they approach the rock. We decided to make the scene complete without the offstage voices in the first place,

---

* If you sing the famous Ride tune to the nonsense words "I'm sick on a seesaw/Sick on a seesaw/Sick on a seesaw/Sick on a train," the strong accent must always be on "sick," whereas it is often wrongly placed on "see"; and the sixteenth-note corresponding to the word "on" must be *really* short. That is precisely how Wagner marked his score.

for there is a great deal of running about to be done by those who are on stage, and it was of primary importance to get their part right. We therefore recorded the entire scene except for the offstage calls and then, after the orchestra had departed, gradually added the approaching voices until the effect seemed right. After about four attempts we felt the result was good enough to give the girls a chance to hear it. They were thrilled, except for one who looked very puzzled at the sound of her own offstage voice, and said: "I sound as if I'm right up there in the clouds!"

"And that," I said to her, "is exactly where you're meant to be."

I did not realize it at the time, but she had probably only sung the piece in productions where Wagner's directions are ignored; in the theater, she had probably always been on stage from the rise of the curtain. (In the Bayreuth production of 1966, for example, no attempt was made to cover even the opening cue. The first call, on stage, is by Gerhilde, and she is answered immediately by Helmwige, who is strictly supposed to be flying through the air but who is at any rate *offstage*. In Bayreuth, Gerhilde and Helmwige stood side by side on the front of the stage, and Helmwige actually made a point of addressing her reply directly to the audience.)

It was my feeling at that session that Nilsson may have sung better than in any other part of the *Ring*. She was inspired; and the G with which she begins the word "*Siegfried*" just before Sieglinde's exit was straight out of heaven, as was Crespin's ecstatic singing of the first, and only, appearance of the redemption motive until the end of *Götterdämmerung*. In the massive buildup to the entrance of Wotan, Wagner had written a part for a thunder *machine* to underline the women's voices, and for this we had rigged up our old *Rheingold* metal sheet, plus a battery of bass drums. As it stretches over many bars, and as there is a lot going on above it, it is the sort of sound you should *feel* rather than hear explicitly; but you certainly notice its abrupt termination under the huge chords as Wotan strides upon the scene. All in all, we had had good luck with the two passages where we had felt we would be most likely to encounter trouble.

Trouble, however, was on the way; and not one of us had a glimpse before it struck. We were aware that the recording of Bruckner's Seventh Symphony, which we had made immediately before *Walküre*, would occupy only three sides, and we wanted to make Wagner's *Siegfried Idyll* for the last side in order to complete the two-record set. We wanted to make it in the form in which Wagner wrote it, which is for thirteen instrumentalists only—or fourteen, to be pedantic, for there is one phrase where a second viola is all but essential. We had the idea of using hand-picked players from the Philharmonic, including their principal strings—but then we ran into difficulties.

The Vienna Philharmonic embodies a number of fine instrumental groups—the Vienna Octet, for example, and the Weller Quartet—and from time to time, with the permission of the orchestral committee, these groups go on tour. In addition, certain "star" members of the orchestra are in demand as soloists, and this is especially so in the case of Willi Boskovsky, who has charmed audiences the world over with his Johann Strauss concerts, during which he conducts and plays the violin in the true Strauss tradition. Our problem with the *Siegfried Idyll* was that we could not coordinate the string group we wanted—some players were ill, and others, like Boskovsky, were away on tour—and by the time we started *Walküre* we had all but postponed the project until the following year. But the Bruckner was good, and it seemed a shame to hold it in reserve for so long.

The orchestra has four concert-masters—Boskovsky, Barylli, Weller, and Sivo—and as we embarked on *Walküre* I suddenly realized not only that Walter Weller was appearing as concert-master at most sessions, but that his young colleagues who made up the Weller Quartet were also playing in the orchestra. This, surely, was the answer to our *Siegfried Idyll* problem: the Quartet was a splendid group and had already made a number of very successful records for us. Accordingly, I asked Professor Wobisch if he had any objection to our using Weller for the *Idyll*, and in the haste of the moment his reply—which was an affirmative—led to serious misunderstanding and later on almost brought *Walküre* to a halt.

What Wobisch meant was that we could use Weller as the concert-master for the *Idyll*, whereas my whole point was that since Weller had a quartet, it was sensible to use it as a unit and not divorce Weller from his regular colleagues who played chamber music with him all the time. From Wobisch's reply I assumed, wrongly, that we had permission to use the Quartet. As we were up to our necks in *Walküre*, none of us even considered the possibility of a misunderstanding, and we proceeded to set up the recording of the *Idyll* on the only day without a *Walküre* session. It was the evening of Sunday, November 14, and to get the right atmosphere for this delicate, intimate piece, we transformed the Sofiensaal.

The instrumental group was in a small enclosure in the center of the hall, and the *Walküre* orchestral setup had been pushed aside. We switched off all the main lights of the hall and brought down some standard lamps from the apartment to add a warm glow to the scene and to illuminate the music stands; and—very unusually for him—Solti was persuaded to conduct sitting down. We wanted to get the musicians completely relaxed, to get them to try and sound as their predecessors must have sounded on that morning in Triebschen when the *Idyll* was first played for Cosima Wagner.

It was an evening of enchanting music. Nobody was watching the clock and the musicians blended to perfection. It was as if a spell had come over the Sofiensaal. We did not need to touch a control: it was pure music-making, pure joy—the sort of session that happens very rarely but more than compensates for whatever struggles one may have had in the past. We parted that night in the knowledge that a very beautiful *Siegfried Idyll* had been committed to tape.

By the schedule there were only five more days left for the completion of *Walküre*. We had still to make the opening of Act Two and continue through the scene with Fricka and to the end of Wotan's great monologue. We had also to make all the latter part of Act Three, between Brünnhilde and Wotan, but we were exactly on schedule, and short of illness it did not seem likely that anything would go wrong.

Then, on November 17, it happened. On that day we planned to record the end of the whole work. (It is always a good idea to try to record the end of any opera at least a day or two before the final session. The end is important, for it gives the listener his final impression; and if you leave it to the last session you have no time for second thoughts.) The session was at 1500 and Hotter arrived for his big scene (the Farewell) in splendid form. Should we not, he suggested, have a crack at it right away, as soon as the session started? He felt in such good form that he would like to try, and Solti agreed immediately. At that moment a deputation from the orchestral committee marched up and demanded an explanation as to why we had used the Quartet, rather than the senior players, for the *Siegfried Idyll*. I was bewildered at first. I explained that I had obtained permission, but they denied this. There was obviously a feeling that we had somehow shown discrimination against certain players, and the resentment had boiled up, though not revealing itself until now, over the past few days.

By that time it was several minutes after the session should have started, but the committee was determined it should not start until a satisfactory explanation had been produced. I still did not grasp the nature of the misunderstanding which had taken place almost a month earlier. The tension in the hall, and outside, was unbearable. I felt desperately sorry for Hotter, who had come in only a few minutes before, full of anticipation for his final scene. Now I could see him pacing up and down as the minutes went by, getting more and more nervous and far from unaware of all the shouting that was going on.

The leading cellist, who had been a friend of ours for years but who was one of those who mistakenly considered himself slighted by the *Idyll* affair, announced that he would leave immediately and would not play the session, for which we needed him badly. Twenty minutes had now been lost, and the mood in which we hoped to make the end of *Walküre* had been hopelessly disrupted. I implored the committee to let us start, as otherwise the opera might never be finished on schedule, and guaranteed that I would give every second of my time between sessions to clearing up the matter. I promised that the *Idyll* would not be released until all parties to the dispute were satisfied; and with that, I was finally able to lead Solti to the podium and Hotter to the stage.

It was hopeless. Every ounce of Solti's professionalism would not break the mood of anger and mystery which hung like a cloud in the Sofiensaal that afternoon. As for Hotter, it was little short of heartbreaking. Nobody could concentrate on what he was supposed to be doing. One faction in the orchestra was seething against another, while the rest, who knew nothing about it at all, were trying to find out what was going on. At the end of the longest, and worst, session of my life we realized that not a single note we had recorded that afternoon was worthy of the rest of *Walküre*, and that we were therefore one whole session behind schedule, with no possibility whatever of getting extra time by the end of the week.

Much later, when I was putting together material for this book, I asked Solti to think back over the years since we started the *Ring* and try to pin down what had been the worst moment for him; and without hesitation he named the *Walküre* session on November 17. In those conditions it is impossible to work, for the very worst sort of dispute is the kind in which one party believes itself slighted, and the other believes itself innocent. I suppose it is the sort of thing which is bound to happen in any relationship sooner or later. So far as the *Ring* was concerned, it had come at the worst possible moment.

Over the years, our relationship with the Philharmonic had grown very close. From our standpoint there are two ways of working with an orchestra. Since the Company is paying an orchestra for its services, you can regard yourself simply as the Company's representative and the guardian of its practical interests—so long as the orchestra turns up and plays and does not waste money, if you care to look at it that way, that is the end of the matter. The other way, which is the one we tried to develop over the years, is to establish a relationship with the management of the orchestra and with the players, so that the making of a gramophone record becomes a joint effort directed towards an artistic aim. With this approach, it became our duty to study the nature of the orchestra from several angles: to get to know its special and distinctive sound qualities and find out how to put them on record; to learn the psychology of the orchestra, in order to create conditions under which it could give of its best; and to try to help the management in a hundred ways, from tracing new or replacement instruments to pointing out that a department in the orchestra, or even a player, is letting the side down. It is only when such a relationship comes into being that properly creative work can take place in the studio.

From about the time of *Rheingold* this sort of relationship between our crew and the Vienna Philharmonic began to grow. (The orchestra had been with Decca for many years before that, but until then there had never been such close contact in the *studio*.) And when this relationship developed, it pleased us that the orchestra began to get a press for its recordings on our label of a kind which had only two precedents in recording history—that of the Philadelphia Orchestra in its heyday, and that of the Philharmonia Orchestra of London during the years immediately after its foundation. Theirs were distinctive records because they conveyed in unmistakable fashion the unique qualities of the orchestras concerned.

Now the same was happening with the Vienna Philharmonic. No matter how good the notices for the many distinguished singers in the Decca *Ring*, no matter how good the reviews for Solti and our own part in the affair, every critic singled out the unique and incomparable qualities of the Vienna Philharmonic as revealed on the records we made. We were proud of what was happening, and wholly in sympathy with the orchestral management's policy of guarding the traditions of sound, and style of playing, which had been handed from generation to generation in the Vienna Philharmonic. This style had no equivalent anywhere, but it was not necessarily invulnerable. Our efforts to help the Philharmonic to make every record, whether of opera or orchestral music, into an outstanding example of the orchestra's qualities, did not go unnoticed by the committee, for in 1959 we were presented, as a team, with the Nicolai Medal, which was a singular and unexpected honor. (Nicolai founded the Vienna Philharmonic in 1842, and the medal has only ever been presented to those artists who have established a close working relationship with the orchestra, or to those who by

John Culshaw, on behalf of the Decca team, accepts silver Nicolai Medal presented by Vienna Philharmonic president Otto Strasser in 1959. Inscription on medal (left below) conveys orchestra's thanks and esteem.

WIENER PHILHARMONIKER
OTTO NICOLAI

UNSEREN
LIEBEN FREUNDEN
VON DER DECCA
ALS ZEICHEN DES DANKES
UND DER ANERKENNUNG
DIE WIENER
PHILHARMONIKER

their special efforts in one field or another have rendered a distinctive sort of service. We never expected such recognition, but it seemed to set the seal on our creative relationship with the orchestra.)

Yet such a relationship is not without its perils; it cannot all be mutual rejoicing. And just as the Philharmonic players were ready to point it out when some aspects of the way we ran sessions were not to their liking, so we felt it part of our duty—not only to them, but to Decca—to mention any serious deficiency in the playing, in so far as it might adversely affect the reception of the recording. Inevitably, this made us a few enemies. We never tried to force our beliefs on the committee, and never suggested that our recommendations should apply to anything but their work in the studio for Decca.

In the three days separating the recording of the *Siegfried Idyll* and that fruitless *Walküre* session, the small faction who were against us and what we were trying to do had chosen an appropriate moment to make trouble. The administrative leader of the orchestra, Professor Helmut Wobisch, who over the years has guided this assertive body of men through many a storm, was in a hospital recovering from a serious illness. His committee was faced with huge administrative burdens, and the orchestra was, as usual, overworked. It was just the right time to stir up trouble by suggesting that we were trying to discriminate against the older string players by forcing them out of recording work. Nothing could have been further from the truth; but nothing was more likely to cause a revolution. Our relationship in the studio, which had taken so many years and so much effort to establish, seemed to dissolve in an afternoon.

The worst of it was that some of the players who had taken offense were those for whom we had the greatest admiration and respect. While I was trying to keep things going in order not to lose time and money, and help Solti and Hotter to regain their shattered nerves, Gordon got on the telephone to Emanuel Brabec, the principal cellist, who had walked out just as the session started. Brabec was a great player and had been an invaluable colleague for years; and to see him, of all people, leave in protest seemed to symbolize the breakdown of a relationship we had tried for years to cultivate. On the telephone Gordon tried to explain the misunderstanding as best he could, and implored Brabec to make the gesture of returning before the end of the session, if only to show his colleagues that he, at least, was not deserting us. We promised him a full explanation; and he came back immediately, too late to save a session which had been on the rocks since it started, but early enough to give pause to a few of the revolutionaries. And when we explained the nature of the misunderstanding—that I had taken the approval to use Weller in the absence of Boskovsky as meaning that we could use Weller's quartet, instead of just Weller the individual—Brabec saw exactly what had happened, and just how the situation had been exploited. Thanks to him, and to the brilliant diplomacy of Professor Strasser and Professor Barylli, the most painful and pointless dispute in all our years in Vienna began to burn itself out.

The orchestra knew that nothing had emerged from that session, and I knew there was not enough time left to finish *Walküre*. Professors Strasser and Barylli came up with a helpful suggestion. It would be possible, the next evening, to hold a session parallel with the performance at the opera, because the work being performed there required a relatively small orchestra. Could we therefore find a part of *Walküre* to record on that evening which did not need the full complement of brass and which might not need the usual doubling on the woodwinds? There was only one possible section: the long Wotan monologue in Act Two; but Hotter was already called for the afternoon session, and I doubted if he would be prepared to attempt two tiring sessions in one day.

I went to see him, and explained the situation. He agreed at once, and so did Birgit Nilsson. (As she has only a few sentences to sing during

Georg Solti is amused by a gift of a padlocked bottle of Scotch given to him by the recording team on his birthday in 1965. Looking on are John Culshaw, Roland Berger, Valerie Pitts (who became Mrs. Solti in 1967) and Solti's good friend John Scott Trotter, the popular bandleader and arranger. Solti was told at first that he would get the key to the bottle only on his next birthday, but the crew relented and gave it to him that evening.

*Birgit Nilsson and Hans Hotter
as Brünnhilde and Wotan in Vienna
State Opera production of "Walküre."*

the monologue, and as she had made a social engagement that evening, she could easily have refused us. Her immediate agreement to come to the emergency session was another example of her consideration and professionalism.) The schedule, of course, had been seriously upset, for even by pushing part of the Act Two monologue into that extra evening session, we still had to find a place to remake the closing scene of Act Three, for which we could not afford to have Hotter in tired voice.

A week or two earlier, when *Walküre* was rolling along so well, it had been very much in our minds that November 19 would be a remarkable day. So far as we could see, at 1730 on that afternoon the Decca *Ring* would be finished at last, and the seven-year saga would be over. We were not likely to go through it again in our lives, and it seemed appropriate to hold a celebration for the orchestra and those artists who would still be in Vienna: Solti, Nilsson, and Hotter. In the subterranean depths of the Sofiensaal are some pleasant tavernlike rooms, and I proposed to get permission to hold a dinner in one of these to which all members of the orchestra and their wives would be invited. Mr. Rosengarten agreed to cover the expense, but we ran into all sorts of catering difficulties at the Vienna end and the plan was modified into a buffet supper with plenty of wine, to be held after the opera performance on the night of the last session.

But now we had a new situation. As I sat for hour after hour with my colleagues trying to fit together the jigsaw of the wrecked *Walküre* schedule, forcing the work of four sessions into the remaining three and seeking a way to conserve the voices at the same time, I knew that the spirit had gone out of any idea for a celebration. The nervous strain was too great. It was a fact that we would not know until 1730 on November 19 whether the *Ring* would be finished or not. The pile-up of material for the final session was little short of absurd: on paper, at any rate, it was impossible. For years we had talked and thought about the day when it would all be over, and how we would celebrate the end of the largest undertaking in record history. Now that it was upon us, I sent the money back to Zurich, because nobody felt like celebrating anything. I was determined we would finish on that Friday afternoon without any compromise in standards; we would reach the end of *Walküre* on that day no matter what the cost in effort and ingenuity. But the mood in which we had hoped to finish had been shattered beyond repair; and our *Ring* venture, like *Walküre* itself, would come to a quiet conclusion.

"You have to remember," Solti said to me months later when we were thinking back to the *Walküre* crisis, "that they love that sort of thing. A crisis brings out the best in them, when they can see you are suffering and fighting the clock. . . ."

To some extent this is true. Except for the minority of committed, interested players, the rank and file of any orchestra finds recording a tedious business, and anything unusual, including a crisis, can only make things more interesting. I do not think this observation applies only to Vienna, although it is true that in Vienna any small point of dispute tends to magnify itself faster than anywhere else.

We were taking no chances for the last *Walküre* session. The night before, I had been through the score time and time again, and had finally worked out the list of material still to be recorded, plus the essential remakes. It was formidable. I made out copies for each artist and each member of the staff, and we glued Solti's copy firmly to his stand. (We were afraid that a member of the orchestra might otherwise remove it. It is a fact that if Solti is ever forgetful enough to leave his baton on the stand during an interval, he will find that the tip has been painted with ink by the time he returns. This has happened so many times over the last ten years that we have lost count. It may sound incredible, but it is true.) The list for the final session, which was far more extensive than that for the equivalent session in *Götterdämmerung*, showed the precise number of minutes to be devoted to the rehearsal and to the recording of each piece. We also fixed a big tickless clock to the conductor's stand, so that Solti could see both the time and the plan at a glance. There was to be no playback at all, and visitors, no matter how distinguished, were not to be admitted.

Tension is clearly written on faces of recording crew as they push to meet deadline for completing "Walküre."

Solti made a brief speech to the orchestra at the start. He said that while he had been glad to learn that the misunderstanding about the *Idyll* had been cleared up, the fact remained that we had lost one whole session on an issue which could just as easily have been raised outside recording time. It was necessary now to make up that time by the utmost concentration. And with that, he got down to work.

As if to make up for what had happened, we had a superb orchestra that afternoon. Although all the accredited members of the Vienna Philharmonic maintain a high standard of skill, there are some players who stand in a class of their own, and on that afternoon they were all present. There had never been such tension in the Sofiensaal, for I think everyone knew that if we fell even five minutes behind schedule there would be no chance of completing *Walküre* that year.

By the interval we had beaten the clock to the extent of four valuable minutes. Hotter and Nilsson had cooperated all the way, and the orchestral discipline was superb. In the second half of the session, almost as if by design to relieve the tension, a mouse appeared in the orchestra and someone put a tuba over it. (Adolf Krypl swore that it was not a Sofiensaal mouse, and that a member of the orchestra had imported it in a paper bag; but wherever it came from, the momentary laughter, the diversion, helped. The pressure could not be relaxed, but the end was in sight.)

We finished at exactly 1730, as planned. The last notes of the Decca *Ring* to be recorded were the last notes of *Walküre*.

There were no speeches. In the control room, before the artists came round, we shook hands; and although I do not remember if we said anything, I am sure that our thoughts went in the same direction, taking us back in an instant to that afternoon in September 1958 when the *Rheingold* E flat pedal first sounded in the Sofiensaal. It seemed like fifteen hours ago, the time of the *Ring* cycle, instead of seven years; but it was all there at last, for the present and future generations to judge. "*Das Ende!*" Hotter said, as he came in, quoting from his Act Two monologue. "*Das Ende!*" We had a drink with him and Nilsson and Solti, and then Gordon and Jimmy and I went into the empty hall. The orchestra had gone. Looking up to our big apron stage in the dimmed lights I could see our three Rhinemaidens flitting here and there pursued by Neidlinger in the opening scene of *Rheingold;* Flagstad in a big picture hat, remonstrating with Wotan; the eighteen anvils and the screaming children; Stolze and Windgassen forging the sword in Act One of *Siegfried;* and Fafner shut in his little room at the back. I thought of Christa Ludwig as Waltraute as she spoke to Brünnhilde with such quiet intensity in Act One of *Götterdämmerung* . . . "*So—sitzt er, sagt kein Wort* . . ."; the sound of Pitz's chorus in Act Two, and Frick's black Hagen, and Fischer-Dieskau when the *Blutbrüderschaft* motive rings out on the horns; the death of Siegfried, so nobly sung by Windgassen; and the rapturous singing of Nilsson in the Immolation scene. And I thought of Hotter, the incomparable Hotter, who had just a few moments ago sung "*denn Einer nur freie dir Braut, der freier als Ich, der Gott!*" with such nobility and sorrow as words cannot describe.

I thought of Solti, working himself to exhaustion, never losing his patience and yet never making an artistic compromise. I thought of my colleagues, and of all those in London and Zurich who had helped and supported us over the years, who had let us have our heads and granted us the money and the conditions not just to make a recording of the *Ring*, but to do the job properly to the best of our abilities.

Standing in the empty hall at the end of the last *Walküre* session, with memories swirling all around us, we felt a strange mixture of sadness and pleasure. For better or worse, it was over. For seven years it had been a major part of our lives, and it would not come our way again.

CHAPTER SIX

Coda

THAT NIGHT, in place of the feast we had planned to mark the end of the *Ring*, we had a simple gathering in the flat: the team, Solti, a handful of friends, and my parents and sister and brother-in-law who, having come to Vienna to witness the end of our seven-year effort, had watched the events of the last few days with something like bewilderment. It was not what they had expected; but then it was not what we had expected, either.

Until the final crisis we had kept pace with the rough-editing of *Walküre*. As each sequence was recorded I had passed a marked score to Jack Law who, as usual, had been willing to work at odd hours of the night or very early in the morning so that by ten o'clock on any morning we were able to hear the rough-edit of the previous day's work. One can sustain this sort of intensity when the atmosphere is right, but not with the sort of tension we had undergone since November 17. The editing lagged, and when the recording was over we had a backlog of some four sessions—about sixty minutes of unedited material. We were determined to do the rough-editing as quickly as possible, but nobody had the heart to tackle the really difficult, detailed work which *Walküre* still required. For the second year in succession we decided that our only way was to return to Vienna immediately after Christmas, thus putting a month between ourselves and the present disagreeable atmosphere.

We were conscious that much of *Walküre* would need even more careful editing than any other part of the *Ring*. This was the one work in the cycle where the critics would be able to make direct comparisons with other complete recordings—the 1960 RCA version made with the London Symphony Orchestra conducted by Erich Leinsdorf (also with Nilsson as Brünnhilde); and Wilhelm Furtwängler's mono recording made in Vienna in the early nineteen-fifties. There was no reason to fear these competitors, but we had taken a chance—and something of a risk—in casting Hotter as Wotan right at the end of his career, and we knew that we would need peace and quiet and a lot of hours to get the best of his performance properly assembled. Yet I also knew that whatever we did, there would be certain critics (I could name them in advance) who would grumble about Hotter's unsteadiness just above the stave and compare him unfavorably with Schorr (who died in 1953). Had we used another, less experienced Wotan, those same gentlemen would have blamed us for depriving posterity of Hotter's classic performance. There are certain games you cannot win, and this is one of them.

On December 26, 1965, Humphrey Burton's film *The Golden Ring* went its full length of ninety minutes on BBC. It was well received in the press and I gather that the BBC was pleased with the viewer-research figures. A week later, when we were back in Vienna for the editing of *Walküre*, the German version went out on the main Austrian network, and as Birgit Nilsson was in Vienna at the time we invited her to see the program. Over the following months the film was shown on both major German networks, in Switzerland, the United States, Canada, Australia, and New Zealand. John Drummond, the assistant producer, went to Scandinavia and prepared a slightly shortened version which was overdubbed with commentaries in the Scandinavian languages. At the same time Decca bought a couple of 16-mm. prints which have by now been shown so often up and down the country that both are wearing out. The remarkable and pleasing thing about all this is that the film is not a slick, snappy "popular" documentary, but a serious attempt to show what really happens during a major opera recording. Even more important, Burton took the considerable risk of including long uninterrupted musical sequences because he believed that the intensity of the performance would hold the viewer's attention. He was right, although there were some who tried, when he was preparing the film, to persuade him otherwise.

Our final playback of the edited *Walküre* was on Tuesday, January 4, in the Sofiensaal. It was not the occasion that *Götterdämmerung* had been, for we had not tried to make *Walküre* into a competing, monumental epic. All along, we had tried to see it within its context, and to conceive it in terms of a listener who, having bought the entire *Ring* on records, might choose to play the four works in sequence on four successive days.

As it turned out there were still a few details to be corrected, and one or two of the effects did not work as I had intended. I had put the thunderclap which marks Wotan's last exit in Act Two far too near the last word of his last line, so that when heard in context it sounded as if someone had lit a fuse and blown him sky high; we had to move it a bar or two closer to the end of the act. And somehow, in our efforts to get the best of Hotter, we had let the final scene of the opera fall apart in a way that was wholly uncharacteristic of Solti. It needed careful re-editing; and when, finally, we were satisfied, the last part of our *Ring* was flown to England to be ready for release in September.

In the summer of 1966 I went back to Bayreuth where our German colleagues had arranged a pre-release playback of parts of *Walküre*. Apart from a flying visit in 1964 when I was looking for steerhorns, I had not been there for many years. New office buildings had reared up all over the town: cold, functional slabs of concrete, emulating Frankfurt and painfully at odds with their environment.

But it was still Wagner's town. There was Wahnfried, glum and shuttered; but you could take an outside pathway to the end of the garden where Wagner and his dog and the ashes of Cosima lay buried. A mile or so away was the railway station where his body had arrived after his death in Venice in 1883; and up on the hill was his beloved Festspielhaus, still in all important senses preserved as he had created it, and still a haunted place for those who believe in ghosts.

I walked up the hill to the theater, as I had done day after day fifteen years ago when we were recording *Parsifal* and one of the versions of the *Ring* which never saw daylight. It struck me that if we had succeeded then, the Vienna *Ring* might never have happened; for in retrospect I do not think we would have sold many copies of the Bayreuth *Ring*, and a failure would have prejudiced the chances of getting enough money for a major studio recording. Now the evidence of our efforts in Vienna was all over Bayreuth: at the station, in shop windows throughout the town, and round the roof of the bookstall next to the Festspielhaus, posters and displays announced the completion of the first recorded *Ring*.

I wondered what Wagner would have thought of his masterpiece becoming available in terms of mass communication. He had built his theater for a devoted minority, to set a standard and an example to be followed by other theaters throughout the world. He had no reason to suppose that more people than could ever be accommodated in all those theaters would eventually have access to his work. Yet even in Bayreuth itself a different application of the idea of mass communication lay behind the controversial productions which Wieland Wagner had staged since 1951. In breaking away from the traditional type of production, Wieland Wagner was trying to rid the music-dramas of their national associations and reveal their universal psychology. Whether one liked what he did or not, the intention was creditable and clear. Consciously or unconsciously, his productions were an attempt to make a vital connection between the stage and a modern audience whose social structure is very different from that of an audience of a hundred years ago. To that extent, if only in terms of the *idea*, he was dealing in a sort of mass communication.

The medium was wrong, however. For all his achievement, he was still working within the confines of the same theater as his grandfather, and with what was basically the same type of equipment. The failure, common to most other opera houses, was in not grasping that theaters, as well as audiences, are subject to change. To convey the *Ring* on the lines he envisaged—and I am not saying that I agree with them— required not only an imaginative but a *technical* revolution. If the philosophy of the *Ring* is to be shown to have universal application and validity, and if its content is to make contact with a wide modern audience, the means of presentation must be that of the mid-twentieth century rather than an extension of whatever was considered adequate in the nineteenth.

Mass communication by means of records and television and radio does not, as some Jeremiahs predict, necessarily mean a lowering of standards; on the contrary, over a long enough period, standards are bound to rise. The better is still the enemy of the good, and the general accessibility of art in all forms is a fine thing, even in its unconscious effect on those who profess to have no interest in it. I am pleased when someone comes out of a *Ring* performance in the theater and comments that although he thinks our recording is splendid, the total experience of hearing and seeing a good theater production is considerably greater. So it should be; but I am equally pleased when someone comes out of an inadequate theater production fuming about its perversity and admitting that the records bring him closer to what the *Ring* is about. Only to that extent do the records present a serious challenge to the theater, for whatever their deficiencies, they mass-communicate a sincere, well-cast, and well-conceived performance which must inevitably set a standard.

I caught a performance of *Walküre*, Act Three, on that visit to Bayreuth in 1966 which seemed to me enough to dissuade anyone with more than a casual acquaintance with the *Ring* from entering the Festspielhaus for a very long time. Except for some splendid singing by Birgit Nilsson, what happened was about as far removed from Richard Wagner's idea as it is possible to get. A sort of crew-cut Wotan pranced about the stage, petulant rather than angry. At the moment of Brünnhilde's last plea ("*Dies Eine musst . . .*") before the farewell, when she is supposed to be clinging to his knees (she refers to them in the text) and he is supposed to be still, and psychologically paralyzed by the conflict between duty and the love for his favorite daughter . . . at that moment, the Bayreuth Wotan was reeling about the stage like a drunken man and throwing his spear in the air; and that was not all. Irrespective of stage considerations, it used at least to be thought that the musical side of things would be in irreproachable hands at Bayreuth. The traditions of Hans Richter, Karl Muck, and Richard Strauss were handed down to Wilhelm Furtwängler, Arturo Toscanini, and Victor de Sabata, among others who appeared at the festivals until 1944; and at the reopening in 1951 the tradition seemed likely to be re-established through the brilliant though greatly differing talents of Hans Knappertsbusch and Herbert von Karajan. Since then, the decline has been spectacular, with the exception of the *Parsifal* performances which Knappertsbusch conducted until the year before his death. (Von Karajan did not return after 1952.)

Orchestrally speaking, the performance of *Walküre* in 1966 would have sufficed in Palermo. It was fast, and sounded as if it had had no rehearsal. The musical light and shade of Wagner's drama was nonexistent. The moments of tension, like the arrival of Wotan, were loud and rhythmically slack; and the moments of emotional release, like the bars preceding Wotan's "*Leb' wohl, du kühnes herrliches Kind!*" or the E major orchestral passage when he finally takes Brünnhilde into his arms, were conducted with a stupefying indifference, as if the conductor could not wait to get back to Salzburg or wherever he was going for his next engagement. A performance of such monumental ineptitude is not to be judged by standards of personal preference for one conductor over another, for one is forced back in protest to the score itself, where the evidence is clear to see. And if by the greater spread of knowledge, whether it be through records or film or any other medium, the time approaches faster when a performance like this cannot happen because it cannot be tolerated, the world of music in general and Wagner in particular will be the healthier.

The trouble is that most of us cannot imagine what we have not experienced. We remain faithful to outdated techniques and methods because they are a sentimental part of our past. We can all of us spot the flaws in a new and challenging technique, and are usually glad to dismiss it because of them. So far, attempts to blend the worlds of the cinema and the theater have failed, and any sort of electrical amplification for voices or orchestra is considered an outrageous interference by technology. (I suppose there were similar cries of horror when acetylene arcs replaced candles for stage illumination.) But if the audience for opera in general and Wagner in particular is to grow, and if that audience is to make contact with the drama in any serious sense, the time is coming when technology must play a greater part even at the cost of a few sacred artistic cows. Just as the conductor is no longer in charge of *every* aspect of a recording session but is nonetheless able to create a more accurate and prepared realization of his wishes because of the facilities provided for him, so I believe that the opera theater of the future will be under the control of men who conceive opera in terms of an expanding communication. In that direction there is at the very least a hope of survival; in the other, the tomb is waiting. Opera as a social event, or as a vehicle for a single star, may not even survive the twentieth century, any more than the court theaters survived the nineteenth: simple economics and the expansion of private forms of communication like records and television will see to that.

The survival of an art form depends partly on its relevance to any given era, and partly on its adaptability in terms of communication. With a few distinguished exceptions, we still approach the presentation of opera with the mentality of the mid-nineteenth century; and when anyone tries to put it effectively where it belongs, which is before the eyes and ears of our own younger generation in a manner that is attuned to and attractive to that generation, the howls of alarm from the elders of the critical establishment can be heard the length and breadth of Europe and America.

Only a few years ago it would have been presumptuous to suggest that any recording might influence the future of opera as produced in the theater. That may still be the case, though I have my doubts. The trend is already to be noticed in some quarters, and especially in Herbert von Karajan's productions of *Boris Godunov* and *Carmen* for the Salzburg festival, both of which have used electrical amplification to create effects like the Kremlin bells in *Boris* and the cheers of the crowd in *Carmen*, Act Four. Whether one considers these were well presented is beside the point: what matters is that they were done at all. It is a fact that many of the aural devices we used to make an effective *Ring* on records could also be made to work in the theater, and I cannot believe it will be long before something like that happens. I am equally sure that before long an attempt will be made to use wide-screen filmed backgrounds (through back projection) for certain parts of the *Ring*. Apart from the advantages of well-photographed natural settings, this is probably the only reliable and effective way of dealing with the various magical incidents which most contemporary productions omit with the excuse that they are not "art." The truth is, of course, that they are considered too difficult, and in any case cannot be accommodated within an abstract setting. (As long ago as the end of the last century, George Bernard Shaw in his days as a music critic repeatedly and bluntly made the same point: you don't have to go to Bayreuth to find out how to make Alberich disappear—you simply ask the producer or stage manager of any provincial pantomime.)

Tradition dies hard, and the birth agonies of any new medium or even a new means of presentation are likely to be protracted. The resistance is rarely from the public, but comes from those guardians of public taste whose judgments are based on nothing stronger than a sentimental recollection of how things *were*. Thus, to return to the world of recording, it is strange that even in the mid-nineteen-sixties only a minority of critics have troubled to equip themselves, or to persuade their employers to equip them, with machines worthy of the records they are reviewing. Most of them, and especially those on English national newspapers, hear records in conditions which I suspect are vastly inferior to those enjoyed by the record-buying public. And the real reason for this is their (possibly unconscious) unwillingness to accept the record as a proper medium for music. It is a commercial product. In its final stages it is mass-produced. It cannot really have anything to do with art. At the very time when they should be chiding the industry for its uneven imaginative approach—one opera done well, one opera done appallingly—they do not seem to be able to hear the difference, or to consider it of any importance when they do. The exception to the rule—a critic like Andrew Porter, who often understands records—contributes importantly to the development of the medium, because one takes notice of what he says, even when disagreeing with him.

The medium, of course, cannot remain as it is. Only twenty years ago the record enthusiast had to be content with fragile, noisy 78-rpm records with a playing time of less than five minutes per side. In that short period of twenty years not only have the long-playing record and stereo appeared, but the quality of amplifiers and speakers has improved beyond recognition. One always tends to assume that the latest development is going to be the last, but the signs of the next stage of record evolution are already beginning to emerge. They are part of what someone has aptly called the "information avalanche" which will doubtless descend upon the next generation, and which that generation will painlessly survive. It is now possible, for the first time, to play any part or the whole of the *Ring* in home conditions in such a way that it is an acceptable substitute for going to the theater. By the next generation, it is not unreasonable to think that it may be *seen* as well as heard.

To imagine this, it is necessary to forget our present, somewhat primitive methods of viewing through the ordinary television set. There is no possible reconciliation between that small picture and the sort of sound which can be produced from a modern recording. (Imagine the second act of *Götterdämmerung* with the chorus spread across an aural spectrum which in the average room today is likely to be several yards wide, while the vision of that same chorus remains restricted to the present width of the largest television screen.) But who supposes that in twenty years we shall still be watching the same sort of box? Is it not likely that the television screen of the future will be more like a picture which you hang on the wall, and adjustable to the size of the room? Or it may be like those roll-up maps which, at school, could be pulled down at will from the ceiling. Whatever form it takes, we can be sure of several things: it will be much less clumsy than our present apparatus; it will be much larger; it will give an accurate color picture, eventually with depth; and it will incorporate stereo sound, coming from its source in the picture.

The listener, or viewer, or whatever one calls him, will either be able to play his own tapes or records over such a system to produce sound and vision, or he will be able to command such a performance to take place by dialing some code through which a computer will channel the performance to him. Nobody has yet quite worked out how he will pay for this, but history has shown that once a demanded facility becomes technically possible, it takes no time at all to find out how to charge for it. What is much more interesting is the question of whether the listener will remain as he is at present—a more or less passive participant who listens to or watches the performance and involves himself emotionally or intellectually according to his desires at the time, while not in any substantial way influencing the proceedings.

One of the objections to recorded vision-in-the-home, and one of the claimed virtues of modern sound recording, is that the man who sees as well as hears an opera performance which is capable of infinite repetitions will soon tire of the visual side. Listening to the recorded *Ring* at present, it is possible to imagine, if one cares to do so, a different setting for each act whenever it is played. A listener can change the imagined shape and size of the characters at will; he can see them as actors on a stage, or as the characters in realistic settings. But once vision is introduced, he is committed to whatever the producer and designer have decreed for that particular recorded production. Worse still, he will become accustomed to the movements and mannerisms of the actors, and with sufficient familiarity will be able to predict them. (It is true that aural mannerisms can also be irritating and predictable, but less so than their visual equivalents.)

The fallacy of this objection to vision-in-the-home is the assumption that the future listener will be as powerless as we are. The breakthrough in this line of thought has been made by the distinguished pianist Glenn Gould, who is an extremist in his conviction that the future of music lies entirely in the home, and that the concert hall and the opera house as we know them will disappear in a few generations. In arguing this way—greatly upsetting the musical puritans by doing so—he points to the growing influence of the listener with his present-day equipment. Twenty years ago you could alter the volume of your records—make them louder or softer at will—which twenty or so years before that was not possible. Twenty years ago you had something called the tone control, through which you could in a primitive way alter the playback characteristic by increasing or reducing the top frequencies. Today, the listener with modern equipment has individual treble and bass controls, plus a mass of filter devices through which he can, if he wishes, produce a sound very different from that intended by the conductor and producer of the recording. And, Gould argues, there is no reason to assume that the listener will be content with this. On the contrary, he is likely, as technology places more and more versatile equipment at his disposal, to demand all sorts of powers to create a sound which *he* particularly likes, irrespective of what the performers involved might think. After all, he is the man who has bought the performance, and he has a right, governed only by his taste and the kind of equipment he can afford, to treat that performance in any way he likes in order to gain from it the maximum musical experience of which he is capable.

Farfetched though it may seem, I can see no reason why a similar, or even more extensive influence, might not be brought to bear upon vision. Equipped with some machine-of-the-future, the opera lover at home could not only adjust the sound to his precise requirements, but also "produce" the opera visually in whatever way he liked. There are, of course, a million professional arguments against a development like this, though most of them are of the "closed shop" kind by which all forms of progress are at first impeded. And such a development can only be imagined or considered in terms of the "information avalanche"—the inescapable fact that people in the majority of countries are maturing earlier with each successive generation, and absorbing "information" of every kind—including music—with an ease and fluency and inquisitiveness that was unthinkable a few generations ago. I am quite incapable of regarding this as an unhealthy or undesirable development. It may well be that there will be fewer amateur pianists and singers; and although the ability to perform on an instrument is, and will remain, an excellent attribute, it is nonsense to try to argue that the amateur violinist of 1905, struggling with a salon piece, knew more about music than the youngster of the 1960's who has thoroughly immersed himself in all forms of music through the gramophone record. It is worse than nonsense: it is arrogant snobbery.

We made our *Ring* for the young generation, though without quite knowing it. No matter how much the establishment may fret and fume over the comparison between what we have done and those relics of the golden era enshrined on single-sided 78-rpm records, the fact remains that the *Ring* on records has been a commercial success—which, in translation, means it has *communicated*—in a way that nobody, ten years earlier, would have thought possible.

The reviews for *Walküre* were, as we expected, more qualified than those for any other part of the *Ring*. They were controversial and even contradictory, which was fine. Most of the discussion turned on the question of Hotter, though not a single one of those who were against him put forward a suggestion of how else we might have cast the part. Interestingly, the American critics—who have probably less experience of Hotter on the stage, and therefore less reason to cherish memories of his standing as an actor—were quicker to appreciate the qualities of his performance than their European colleagues. Howard Klein, in the New York *Times*, went overboard not once but twice to proclaim that the impact of our *Walküre* recording had been so great that it had made him rethink his whole approach to the task of reviewing opera on records.

In the second week of November 1966, I went with Solti on a short promotional tour to present excerpts from *Walküre* to audiences in London, Manchester, and Cambridge. In each city there was a capacity audience: indeed, so large was the audience in the Guildhall, Cambridge, that our effort had to be relayed to a second hall by closed-circuit television. During those three evenings we had plenty of time to look at our audiences, and it is exciting to say that in all three cities the younger generation was overwhelmingly dominant. More than that, the questions that were thrown at us in the second half of the program showed an intelligence, a perception, an awareness of what we had been trying to do in making such records, which was in itself encouraging and stimulating. Not that we were spared criticism—but it was always penetrating criticism of the kind which reveals at once that the critic has done his homework, and thought through to the point where his objections are clear and stripped of prejudice or sentiment. One saw, very suddenly, the enormous gulf separating this sort of audience from the metropolitan musical intelligentsia; one suddenly grasped the narrowness of what is generally considered to be the musical world, and realized the untapped potential for music in general and opera in particular once the trappings of outmoded traditions and methods of presentation can be surmounted. These were audiences thirsty for knowledge and experience, yet uninhibited about expressing strong viewpoints; ready to consider anything new or anything old, but unwilling to be led by the nose and be told what to think in the name of hallowed tradition. These were young people who already knew a lot about the *Ring*, though most of them had probably never seen it in the theater. Perhaps I am being sentimental, but I think their faces and their questions would have delighted Richard Wagner.

You cannot live with the *Ring* for seven years without its creator seeming to become someone you know very well. All the same, if we could be taken back in a time machine to the period one hundred years ago and allowed to watch Richard Wagner at work, I am sure we—to say nothing of Wagner—would have a shock. (His Leipzig accent, which was evidently very strong, would be the first surprise.) Our imaginary figure would dissolve before the actual presence of the most committed and ruthless revolutionary in the history of music. The life of Richard Wagner makes fascinating but often disagreeable reading, for it is far easier for us to assimilate the flaws in his character than to grasp the immensity of the opposition he encountered. A lesser, more tolerant, *nicer* man would have quit or committed suicide long before Wagner allowed his presiding demon to drive him into the composition of the *Ring* at a time when there seemed not the slightest possibility of its ever being produced on the stage.

The enemy he faced is still with us, though less securely entrenched. It is any mentality which resists change in any form, save possibly that of a comfortable extension of prevailing fashion. It is any mentality which assumes that the value of a work of art is somehow necessarily in inverse proportion to the number of people who like it; or that the transference of a work of art from one environment or medium to another (from the church to the concert hall, from the opera house to cinema, television, or the gramophone) *necessarily* causes irreparable damage. Yet all that really happens is an alteration of emphasis; and this alteration, being unfamiliar, is therefore deemed undesirable or dismissed as a trick. (In Basil Coleman's 1966 production of Britten's *Billy Budd* for television, the camera stayed in close up on Captain Vere's face when Billy was hanged. What one saw and experienced could not possibly happen in the theater; it was not *better* than the theater, but entirely different. It was wholly valid within the television medium because of the sensitivity of the direction and the ability of Peter Pears to convey, facially, the agony of Captain Vere.)

Our lines of communication are changing. There are still a few who insist that the proper place for opera is in the theater before or after an elegant dinner, and that if the hobbledehoy insists on admission he should be sealed off in the upper tiers, or preferably sent home to listen to records or to watch television. The sickness of opera has been, and is, that it is a very expensive and exclusive closed shop. (In some places it is worse than others: witness the appalling decline of La Scala, Milan.) Richard Wagner abhorred this attitude a hundred years ago, and we are only now beginning to make the slightest progress towards a change. If, by as much as a fraction, the *Ring* on records has contributed to that change, then I believe that all of us connected with it have reason to be pleased.

It has not been easy to recall exactly what took place in the Sofiensaal over the years covered by the *Ring* recording. I have found it increasingly difficult to remember what this or that artist did or said as a person, and I have only been able to write this book by dint of constant references to notes, letters, and all kinds of memory-joggers which, fortunately or otherwise, were preserved. By the end of each recording, in my mind at any rate, Wagner's characters had taken over completely and had assumed lives of their own. I do not visualize Fischer-Dieskau, but Gunther; I do not think of Nilsson as Brünnhilde or Flagstad as Fricka, but of Brünnhilde and Fricka. This does not often happen with opera recordings, even with the good ones. I tend to think it is the single most important quality about the *Ring* we have made, and the one which—mercifully—defies analysis.

Perhaps it came from spontaneity; perhaps it came from its opposite: the occasional overthoroughness with which we managed to upset both the artists and the administration. Perhaps it came from neither, but from the happiest of coincidences: the coming together of a great Company, a great orchestra, a great conductor, the finest cast that money and effort could assemble, and a team of enthusiasts who loved Wagner and found nothing irreconcilable between his work and the medium at their disposal. The future is sure to bring more recordings of the *Ring*, not only in the present form but in whatever manner posterity chooses to hear, and possibly see, opera in the home. We tried to set an example; we tried to do our best. What will remain is something much more than a transcription of voices to enable posterity to make its comparisons between the living and the dead: it is a record of Wagner's characters as they were recreated and brought to life in a new medium ninety years after the first complete performance in Bayreuth of *Der Ring des Nibelungen*.

As this book was going to press there were several last-minute developments which seem worthy of inclusion. Our recording of *Die Walküre* reached the No. 1 position in the *Billboard* charts of Best Selling Classical L.P.s in the second week of January 1967. A few weeks later the American National Academy of Recording Arts and Sciences (NARAS) honoured our entire *Ring* with a special "Grammy" award. (This is the recording equivalent of an Oscar in the cinema.) During the celebrations marking the 125th Anniversary of the Vienna Philharmonic Orchestra in March 1967, the orchestra presented Georg Solti with its Ehrenring, and at the same ceremony Decca presented the orchestra with copies of the *Grand Prix du Disque Mondiale* awards which had been won for each successive part of the *Ring* recording. Finally, at our instigation, Deryck Cooke wrote and recorded a brilliant and penetrating analysis of the *Ring* motives, illustrated with nearly three hundred musical examples which—with a few specially prepared exceptions—were drawn from the complete recordings.

Ring Chronology

APPENDIX A

Whenever things were going badly during the *Ring* recording we frequently had to remind ourselves that our troubles were as nothing compared with those encountered by Richard Wagner in getting his work on the stage. In his *Life of Richard Wagner*, Ernest Newman provides an enthralling and indeed heartbreaking account of all that happened; and to put matters into the correct perspective, I felt it might be useful to provide the following summary of Wagner's work on the *Ring* between its inception and the first complete performance at Bayreuth.

1848   Wagner writes the poem of *Siegfried's Death* (later to be the basis for the text of *Götterdämmerung*).

1851   Poem of *Young Siegfried* written (later to be the basis of *Siegfried*).

1852   Texts written for *Walküre* and *Rheingold*. Earlier texts revised to become the basis for *Siegfried* and *Götterdämmerung*.

1853   The above texts privately printed and called *Der Ring des Nibelungen*.

1853   Composition of *Rheingold* begins (completed early 1854).

1854   Scoring of *Rheingold* completed. Composition of *Walküre* started.

1856   Scoring of *Walküre* completed. Composition of *Siegfried* started.

1857   First and second acts of *Siegfried* completed.

1865   Composition of *Siegfried* resumed at opening of Act Three.

1869   Completion of *Siegfried*, Act Three, except for scoring. Composition of *Götterdämmerung* started. First performance of *Rheingold* at Munich.

1870   Composition of *Götterdämmerung* continues. First performance of *Walküre* at Munich.

1871   Scoring of *Siegfried* completed.

1872   Composition of *Götterdämmerung* completed.

1873   Scoring of *Götterdämmerung* started.

1874   Scoring of *Götterdämmerung* completed.

1876   First performance of *Der Ring des Nibelungen* (Bayreuth, with Richter conducting).

The Recordings

APPENDIX B

The Casts

DAS RHEINGOLD

WOTAN	GEORGE LONDON
ALBERICH	GUSTAV NEIDLINGER
LOGE	SET SVANHOLM
FRICKA	KIRSTEN FLAGSTAD
MIME	PAUL KUEN
FASHOLT	WALTER KREPPL
FAFNER	KURT BÖHME
FREIA	CLAIRE WATSON
FROH	WALDEMAR KMENTT
DONNER	EBERHARD WÄCHTER
ERDA	JEAN MADEIRA
WOGLINDE	ODA BALSBORG
WELLGUNDE	HETTY PLÜMACHER
FLOSSHILDE	IRA MALANIUK

Vienna Philharmonic Orchestra / GEORG SOLTI

DIE WALKÜRE

BRÜNNHILDE	BIRGIT NILSSON
WOTAN	HANS HOTTER
SIEGLINDE	RÉGINE CRESPIN
SIEGMUND	JAMES KING
FRICKA	CHRISTA LUDWIG
HUNDING	GOTTLOB FRICK
HELMWIGE	BERIT LINDHOLM
ORTLINDE	HELGA DERNESCH
GERHILDE	VERA SCHLOSSER
WALTRAUTE	BRIGITTE FASSBAENDER
SIEGRUNE	VERA LITTLE
ROSSWEISE	CLAUDIA HELLMANN
GRIMGERDE	MARILYN TYLER
SCHWERTLEITE	HELEN WATTS

Vienna Philharmonic Orchestra / GEORG SOLTI

SIEGFRIED

SIEGFRIED	WOLFGANG WINDGASSEN
BRÜNNHILDE	BIRGIT NILSSON
WANDERER	HANS HOTTER
ALBERICH	GUSTAV NEIDLINGER
MIME	GERHARD STOLZE
FAFNER	KURT BÖHME
ERDA	MARGA HÖFFGEN
WOODBIRD	JOAN SUTHERLAND

Vienna Philharmonic Orchestra / GEORG SOLTI

GÖTTERDÄMMERUNG

BRÜNNHILDE	BIRGIT NILSSON
SIEGFRIED	WOLFGANG WINDGASSEN
HAGEN	GOTTLOB FRICK
GUNTHER	DIETRICH FISCHER-DIESKAU
GUTRUNE	CLAIRE WATSON
ALBERICH	GUSTAV NEIDLINGER
WALTRAUTE	CHRISTA LUDWIG
WOGLINDE	LUCIA POPP
WELLGUNDE	GWYNETH JONES
FLOSSHILDE	MAUREEN GUY
FIRST NORN	HELEN WATTS
SECOND NORN	GRACE HOFFMAN
THIRD NORN	ANITA VÄLKKI

Vienna Philharmonic Orchestra / GEORG SOLTI

Acknowledgments and Credits

The editors of Time-Life Records are particularly indebted to author John Culshaw, presently head of BBC-TV Music, for his invaluable help and wise counsel in assembling the illustrations for this book.

Particular thanks also are due to the following persons for assistance (in production): Wolfgang Wagner, Dr. Herbert Barth, Heinz Eysell and Frau Gertrud Strobel, Bayreuth; Sir Georg and Lady Valerie Solti; Adolf Krypl, Manager, Sofiensaal, Vienna; The Vienna Philharmonic Orchestra; Peter Goodchild, Gordon Parry, Christopher Raeburn and Jack Law, Decca Records Co., Ltd., London; Terry McEwen and Hans Boon, London Records, New York; Mrs. Beryl Kathleen Jennings Turner, Gananoque, Ontario, and Mr. and Mrs. Arthur V. Dusenberry, Phoenix.

Photographer Dmitri Kessel was ably assisted by Pepi Martis and Jacques Minassian, Paris.

Time Inc. departments and other staff members who also were extremely helpful: Robert Parker, Margot Hapgood, Franz Spelman, Rosemary Young, Susie Marquis, Leny Heinen, Traudl Lessing, all of the Time-Life News Service; Sarah Cothran, Picture Collection, and George Karas and Herbert Orth, Photographic Laboratory.

Photographs by Dmitri Kessel were taken for Time-Life Records.

Photographs by Hans Wild are used with the courtesy of The Decca Record Company Limited unless otherwise indicated.

Cover — Photographs: Georg Solti by Hans Wild; background by Al Freni
viii — Derek Bayes
2 — Bettmann Archive
3 — Opera News
6, 7 — t.l. & t.c. Brown Brothers; b.c. & t.r. Culver Pictures
8 — Eric Schaal
9 — The New Studio
14 — courtesy John Culshaw
15 — courtesy Sir Georg and Lady Solti
18 — Sabine Toepffer
21 — courtesy Beryl Kathleen Jennings Turner
24 — Dmitri Kessel
26 — Bildarchiv Bayreuther Festspiele
29 — t. Rudolf Betz, Bildarchiv Bayreuther Festspiele; c. Siegfried Lauterwasser, Bildarchiv Bayreuther Festspiele; b. Schwennicke, Bildarchiv Bayreuther Festspiele
31 — Eduard Renner, Bildarchiv Bayreuther Festspiele
32 — B. Schmitz-Sieg, courtesy John Culshaw
36 — Elfriede Hanak
39 — courtesy Mr. and Mrs. Arthur V. Dusenberry
44, 45 — NBC Artists Service exc. b. Opera News, r. Hugo Wickman
46, 47 — l. & t.c. Opera News; b.l. Jan Greve; b.r. Associated Press

51, 52 — Bildarchiv der Österreichischen Nationalbibliothek
54 — Molden
55 — Farrell Grehan
59 — Gustav Schikola
61 — Gustav Schikola
63 — t. Hans Wild; b. Culver
64, 66 — Elfriede Hanak
68 — Dmitri Kessel
69 — Ralph Crane
70 — Pierre Boulat
71, 72 — Dmitri Kessel
73 — Dmitri Kessel exc. b.c. David Johnson
74, 75 — Dmitri Kessel exc. b.r. Pierre Boulat
76 — Dmitri Kessel
83 — Eugene Cook
87–94 — Hans Wild
95 — t. Hans Wild; b. Hans Wild, courtesy John Culshaw
98 — Hans Wild
99 — t. Siegfried Lauterwasser, Bildarchiv Bayreuther Festspiele; b. Eduard Renner, Bildarchiv Bayreuther Festspiele
101 — Hans Wild
102 — Foto Fayer courtesy Decca Record Company Limited.
105–115 — Hans Wild
126 — courtesy Mr. and Mrs. Arthur V. Dusenberry
132, 133 — Foto Fayer
137 — Hans Wild
138 — Gustav Schikola
140 — Siegfried Lauterwasser, Bildarchiv Bayreuther Festspiele
142, 144 — Wilhelm Rauh, Bildarchiv Bayreuther Festspiele
145 — Gustav Schikola

147 — Siegfried Lauterwasser, Bildarchiv Bayreuther Festspiele
150 — Hans Wild
151 — Eleanor Morrison, courtesy London Records
153 — l. Schwennicke, Bildarchiv Bayreuther Festspiele; r. Hans Wild
155 — Gustav Schikola
160 — Jack Law
161 — Dmitri Kessel
162 — Ralph Crane
163 — Dmitri Kessel
164 — David Lees
166 — l. Bildarchiv der Österreichischen Nationalbibliothek; r. Franz Votava
169 — courtesy Decca Record Company Limited
170, 173 — Hans Wild
175 — Jack Law
176–201 — Hans Wild
205 — Elfriede Hanak
206 — Hans Wild
213 — Tony Altaffer, courtesy Decca Record Company Limited
214, 215 — Dmitri Kessel
216 — Elfriede Hanak
218 — Louis Mélançon
219 — Cecil J. Thompson
220, 221 — courtesy John Culshaw
223 — Wilhelm Rauh, Bildarchiv Bayreuther Festspiele
224, 225 — courtesy John Culshaw
227, 229 — Elfriede Hanak
230 — Derek Bayes
234 — Jack Law
238 — Elfriede Hanak
245 — Gustav Schikola
247 — courtesy Sir Georg and Lady Solti
248 — Elfriede Hanak
250 — Hans Wild

Abbreviations: b., bottom; c., center; exc., except; l., left; r., right; t., top

Index